INSHORE CRAFT OF GREAT BRITAIN

INSHORE CRAFT
OF GREAT BRITAIN

In the Days of Sail and Oar

by EDGAR J. MARCH

VOLUME TWO

David & Charles : Newton Abbot
Fishing News (Books) Ltd, 110 Fleet Street, London
International Marine Publishing Company, Camden, Maine, USA

0 7153 4981 3
USA ISBN 0 87742 003 3
LOC 74 117924

Set in 11 on 13 pt Baskerville
and printed in Great Britain
by Latimer Trend & Company Ltd Plymouth

CONTENTS

LIST OF ILLUSTRATIONS

LIST OF DRAWINGS

CHAPTER ONE

THE KENT COAST

IN Victorian and Edwardian days, half a century ago, bawleys from Rochester and Queenborough worked the grounds at the mouth of the Medway and the deeps frequented by the Leigh men, seeking any saleable fish, especially shrimps, for which there was an unceasing demand from the Medway towns and Sheerness. At times they slipped through the Swale to fish for sprats in the vicinity of the Girdler and Margate Sands. (Picture, p 20.)

The Rochester boats lay at moorings in a reach at Strood, often with topmasts housed and nets hung up to dry, a picturesque sight from the train crossing the Medway. And always there were a number of russet-sailed spritsail barges alongside the wharves, or working up and down the river, some bearing on their topsails the insignia of many a cement company before nearly all the firms merged and the barges carried the Blue Circle emblem. (Picture, p. 37.)

Round in Whitstable were a few bawleys bearing the Faversham registration, including three or four with mizzen masts on which were set small standing lugsails. Two of these boats, *Mary* and *Jessie*, were eventually sold to Margate men who found the mizzen mast useful when hauling up the after end of the trawl beam. Photographs in my collection show *Mary* setting a huge topsail with a yard almost the length of the gaff; alongside is *Jessie* with the more usual jib-headed sail. The mizzen mast was stepped against the transom and the sail sheeted to the end of a long outrigger. (Picture, p 17.)

Whitstable has been renowned for its oysters for over 2,000 years. During the Roman occupation of Britain thousands were

sent to Rome where emperors, senators and the well-to-do were
very partial to the succulent oyster as a prelude to their epi-
curean banquets. For centuries the rights of dredging were
vested in the Lord of the Manor, and sons of strangers were ad-
mitted as Free Dredgers after an apprenticeship of seven years.
In 1792 that portion of the Manor covered by the sea was sold
to Thomas Foord who conveyed it to The Company of Free
Fishers and Dredgers of Whitstable the following year, being
empowered by Parliament to purchase the exclusive right of
fishing from the previously 'customary tenants, then only 36 in
number . . . had to borrow £20,000, subsequently increased to
£30,000 for the purchase of ground and for stocking it with
brood'.

By 1863 the debt had been paid off, the stock was valued at
£400,000, and about £90,000 worth of oysters had been sold
the previous season. Over 100 'yawls' were employed and the
Company numbered 408 of whom 340, all Whitstable men,
were members, the rest being widows. An independent body of
men, they met in the Duke of Cumberland public house where
profits and dividends were paid out. The Company was
governed by a Foreman, Deputy Foreman, and Treasurer
elected by the whole body, and a jury of twelve nominated by
the officers. The only persons having the right to become
members were the sons of dredgermen. A 14-years-old apprentice came into his birthright at 21 and could attend the Water
Court held on the second Thursday in July when all met and
voted by ballot to revise byelaws, approve nine watchmen with
three 'watching' boats, and elect the foreman of the ground and
his deputy, who, with the 12 jurymen, made the Board of
Management for the following year. If a Freeman died without
male issue his share went into 'the common stock', but his
widow received a reduced payment out of each day's fishing
profits until her death. The aged and infirm had a superan-
nuation of about one-fifth.

With the large families of those times there was soon a rapid
rise in the number of Freemen, and in 1881 only the eldest sons

could be enrolled at the age of 21. As only the services of a
certain number were required to work the fishery, a great many
non-working members had to find other occupations, but they
still received one-third of a member's share of the profits, the
additional two-thirds going to the working dredgermen. This
new state of affairs became unworkable and in 1895 certain
gentlemen proposed to raise sufficient capital to buy the rights
of all members willing to sell, and an Act was obtained the following year enabling this to be done. The promoters, however,
failed to raise sufficient funds, and after three months the Company had possession of the Act and a complete reorganisation
took place. The nominal capital had been fixed by the Act at
£250,000. Each member of the old Company was allotted
twenty £10 shares, amounting in value to £120,000. The same
amount went to those sons of members who were 14 years of age
and enrolled on the books at the time of the passing of the Act,
on their attaining the age of 21 and being unmarried. Every
widow retained the previous advantages and had a life interest
of seven £10 shares which reverted to the Company at her
death. The Company thus became a public one, managed by
five directors with a secretary.

According to the 1865 Fisheries Report, the officers and jury
decided the quantity of oysters to be dredged up and sold in the
market, the amount of brood to be bought, and how much was
to be paid for work done. In 1858, some £15,000 was spent on
young brood from Essex where the oyster was more prolific, but
its quality improved rapidly on being transferred to fatten on
the Whitstable beds; hence much business was transacted between the two counties. The local beds 'are the most productive
in the world and, although small, are protected by a spit of
sand from easterly winds . . . 1½ miles long, the ground inside is
2 miles each way, depth 4 to 6 ft at lowest tide'. The Flats, being
common ground, were frequently worked by Colchester smacks
dredging there for brood and delivering their catches at Whitstable.

The Report continues:

The rate of wages varies according to the quantity sold and the price; on the average of the last 18 years the rate has been 23s per week, the last few years being considerably more and a bonus was divided in 1863 of £20, 1864 £16, so the amount received by each member was £100. Widows receive one-third. Between £33,000 and £34,000 was paid over to members in the year; for this the average work performed by dredgermen during the open season (for sale) was two hours a day, in close season; when dredging and clearing ground, moving and separating oysters, four hours a day. The rest of the time is spent dredging the 'Flats' for brood, which they sell to Company for laying down and in good years they make more by work outside than in wages. Always the practice of the Company to observe close time, ceasing on a day fixed by the jury, usually about 9 May, commence 3 August, during which time the men clean ground, preventing accumulation of mud and weeds, killing mussels and five-fingers, separating large oysters from small. The large are set apart on a ground from which the market will be supplied.

The men dredge constantly except for about one month, June or July, when 'spat' is observed settling on the beds . . . has been no good spat since 1858, Mr Nichols, the foreman, said one good fall in every six years, good being followed by one or two seasons of moderate, one good will supply enough brood for six to seven years. The purchase of brood from open grounds has always been by far the largest portion of business of the Company.

In 1852 the Company obtained from flats and Essex beds 63,853 wash at a cost of £15,240, average price 5s a wash, and sold £49,671 worth of 'natives', average price £2 2s per bushel . . . lowest price paid was in 1858—at 4s 3d, highest 18s in 1863–4. Highest sale, 1862–3, brought £90,892 at £2 8s per bushel; lowest sale 1857–8, £7,681 at £2 2s per bushel. . . . A heavy gale will roll up oysters in a ridge 3 ft deep, great injury done if not worked to spread out again and the mud goes away. If settled on ridge soon kills oysters and if allowed to remain would cause eddy and fresh deposit of mud all round. Five-fingers come in like flocks of gulls, one kind will eat oyster itself. If dredged will roll themselves up and float away, some days 10 bushels caught, next none.

The price of natives in 1826–7 was £1 per bushel, rising gradually to £2 2s in 1840–1, jumping to £3 four years later, then dropping rapidly to £1 11s in 1850. It then increased again, rising to £3 8s in 1863 and in the following year it was up to £4 10s. These violent fluctuations show clearly what a chancy business was the cultivation of oysters, even in those days of golden sovereigns!

The oysters were carried to Billingsgate in hoys, 14 being constantly employed. To avoid too great fluctuations in price, the two salesmen telegraphed the number of bushels to be caught each day, divided among all the effective members. Crew numbered three and they had to dredge the daily 'stint' and no more. Their usual dress was long worsted stockings over trousers, heavy boots almost reaching to the waist, guernsey, oilskins and sou'wester. Nearly all the men were related, and 'all equal'.

The growing grounds, settled by foreman and jury, were marked with poles.

The nets (continues the 1865 Report) are trellis work of un-dressed buffalo hide, washed almost white, iron knife-like bar for scraping at the mouth . . . dropped in, when hauled each net may have 800 oysters, emptied on deck, nets cast over again and sorting begins, all sizes and different stages of growth, some like blocks of flint, a mass of 30 or more shells, some covered with pearly counters the size of a shilling, infest oysters less than a year old, some covered with red pimples 'quats', two years old about the size of a half-crown, only four years old picked out and thrown into baskets, will live about ten years, best at five, age told by layers outside bottom shell. Perfect yellow circle at small end of fan is one year, then three successive brown pearly semi-circles represents three other years, and rough fringe round outer edge is one year more. Four years for general eating. When the sorting is finished, baskets serving as measures are filled with picked oysters and refuse swept back through trap holes in bulwarks. The vessel shifts its mooring once or twice in course of a morning's dredging to mix the hauls, so that eaten not spoiled by feeding on one quality and that perhaps the best. The baskets are rowed to market hoys which hold about 100 bushels or 160,000 oysters, contents tipped into a long, wet hold. Inspector checks quantity and quality, money sent down by two salesmen in London to Canterbury bank, and sum is drawn out and divided by jury of twelve.

Such was the oyster fishery a century ago. In 1901 the Company employed about 120 men, and 300 dredgers and flatsmen were engaged in 80 smacks. During that summer there was an extraordinary fall of spat. The flatsmen worked several tides on a small piece of ground off Bishopstone, surrounded by sandstone rocks. One day it was blowing hard easterly, and when there was enough water several deep-keeled Colchester smacks came in and worked until high water, hauling their dredges from four fathoms. On this one tide they delivered 10 washes of brood per boat to the Company's store.

The dredge, of triangular form, is made of wrought iron, with a ring passing through a hole in the heel, or 'rest', which hooks on to the bulwark when the dredge is about to be lifted on board. The three iron bars radiating from the heel are called 'limbs', the cross tie the 'warbin'. The ends of the two outer limbs are joined by a flat bar with a blunt edge, the 'bit', which

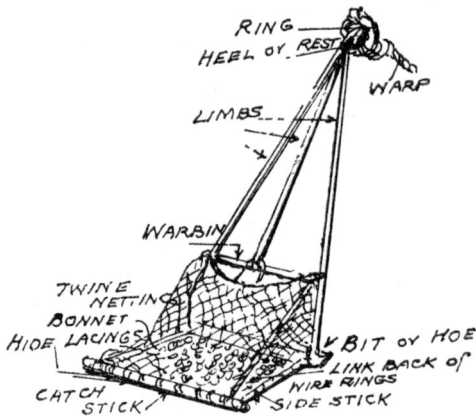

Sketch of oyster dredge

scrapes up the oysters and much else. The dredges used on the flats have a 'link back', or 'ground' of wire rings, made by the men, but on the beds this would be too rough, and hide is used instead. The upper netting of twine is fastened to the dredge by hide lacings; the 'catch-stick', to which the link back is fas-

Page 17 (above) Hauling dredges, a rare photograph of an early clench-built yawl with stump topmast. Note crutch for main boom; (below) *Ellen Jane*, 28 F. Note the huge gaff topsail. The yawl to leeward sets a jib-headed topsail

Page 18   (above) Casting an oyster dredge overboard;
(below) washing oysters before culling

Page 19 (*above*) Sampling the quality of the oysters;
(*below*) Excellent! The verdict of the connoisseurs

Page 20 (above) Yawl 87 F off Herne Bay. Reefed down in a hard SW blow, the small jib is set but bowsprit is not reefed; (below) *Iverna*, 7 RR, June 1893. A Medway bawley built by George Gill at Rochester in 1893 and still working in 1957. Cost, £140 ready for sea

tened, is of holly, the two side sticks, oak. Between the catch stick and the twine net are three rows of wire netting, the 'bonnet' to take the weight and pressure when the net is filling. Dredges weigh from 18 to 24 lb, with 5 lb extra for the rigging.

The bass warp is fastened to the ring by a fisherman's bend and, to save the rope from chafing, the ring is bound round with canvas, the 'puddening'. The warp is coiled on deck, with the end buoyed, and is secured to a cleat only by a short length of twine, the 'stop, which breaks if the dredge becomes fast. The buoy then marks the spot, enabling the boat to pick up the lost warp.

Each smack worked a 'fleet' of five or six dredges, the two heaviest from the bow, two of medium weight from amidships, and the two lightest from the stern. The smack sailed or drifted with wind and tide, the skipper steering to keep as nearly broadside to the tide as possible.

After hauling, the contents of the dredge were shot out on deck and culled. This involved chipping oysters off the 'cultch' with a knife, the 'cultick', sorting out any saleable fish and then 'shading' the rubbish overboard. When working over the beds only three dredges were used, each having hide in place of wire rings to prevent damage.

Although called 'yawls' locally, the smacks were cutter-rigged and varied considerably in size. Some had pole masts, others a long topmast on which a jib-headed or gaff topsail was set. The sails were either left white or tanned, often with a pleasing shade of ochre. I well remember what a beautiful sight it was to see the fleet at sea on a bright summer day. Several of the old yawls were clench-built.

Builders stamped their individuality on many details, and as owners had their own ideas for arrangements of fittings and gear scarcely two were alike. There were slight differences in the shape of sterns, bowsprits were set to port or starboard of the stem, some smacks had one main hatch, others two. A few were copper-sheathed. The earlier fashion was for a straight keel, but in later years most of the yawls drew more water aft

B

than for'ard. The position of the sliding hatch to the companionway might be before or abaft the mast, on the centre line, to port or to starboard. Hulls were black and rarely any other colour than white inside the bulwarks.

Framing differed according to the timber available; usually two timbers sided together, but at times short lengths were sided to one another. Stanchions were either a continuation of the frame, or a separate timber sided to the top of the frame. Hulls were strongly built to withstand the constant bumping as the smacks dried out or refloated, with little shelter in certain winds. The anchorage was landlocked from the south and west, open from the north, and protected on the east by 'The Street', a bed of shingle running upwards of a mile seaward which usually dried out at low water.

Trawling was also carried out by some smacks, and I give particulars of gear used by L. Kemp, great-grandfather of W. Harvey. Three sizes were then in use, small 12 ft, large 15 ft, shrimp 18 ft beam. The triangular net was 15 ft in length, with a buoy fastened to the cod end. Meshes varied in size, being fine for shrimps, and larger for dabs and cod. Instead of rope, a leather thong was often used for the ground rope. I saw and measured up a pair of head irons over 200 years old of similar pattern to that used by Brixham trawlermen; also the 'painter's devil' which, filled with charcoal, was used for 'breaming', the name for removing old paint and tar from the hulls.

I have known Whitstable since boyhood when, years before the first world war, we used to go there by train on school outings. Then the place was full of interest, the harbour packed with brigantines, schooners and spritsail barges, while out in the offing yawls where working the tides. Along the shore was many an ancient tarred shed and sail-loft and, towering above everything, the coasters hauled up on the slips for repairs or refit. Everywhere was the tang of the sea, Stockholm tar, old rope, and perhaps mud—but what a nostalgic mixture it made, and how much better than petrol fumes!

In the mid-nineteenth century Whitstable had six shipyards,

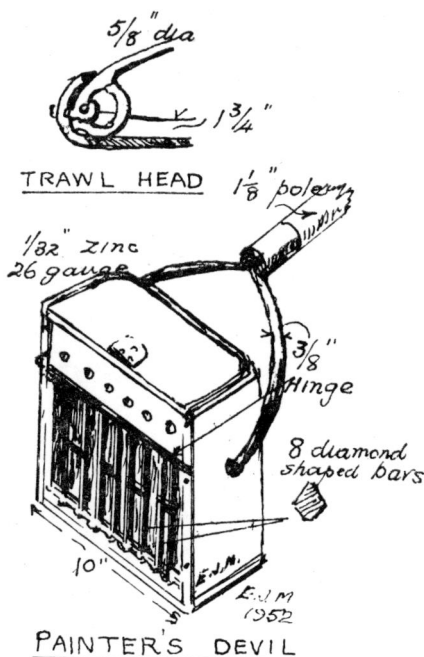

Sketch of iron trawl head and painter's devil,
measured at Whitstable, October 1952

four sailmakers, one ropemaker and five shipsmiths, and ships
of 300 tons and more were slipped down direct into the sea on
launching days.

I have before me, written on blue foolscap paper, in ink as
black as the day it was penned, the specification form for the
hull of a new watch boat of the following dimensions:

Length of keel, 36 ft; 13 ft beam; 6½ ft depth of hold, to be 1 ft
rise in floor, the same to be carried out in proportion to bearings
of boat.

Keel to be of English elm 6 in sided to be moulded not less than
12 in aft and 9 in forward. The same to be well housed as to
show not more than 5 in below keelson at midship. The
bottom of same to be of square edge for fixing of false keel of
2½ in substance fore and aft of the same material as main keel.

Stem of English oak 5½ in sided moulded 10 in at base and 8 ½ in
at top.

Sternpost. English oak $5\frac{1}{2}$ in sided, moulded 10 in base and 9 in at top with solid square attached of 3-in oak planking of proportionate depth, to be fastened with clench bolts to sleepers or fashion timbers.

Dead Wood. English elm with connecting knee of oak.

Kelson. English oak 7 in sided, moulded 9 in. The whole of the above to be fastened through each floor to main keel with not less than $\frac{7}{8}$ in yellow metal bolts.

Apron. English oak sided 6 in, moulded 5 in, and fastened to stem with not less than $\frac{3}{4}$ in yellow metal bolts.

Framing of hull to consist of 12 double-framed timbers with single oak ditto to be so fixed as to leave an opening not more than 7 in. Floor timbers to run fore and aft. Floors $4\frac{1}{2}$ in, futtock $3\frac{1}{2}$ in, and 3 in sided, moulded at throat 7 in. Bilge $4\frac{1}{2}$ in. Top 3 in to be all of oak.

Deck. Beams for main cuddy to be sided 6 in, moulded $4\frac{1}{2}$ in.

Framing fore and aft. Framing of oak 6 in by $3\frac{1}{2}$ in, with deck carlings in proportion. All the beams to be dowled or dovetailed to shelf, to be $4\frac{1}{2}$ in moulded and sided. Mast, cuddy and transom beams to be kneed.

Shelf. Fore and aft of oak $5\frac{1}{2}$ in, moulded 3 in thick.

Wale. $2\frac{1}{2}$ in oak, 14 in depth to be fastened with metal spks. All bolts through the same to connect knees or shelf to be of $\frac{5}{8}$-in yellow metal.

Plankshare of oak and decks of yellow fir of $1\frac{3}{4}$ in substance to be fastened with metal or galvanised spikes.

Planking from wale down to bilge of pitchpine not to exceed 7 in width and from bilge to keel of beech or elm not more than 8 in width, $1\frac{3}{4}$ in substance to be double and single fastened with $4\frac{1}{2}$- and 5-in metal spks.

Inside Lining. Clamp fore and aft $1\frac{1}{4}$-in oak, 7 in width from clamp to bilge, $\frac{3}{4}$ in yellow fir the edges of which to be . . . or so fayed in way of cabin to prevent draughts fastened galvanized. Bilge strakes two oak planks 2 in thick, 7 in wide, fastened galvanized spikes. Bilge to kelson 1-in fir.

Rail to be 17 in depth to top, 4 in wide, 2 in thick, of oak or American elm. Stanchions $2\frac{1}{2}$ ft as under $3\frac{1}{2}$in square at plankshare. Washstrake 1-in oak. Bulwark $\frac{3}{4}$-in fir fastened galvanized nails.

Cuddy. 7 ft long, 3 ft wide, 18 in deep, of 3-in oak with slide on top.

Fore Hatchway. $2\frac{1}{4}$-ft square oak comings, 8 in deep, of 3-in oak plank. Hatch oak framed of $\frac{3}{4}$-in fir.

Main Hatchway. 2¼ ft square with 3-in oak comings of 8 in deep. Hatch oak framed and ¾-in fir.

Windlass of English oak 8½ in at ring, to be fitted with cheeks, jumping pall ring and all ironwork complete.

Hawsepiece to fix one found.

Cabin. 18 ft in length, two bulkheads of 1-in fir tongued and grooved. Plain locker fore and aft. Flooring 1 in fir.

Rudder. Post of oak and back of fir, to be fastened with yellow metal bolts and braces and bolt of same material.

Stern of elliptical shape.

The difference in price of metal or iron fastenings as above specified to our own calculations would be about £9 or £10.

CONDITIONS

The work to be completed and launched by 1 August next or to forfeit and pay seven shillings per day for every day during which the work shall be completed after that date.

Not to advance more money than seventy-five per cent of work done, the remainder to be paid seven days after launching.

We do not bind ourselves to accept the lowest or any tender.

Tenders to be sent in to the foreman on or before 10 April 1875.

Note: The spelling is as in the original document.

A very complete specification was also given for the rigging, detailing sizes of ropes, deadeye lanyards, sails, halyards, lacings of mainsail to gaff, reef points, shrouds, stays, sheets and clewlines. Topsails were usually set to port but there was no hard and fast rule. The number of hitches to lace sails to spars was also specified; in fact nothing whatever was left to chance, or to provide a point for argument.

In 1880 the Whitstable Fishery Co owned the *Thomas Foord*, 40 ft long, 13 ft 3 in beam, depth 5 ft, and the *Royal Native*, registered on 8 February 1879, length 44 ft, beam 13 ft.

When I last visited Whitstable in 1952 the old smack *Royal Native* lay derelict on the beach and I made some hurried sketches of her gear in 70 minutes, all the time I had to spare. Peak halyards went to starboard, throat and topping lift to port; its Spanish Burton purchase to starboard. The deck had been doubled in places. The colour scheme was: gaff, boom, blocks, bulls eyes, heel and end of bowsprit, white; mast yellow; white inside bulwarks; rail and hull black; stanchions mast colour; crutch white; black socket. The bowsprit had two fid holes for reefing.

Previously, I had had some interesting and valuable chats with men who knew the days when sail was supreme. Mr M. Luckhurst told me that the smack *Stormy Petrel*, built by Charles Perkins, cost £245 ready for sea, with fishing gear. She finished up as a watch boat moored near the forts.

Mr John Warner, who had several yawls built for him, started with the Seasalter Fishery at the age of 19 as skipper of the *Three Brothers*, 'a heavy old tub, built for a cattle boat', still had rings in the hold for tying 'em up'. (Picture, p 40.)

St Agnes, 20 tons, launched in November 1906 by John Collar, cost £290 ready for sea, but with no fishing gear. In May 1945 he sold her for £600 for conversion to a yacht.

> Beautifully built, no repairs, never recaulked, blacked twice a year when tar was burnt off and retarred . . . the Whitstable Shipping Co built *Thistle* for £265 complete. . . . *Rose & Ada* built by Collar for Emptage to same lines was four inches longer than *St Agnes*, but my boat was the faster. *Clyde* I bought after the war, had been built by Aldous at Brightlingsea on speculation, gave £250 for her, hull, spars and sails, oak framed, pitchpine planking, Oregon pine deck and spars . . . sold her for a yacht.

Goldfinch made most of the sails, charging in 1914 £20 for a mainsail, and £40 between the wars. A full suit consisted of two gaff topsails, four jibs, two foresails, one mainsail and cost £75 to £80 . . . 'frequently a summer and winter mainsail, three or four reefs'.

> Before the war, a good year grossed £280 for oystering, average £200, skipper received 2s in £ extra, three hands, four shares and one to the boat . . . best year I gave a skipper £30; 25s a week was good money for a week's work when I first had her, worst year's earnings £1 a week.

During the 1914–18 war John Warner bought the snib-bowed Ramsgate smack *Vic* for £250 and carried coal from the Humber to St Valerie, selling her after the war for £500 for

Icelandic cod fishing. In partnership with five others, he purchased the Folkestone brigantine *Aneroid* for £425, built of
softwood by Ramsey at Prince Edward Island in 1874. For four
years she ran to France, 'earning good freights up to £4 a ton
. . . when offered £3,000 we sold out, but captain remained in
her'.

He chatted on:

> Had no ill luck, except for *Kent* run down and sunk by the
> paddle steamer *Eagle* . . . a clear day, she was coming up from
> Margate, light easterly wind, kept altering course but had me in
> the end, cut down to the mast. . . . I gave £70 for her . . . old
> timbers rotten, had been doubled twice and lengthened twice . . .
> got full compensation . . . was near the Girdler Buoy. . . . Once
> 140 boats in oyster work, now one power will do the work of ten
> sail, but sail best for working dredges as spread out, power all
> keel dredging.

Rose and Ada, built by Collar, had an overall length of 46 ft
8 in, and a beam of 13 ft 3 in. The hull had a moderate rise of
floor and rounded bilges. Below deck was a hold 25 ft 6 in long
with two hatches; a companionway to port gave access to the
cabin which extended from the mast to the stem, with locker
seats along each side, and a coal stove.

On deck was the usual wooden windlass, the bowsprit was
set to starboard of the stem, to port was a roller. The bulwarks
were about 1 in clear of the deck and there were four freeing
ports a side, 1 ft 6 in by 6 in. Immediately inboard were trays
with the deck protected by sheathing boards to save the planking from being scoured by oyster shells.

The sail plan consisted of a mainsail with three lines of reef
points—a few men liked four—a jib-headed topsail, foresail
and three jibs. The balloon for light weather had its head about
5 ft from the topmast sheave or block, the working jib to about
halfway up the masthead, and a small storm jib.

The mast was 27 ft 8 in from deck to hounds, masthead 7 ft
3 in, topmast 27 ft 3 in, bowsprit 26 ft overall, 21 ft outboard,
gaff 25 ft 6 in and boom 33 ft 6 in. Three shrouds a side were
set up with deadeyes and had a pinrail across.

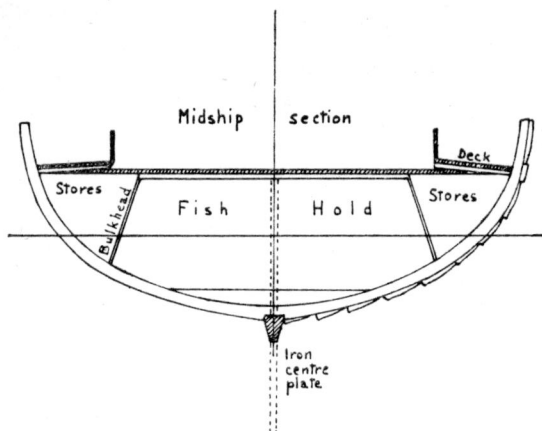

Midship   section

Deck

Stores   Fish   Hold   Stores

Iron
centre
plate

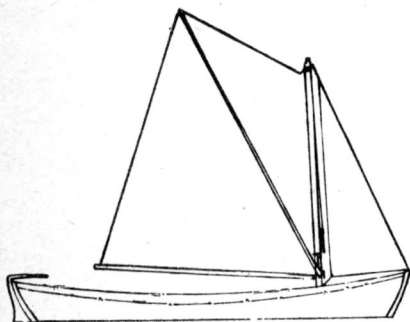

Doble "Louise" (similar ship)

Mast overall   13' 2"
Boom   11'
Sprit   15'

Heel of sprit is sweated up mast on hoop with tackle to mast head. Fores'l set flying, sheet lashed to ring on horse . Some dobles do not carry a main horse .

In March 1933 there were 17 dobles in the Medway fishing between Rochester Bridge and Rainham, but only about 3 still sail. Some dobles carry centre plates lowered in the fish hold.

Midship section and sail plan of Medway doble,

Whitstable boats were registered at Faversham, letters FM, later F; *Rose and Ada* was F 105.

The Seasalter & Ham Oyster Fishery Co had beds farther seaward, the Faversham Co higher up the Swale. In 1864 the Herne Bay Co acquired rights to a ground, 7 miles long and 1 mile wide, between Whitstable and Margate, after strong opposition as it was a public ground for brood.

An interesting survival from the past which could be seen around the Medway and occasionally in Whitstable harbour, was the 'doble', practically identical in type to the Thames Peter-boat, double-ended, half-decked with a fish well amidships. A short mast stepped well forward carried a spritsail, the heel of the sprit being sweated up the mast by a tackle to the masthead. A small foresail was set flying, the tack to stemhead and sheet working on an iron horse. One or two dobles still worked under sail after the first world war, but about 15 had motors; all had oars working in thole pins.

Farther along the coast the longshore men from Westgate-on-Sea made a living chiefly by taking summer visitors for trips, especially when warships lay in Margate Roads for days at a time. In winter, they went drift-netting for herring and sprats, a bitterly cold job in open boats, but the fish brought round to our door next morning were marvellous, and a common price for herring was 24 for a shilling. The two big herring punts were *Edith Mary*, and *Enchantress* owned by Chris Case—my friend from boyhood until his death during the last war—who taught me the difference between all the rigs of sailing vessels in the days when they could be seen every day in the offing. The other belonged to Walter Miller. Both boats were 18 ft long, 6 ft beam, and 3 ft deep. As a schoolboy I used to walk to Margate, where Chris kept his boat in the harbour, and sail back with him, when he told me many things. A deeply religious man, he never took his boat out on Sundays. His fine, bearded face gave him the look of an apostle, but he would never be photographed, despite all pleas from visitors—'toffs'.

When analysing the hundreds of entries in an old ledger belonging to G. W. Finnis, sailmaker, Deal, I found an entry in 1894 for a gaff mainsail, mizzen, staysail and jib for Mr Armitage, Westgate, the bill amounting to £5 18s 6d for a complete suit of sails. I believe this was *Edith Mary*, later owned by Walter Miller. Another was for Mr Case in 1897, a gaff mainsail made from 29½ yd of canvas at 1s 8½ a yard—£2 8s 6d. The dimensions of the other sails are given, but no prices. *Enchantress* was sold for conversion to a yacht after the death of her owner, having given him about 50 years service.

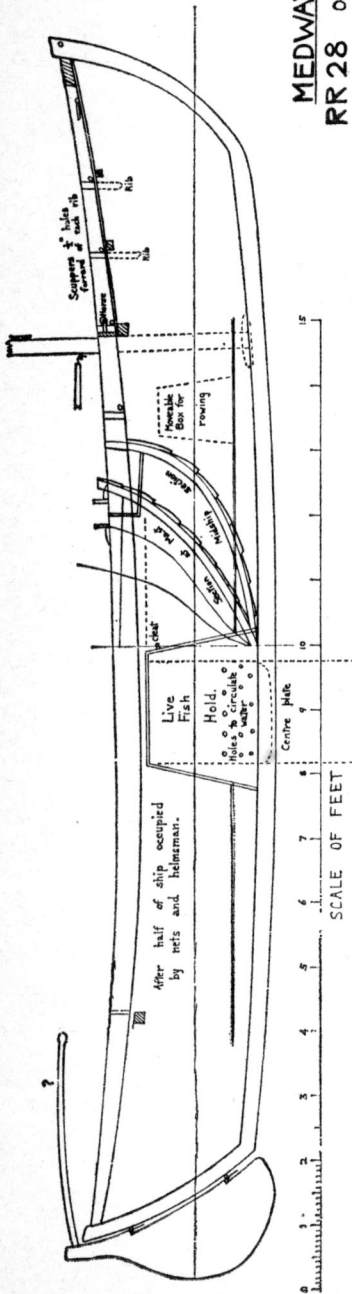

MEDWAY "DOBLE"

RR 28   Owner. Fred J.Wadhams.

Measured at Strood pier 4/3/33.

These craft are very similar in type to,
if not the same as, the Thames "Peter Boats."
No sail plan can be traced, but the sprit
of this boat was still aboard and measured
14'.10" overall.

This plan is not authoritative but is
compiled from careful measurements
and photos of the ship.

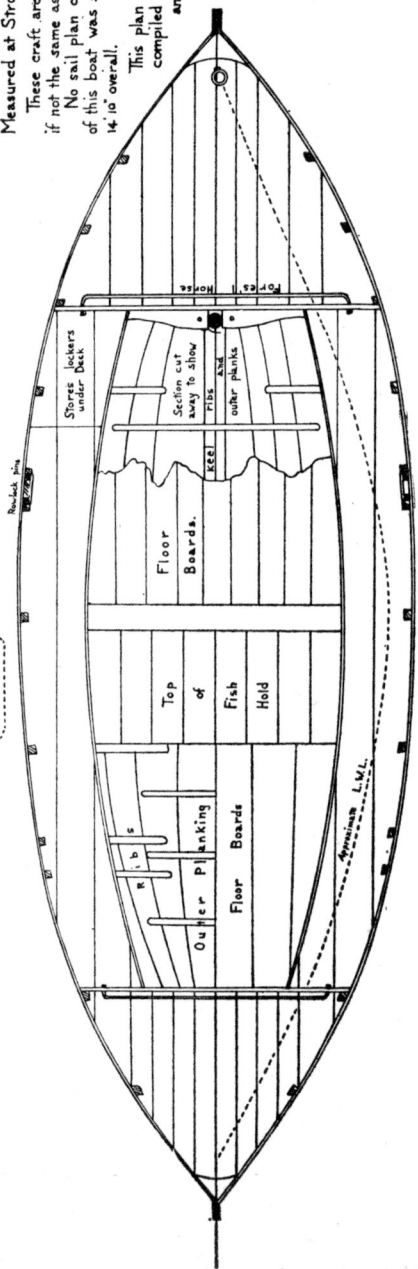

Scuppers ⅜" holes in each rib

Rib

Rib

Removable thwart for rowing

Live Fish Hold.

6 circular Holes to circulate water

Centre plate

After half of ship occupied by nets and helmsman.

SCALE OF FEET

Rowlock pins

Stores lockers under Deck

Section cut away to show ribs and outer planks

Keel

Floor Boards

Top of Fish Hold

Outer Planking

Floor Boards

Rib

Approximate L.W.L.

FOR'CES HORSE

Plans of Medway doble, RR 28, measured at Strood,
March 1933 and drawn by F. T. Wayne

Margate was the most southerly port for bawleys, with quite a fleet in their heyday, and often when walking to school along the cliffs to Birchington I could watch them trawling for shrimps, their lofty topmasts high above the chalk bastions. In my nostrils was the scent of the lucerne fields, once so well known to homeward-bounders; some summers the red trifolium made a glorious splash of colour, especially if mixed with the blue of the lucerne, fields now buried for ever under bricks and mortar. In the bays were lines of bathing machines, drawn in and out of deep water by patient old horses, the ladies modestly entering the water by steps at the back, safe from all eyes, and clothed from head to foot in serge bathing suits, perhaps daringly edged with white!

Sail held its own long after the war, as the men considered the fumes from a motor would contaminate the shrimps. The last was *Providence* R 225, built for Letley Bros by S. Taylor of Milton Creek, who was responsible for many a bawley and came to Margate in February 1909. After the second world war *Providence*'s sails went and a motor was at last fitted; she was sold a few years later and finally lost in the estuary after striking wreckage.

Prices for repairs done by L. C. Brockman were amazingly cheap. In September 1912 he made a new pitchpine mast for Shrubsall's bawley *Jessie*, 34 ft 6 in long, 9 in at deck, 7 in at masthead, with lower cap of oak, two oak cheeks 2 ft long (6s 3d), jib halyards (5s), three 12-in belaying cleats and fastenings (3s 6d), three 12-in mast hoops (4s 6d), total for the complete mast being only £7 4s 0d, with a 10s allowance for the old mast. A tumbler for the gaff cost 2s 6d, an 18-ft trawl beam 18s, and scarfing 2s 6d. For the bawley *Magnet*, Mr Letley, he supplied 4 lb of oakum for 1s 4d, 5 lb of pitch for 1s, and six hours labour was charged at 6s.

In May 1952 I had a chat with Bill Wyatt, aged 92, at West Mersea, and he told me he could make a mast for an oyster smack by himself complete in 3½ days at a finished cost of £10 to £12.

The Margate boatmen were fearless seamen in their big luggers, and saved hundreds of lives before any lifeboat was stationed there. In 1803 the East Indiaman *Hindustan* was wrecked on the Margate Sand, the lugger *Nelson* saved 127 lives and her crew received 500 guineas from the East India Company.

On the stone pier was a memorial tablet to commemorate the loss of *Victory*, a lugger on 6 January 1857; before daybreak she went to the assistance of an American ship, *Northern Belle*, 1,100 tons, stranded on Foreness Rocks while on passage from New York. The lugger was lost with all hands, nine, the oldest John Smith, 63, the youngest Fred Batt, 22; two Emptages also were drowned. Such a disaster had never been known before and £2,100 was raised for the relatives.

A furious NE gale had been roaring all Sunday, 12 February 1860, and at sunset heavy clouds betokened a very dirty night; the wind continued to gust with increasing violence with thick snow squalls. Before dawn, the lugger *Eclipse* put to sea on the lookout for any disaster and saw a vessel ashore on the Margate Sand. She was the Spanish brig *Samaritano*, 170 tons, bound from Antwerp to Santander with a valuable cargo, and had driven ashore about 5.30 am. The lugger spoke a Whitstable smack, borrowed two men and a boat, then boarded the wreck as the tide fell, six Margate men and two from Whitstable gaining her deck. The gale increased as the tide rose, the brig began to pound heavily, and when she finally started to break up the men cut away the mainmast and took refuge in the fore rigging. The smaller lifeboat was launched from Margate, but soon lost her buoyancy and filled to the waists of the men, the valves in the air boxes having been left unscrewed. Despite this handicap, the lifeboat succeeded in getting within a quarter of a mile of the wreck; then she was forced to run for the shore, and after four hours drove into Westgate Bay where her crew were rescued by the coastguards. The surfboat *Friend of all Nations* was launched, but the tiller broke and she was driven ashore a mile away. The luggers *Nelson* and *Lively* then put off.

The former had her foremast swept clean overboard, *Lively* got to sea but could not cross the sands owing to the furious breaking seas in which no open boat could live.

Express messages were now sent to Ramsgate as fast as a horse could gallop, and soon after noon the lifeboat left in tow of her tug *Aid* at the end of a 50-fathom 5-in hawser. The seas were so mountainous and the strain so terrific that eventually the rope parted; but a new line was got aboard near the Brake Sands. The bridge of the tug was constantly swept by seas and sheets of spray, the men crouching behind flimsy canvas screens, fighting for breath. Now the tug was high on a crest, then plunged into the trough, disappearing from the view of the lifeboatmen who grimly sat in their cork jackets waiting the time when they must cast off and face it alone. Inch by inch the tug battled on, towing the lifeboat as far as the Woolpack Sands; here she left under double-reefed foresail and mizzen, anchoring 40 yards from the wreck after a fight which had lasted over four hours. The coxswain then veered down and the crew of the *Samaritano*, master and eleven men, jumped from the wreck, making 32 in the lifeboat. Efforts to get in the anchor having failed, the bowman tried to cut the cable, but only one strand of three had been severed when the foremast and sail were blown out of the boat. The cable was payed out fast and the lifeboat swept back towards the wreck until her stern grazed the bows of the ship. The cable tautened, and again efforts were made to haul it in; but would the severed strands hold? The mast and sail, dragging alongside, were most difficult to get on board, and when this was eventually done it was found that the mast had broken off 3 ft from the foot and a new heel had to be chopped before the mast could be stepped. Great was the relief of all when the cut part of the cable came inboard; sail was set, the lifeboat drew ahead as the cable was payed away, and when clear of the wreck the cable was cut after over an hour's intense anxiety. The boat then made for the tug sheltering behind the Hook Sand off Reculvers, the crew were transferred and the long tow home started in Stygian darkness. The wind came aft when the Foreland was reached and all were soon safe in Ramsgate.

It was indeed a noble and thrilling sight to see one of the two Margate lifeboats beating up to a barge in distress in the Gore, spray flying over everything, brown lugs taut as a drum, the red, white and blue hull diving into and out of the blue-green seas, crested with white horses, the men still as statues until the moment came to go about and the dipping lug was lowered and rehoisted on the opposite side of the mast. What must it have been like on a wild, dark night among the breakers leaping over the sands!

The largest vessel built at Margate was *Moss Rose*, constructed by W. H. Huggett in a field a considerable distance from water. Designed and owned by E. S. Whitehead, she was 52 ft 9 in long, 17 ft 5 in beam, 7 ft 1 in depth, 34·79 registered tons. When the day came for launching she was put on a trolley astern of a steam roller. The immense weight and friction soon had the well-greased axles getting hot, and a crowd of men and boys enjoyed themselves flinging buckets of water over them to keep them cool; and if one or two missed their mark and hit the face of a spectator it all added to the fun. Soon the steam roller found the task beyond her powers and ground to a halt. What to do now? Believe it or not, Lord George Sanger's famous circus was in the town and the circus king lent his biggest elephants for the task. Led by 'Ajax', they were hitched to the trolley and made light work of getting *Moss Rose* to the water. As a pleasure yacht she was unique in being bawley-rigged and, proving successful, Huggett built another monster, *Sunbeam*, capable of going trawling during the winter months when visitors certainly did not want to go for a sea trip. *Moss Rose* proved so popular that her transom stern was fitted with a 'lute' stern, or false counter, by Collar & Sons at Whitstable, increasing her length to 55 ft 5 in. I often saw her well out at sea with a full load of passengers. She was licensed to carry 145, and when it fell a breathless calm I wondered what the landladies had to say when their guests turned up hours late for lunch, or were well after locking-up time if on an evening cruise. In 1906 she was packed to capacity and more when the last away from HMS *Bulwark*. It was then the habit of certain boatmen to take crowds off but not trouble to run out empty to bring them ashore; the only thing to do was to pack in everyone possible and then use the warship's boats.

I knew Mr Whitehead, the owner of *Moss Rose*, quite well, and he was a character if ever there was one. He never went to school but was apprenticed to a Ramsgate smack-owner in March 1870 when under twelve, but ran away to go in deep-water ships. Later, as second coxswain of the lifeboat *Quiver*, he was awarded the BOT silver medal for his part in the rescue of the crew of the brigantine *Druid* in 1893. He next had a ship chandler's shop, and I often dropped in for a yarn, as he could spin many a good one. Once I asked him some questions and thought he was pulling my leg when he replied, 'I'll ask my dad.' White-haired, with twinkling eyes and well over 70, this seemed a bit tall, but sure enough it was true; he wanted to out-live his father who died at the age of 96, but slipped his moorings in 1944 when only 86. He owned *Moss Rose* for more than 30 years without any serious mishap, other than children falling overboard at times. Her hulk now lies up the river Stour at Plucks Gutter.

Another boat-builder, L. C. Brockman, was a fine craftsman who was entrusted with any repair work required by the life-boats. When he died, I rescued his old ledger from the dustbin where it had been consigned as of no value, the pages torn but containing invaluable information for me. The old chap was better with a tool in his hand than a pen; his spelling was phonetic, and difficult to read but clear if said aloud. 'Frind to Hall Nashians' was the name given to the entry for repairs to the surfboat.

The elaborate specifications prepared by the Institution's officers for repairs to end boxes in No 1 lifeboat, and calling for an estimate, is rather cut down to size by the amount of the bill, £1 7s 6d.

Lifeboat work apparently caused the old chap many a head-ache as he was faced with unfamiliar words: '4 ft Amaricktin ealm 5 in by ¾ in, 2s; 8 ft ¾ × 6 Undura mugany 4s.'

Other items are 56 lb white lead, £1 9s in 1916 (but 12 lb cost 12s two years later); 30 ft 'yelow pine' ½ in × 9 in, 10s; 3 gallons black varnish, 7s 3d (in 1918 the price for 3 pints was 1s 6d); a new mast, 23 ft 6 in, £4 15s with labour. The total bill, charging his labour at 1s per hour and that of a labourer at 8d, came to £59 0s 6d.

His ledger showed that 9 October 1909 he started building the galley *Perseverance*, for Ladd & Co, she was 28 ft long, height of stem 4 ft 9 in, stern post 4 ft 11 in, tuck 1 ft 10 in, breadth 4 ft. She was built by one man and a boy in 591½ hours at 7¾d per hour, and complete with mast and yards cost £18 9s 8d.

Other craft recorded in the ledger include:

    Boat 18 ft 8 in long, 392½ hours complete
      „   15 ft long,   151½   do   do
      „   27 ft 2 in overall, 7 ft 7 in beam, 645½ hours
           8d per hour £21 10s 4. Boy 4d, £10 15s 2d.
           Total £32 5s 6d.
    Boat 18 ft long 'whin built caust' £30
         24 strakes of 'plinking' 432 feet Net.

In July 1912 *Perseverance* had a new mast, 27 ft long, 6 in in the butt, which cost 18s; a yard, 15 ft 6 in 'and varnishing' was charged at 10s. In January the following year another mast was 4s 6d dearer.

A 10-ft boat of 4 ft 6 in beam, complete with ash oars, rudder yoke, keel and stem band was built for £10 10s, 'extras' being 3s 6d for a 7-lb anchor, and 2s 9d for a boathook and staff.

A 13-ft boat, complete with oars and rowlocks, for £13 suggests that he was building small boats for £1 a foot, a usual price for most builders in those days.

The following were the prices for materials for a boat of 30 ft 8 in, 'lanketh' 8 ft 6 in beam, 'senter deep' 4 ft 1 in, 16 strakes a side.

Page 37 (*above*) Bawleys at Strood. Note doble alongside RR 43 in foreground with topmasts housed and nets drying; (*below*) Folkestone harbour, *c* 1914. FE 65 is *Dorothy Louisa*. Note foremast stepped well forward and long bowsprit and outrigger

Page 38 Wrecks on Deal beach after an easterly gale on 12 February 1870. The ship far left is completely wrecked. Centre is *Star of the Ocean*, 177 net tons, built as a brig by Lungley at Southampton in 1863. Refloated, she was rigged as a brigantine. To right is *Republique*. There are 45 vessels in the background. In 1871 24 vessels were lost on the Goodwins; in ten years, there were 109 wrecks

Page 39 South End station, *c* 1865, with sets of boats on their stages ready for instant launching. In foreground, a second-class lugger, then a fore-peaker, another second-class and fore-peaker and, beyond, the great galleys. Note steep angle of shingle beach, greased woods under bows, haul-off warps to anchors well to seaward, ruffle chains and long outriggers. Ninety-two vessels are sheltering in the Downs in the background

Page 40 (right) Three Brothers. Built as a cattle boat, she was still registered in 1910. Note short headstick on topsail and four lines of reef points;

(left) Pilgrim, DL 19, at Kingsdown. Built by John Bayly in 1872. Note 22 strakes of planking, stem rope through hole in forefoot, mast tabernacle, bilge keel, traveller and tye on foremast

	£	s	d
Keel 'pic' oak 27 ft, 6 in × 3¼ in		16	3¾
'Sturn' post		10	6
I knee		4	
'Sturn squair'		9	
'Aparn'		I	6
6 × 2-in long arm knees		8	4
8 × 1½ in do		6	0
'Brist' Hook		2	6
7 Frames cut out	2	I	6
2 'Bemes' 4½ × 4		9	6
Moulding 65 ft 4 × 1¾		16	3
Top strakes oak 6 × 6 in		12	2¼
'Garbard ealm' 6 × 1 in		12	2¼
50 × 15 ft oak timbers 1¼ × 7	2	7	5
448 ft Pitch 'pin' 5 × 1 in	4	13	4
448 ft do 6 × 1 in	5	12	
'Resings P. pin' 2½d gunels 'P. pin', 60 ft		12	6
Kelson 20 ft, 6 × 1 in 'ealm'		4	2
Labour up to 27 Nov 1915 14 'weekes' 2 'pund' per week	28		
Copper		10	

With sundries, the bill amounted to £64 6s 4¼d.
For another boat, his charges were:

	£	s	d
Mizzen 'tabernackle' and step, 2 oak knees, labour, wood and bolts		15	6
Fore 'tabernackle' complete		18	6
'My selph'		4	6
36 ft fir, 6 × 1 in, best 'yelow p.'		14	4
54 ft fir do		7	10
New fore mast 24 ft long, 6 in butt, galvanised sheave, capper and pin	I	2	6
New fore yard		7	6
Mizzen boom and yard		8	
Making mizzen mast		4	
Cost of copper to complete boat	12	12	11

This would be for a 'punt' rigged with fore lug and a standing mizzen lugsail.

For a boat 32 ft long, 8 ft beam, 4 ft depth, he estimated the
c

cost at £86 10s in December 1912, subject to extras as required by owner; these finally amounted to £28 13s 9d.

> To be built on same lines as model as near as possible. To be built of oak, elm and pitch pine. Planking to be one inch in thickness, other material to be suitable for size of boat. To be carvel built, to be copper fastened suitable to owner's wish, wood work the same. One coat of paint or varnish as required.
> Money to be paid as required leaving a balance of Ten pounds in hand for the satisfaction of tightness. The Boat to be taken from Workshop to Harbour at owner's expence with our help and material. This estimate is clear from all Iron & Brass work.

The scantlings for a similar boat, 30 ft long, were:

Keel	English oak,	3 in × 5 in
Stem	do	3 in × 6 in
Stern post	do	3 in × 6 in
Deadwoods	do	sided to form of boat
Timbers	do	$\frac{7}{8}$ in × $1\frac{1}{4}$ in
Rising	do	$1\frac{1}{2}$ in × 2 in
Gunwale	do	$1\frac{1}{4}$ in × 3 in

Outside planking pitch pine, $\frac{3}{4}$ in finished

Transom	English oak,	3 in × 8 in
Deck beams	Pitch pine,	2 in × 3 in

Deck of 1 in × 6 in fir, covered with canvas
Fastenings of copper nails clenched over roves, deadwoods fastened with $\frac{1}{2}$ in metal bolts.

All woodwork painted three coats, approved colour.
All seams to be caulked and stopped with putty.
Boat to be fitted with stem band, skeg band and keel band of iron.
Hawsepiece for chain cable.
Four chain plates.
The boat to be decked 12 ft from forward.

Most of the longshore boats and luggers were varnished, a style much favoured by all fishermen as showing up any defects; 'paint covered a multitude of sins'.

These scantlings were probably typical of luggers built in Kent. Few particulars seem to have survived the passing of time, hence their value. Combined with other data for sails made at Deal, a very fair idea can be obtained of these splendid sea boats. The pity is that no lines were ever taken off when the opportunity was there; any moulds were consigned to the scrap heap. The boats had to be fast and weatherly, able to face most seas, carry heavy anchors at times, and in the summer take visitors for a trip round the lightships. Later, many were built to take motors, but the sailing lugger barely survived the first world war.

Rates of pay for Brockman's men were 7d, 8½d and 9d per hour, boy 4d; by the end of the 1914–18 war the rate was 1s an hour for men.

The following items for repairs, selected from the ledgers, show how low the prices now appear:

	£	s	d
New gaft for *Moss Rose*, 30 ft 3 in	1	5	0
For coastguards, Kingsgate, pair 9-ft ash oars		12	
Copper nails, 1s 6d lb, 2½ in, 7 for 4d			
6 in, 7 for 1s 9d			
Keel, oak 14 ft 3 × 2¼ in		5	6
Mahogany backboard cut to shape		5	
7-lb galvanised anchor		3	6
Thwart pitch pine 3 ft 6 in, copper nails and labour		2	
240 ft board, 6 × ½ in	2	15	
Punt stem, 4 ft 4½ × 2¼ in oak		3	6
Oak knees, 1s 4d each; oak floors, 4½d each,			
top timbers, 3d each; 31-ft keel piece, 11s 7d.			
Fudicks, 1s each.			

For *Early Bird* 'wery' (? wherry), 16 floor timbers, 1s 4d each; 36 top timbers, 1s each; 58 ft planking elm, 6 × ½ in @ 1s a ft, £2 18s; 'carking garbard' seam, 2s; 20 ft capping, 4d per ft.

	£	s	d
Planking 52 ft 'ealm', 6 × ¾ in		19	6
2-in oak knees, 10d each			
70-ft elm 'bat bard', ¾ × 7 in	1	15	
27 ⅜-in gal dumps, 4 in long		5	7½
14 lb rope @ 9d lb; 20 lb paint 15s			
2 pair brass tack hooks, hand made		9	6
'Yelow pin' best, 36 ft 6 × 1 in		14	4
Fir do do do		7	10

And, when fitting out boats for trawling during the war:

	£	s	d
April 1915 'for traling'			
'10 fathams of white lin for led lin'		1	8
Oak 'tral' beam cut to 'linkith' 20 ft	1		
New warp 55 'fathams', 'bridels' 8 'fatham', sold as agreed	2	15	

Following the death of Mr Brockman after the second world war, the boatyard was put up for sale with his tools and gear. I went along expecting reasonably high prices would be realised as tools were in short supply, but everything went for 'old rope'; 36 planes of every type from large jack to small moulding went for £2 18s; oars for 1s each.

As the auctioneer's voice rose and his hammer fell on these lots of tools, sweat-darkened by the hands of one now gone to his rest, I thought of all the years they had helped him to earn an honest living, how his fingers had grasped the planes and chisels to form sweet curves and lovely shapes as a boat grew into life. Now they were sold for a few shillings to men out to secure a bargain, and some lots failed even to find a bidder. Rheumy-eyed old men, who in their youth had ordered boats from the yard, or had repairs done, stood silently by watching the tools passing into alien hands, never again to be used in the building of luggers which were once the pride of their owners. Men whose hands had steered their boats on many a wild night, trusting to the dead man's craftsmanship, and the use of trustworthy materials fashioned by simple tools applied so skilfully that the elementary forces of nature could be met with confidence year after year until, in many instances, generations passed. And still the work of the craftsman remained, a lasting tribute to an honesty of purpose worthy of the highest commendation.

How much times have changed was forcibly brought home to me when I read that an 8-ft dinghy, then built complete for £6, can now cost over £50. I doubt if the materials will last many years; yet many a boat I knew in boyhood was still giving ex-

cellent service fifty and more years later, and they were not
new when I first knew them.

To turn aside from humble craft to those beautiful gigs built
for the big racing cutters in the 1890s. A set of three, 'planked
without a scarph, not a knot or blemish', 27 ft long, was built
for £90 by a Scottish boatbuilder.

The Margate Roads afforded good anchorage, bottom sand
and mud, 6 to 8½ fathoms, well sheltered in southerly winds.
Many a time have I seen anything up to 100 sail waiting a slant
to go down Channel, but if the wind flew northerly it was 'up
anchor and away' before perhaps being driven on a lee shore.
Sweeping for lost anchors was a worthwhile job for the local
luggers, who also took out any stores required, a service known
in Ramsgate, Broadstairs and Margate as 'foying'.

Thanet has always been noted for the quality of its farming.
In the middle of the eighteenth century it was stated:

> Agriculture is carried on here to a degree of perfection hardly
> to be found elsewhere . . . no labour or expense is spared to keep
> the corn clean, so that (with exception only to the fields of a few
> slothful people) there is hardly a weed to be seen. . . . Common
> people are a sort of amphibious animals, who get their living both
> by sea and land, as having to do with both elements, being
> fishermen and husbandmen, and equally skilled in holding helm
> or plough, according to the season of the year. They knit nets,
> catch cods, herring, mackerel etc. go voyages, and export mer-
> chant dyes. The very same persons dung the land, plough, sow,
> reap and carry in the corn. They work hard and live hard and are
> truly industrious.

A similar standard could have been claimed for many of the
farms I knew in the years before the first world war, and without
the use of 'pesticides' the fields were clean.

Round the Foreland lay Broadstairs, a pretty little place
where herring punts took out summer visitors and caught sprats
and herring in the autumn and winter. I have in my collection
a perfect model, scale ½ in to 1 ft, of *Invicta* and impossible to
fault. An inscription underneath the base of the sea reads:

> This scaled model of our boat, the *Invicta*, (launched at Mar-

gate 22 March '83) with all the details, was made by W. W.
Banting between Saturday Oct. 20 '83 and Saturday Mar. 29. '84
from drawings and measurements taken during the month of
September '83 at Broadstairs.

This 'punt' is 19 ft overall, with a beam of 6 ft 6 in, and is
fitted out with a summer suit of sails consisting of a loose-footed
mainsail, a gaff 12 ft overall, standing lug mizzen, yard 6 ft, and
outrigger 8 ft 9 in. The mainmast is 22 ft 9 in in height, mizzen
mast 11 ft 9 in, and bowsprit 12 ft (6 ft 9 in outboard). Other
gear includes a wire forestay, staysail and large jib, 'spitfire'
and spinnaker, or balloon jib.

In the winter, the rig was the normal fore and mizzen lug,
foremast 16 ft 3 in, mizzen 10 ft 6 in, foreyard 11 ft, mizzen
yard 6 ft 3 in, outrigger 9 ft 10 in.

Every tiny item is beautifully made, including brass rowlocks, fenders, anchor, oars 12 ft with blade 4 ft by 6 in wide,
leathered and coppered, a tiny binnacle with sliding doors, a
fish box, and in a drawer under a thwart are two spare hoops
for the summer mainsail. The brass tiller, 4 ft 9 in long, has a
half circle kink to port to clear the mizzen mast, a boat hook
8 ft long, perfect blocks including sister hooks, in fact a complete outfit.

Never have I seen better-made sails. The standard of all
Banting's work can be judged by his sewing the boltropes to the
edges of the sails through every 'contline'—strand. Cringles are
turned in properly, lines of reef points are correct. There is a
wonderful trawl with a beam 10 ft 9 in long fitted with iron
heads, the net, 18 ft long, even has a few fish in the cod end, and
the ground rope is served with old rope for additional protection. Each rope is correctly stranded.

The hull is clinker-built, every plank fastened with tiny
copper nails over rooves, floors, frames, bottom boards and
mahogany backboard with the name INVICTA in gold. Below
the waterline and up to the level of the bottom boards is black,
and all planking etc is bright varnished—a wonderful replica of
the original boat.

With the North Sand Head of the Goodwins lying only five miles to seaward, luggers manned by Broadstairs boatmen cruised in the vicinity in bad weather, as did the men from Ramsgate and Deal, rescuing many a shipwrecked crew or picking up a salvage job. The Knock Sand, about 18½ miles from the North Foreland, and the Galloper some 30 miles distant, were more the cruising ground for Margate and Essex salvagers.

Frequently, during hard sw gales, vessels unable to make the Downs were forced to anchor in exposed places, and at times were in sore need of assistance. Then was the chance to put a local man on board to pilot a ship into Dover or Ramsgate harbour, or to run up the coast to a more sheltered anchorage.

Even on a bright sunny day the breakers, clearly seen from the cliffs, rise and fall like contending fighters, awe-inspiring to watch. How much more terrifying to be among them in the blackness of a winter night. The sight of a ship ashore, or rockets bursting in the sky, sent men hurrying to the shore to get the luggers afloat. On reaching the sands, perhaps they would find a brig almost high and dry, but there was a chance that she might be kedged off as the flood tide made. Her crew would rig tackles from the foreyard, hook into one of the bower anchors and slew it aft, then shift tackles to the mainyard and repeat the process, finally getting the anchor over the stern into the waiting lugger with the cable clear for running out. The frail boat then took the anchor as far out as possible and dropped it overboard, using a tackle from the foremast, returned and put every man available on board to help man the windlass. Every time the brig lifted they would heave-in, and with luck she might come off. But if she had already made a bed for herself in the sands, then she would probably pound to pieces if the wind increased.

Or, a tug might come up; then the towrope would be taken into broken water by the lugger. These were ordinary jobs, undertaken without great risk, but how different were the many other services rendered by the luggers to vessels in distress.

After a lifeboat was stationed at Broadstairs it was often a race between her and the luggers to be first at a wreck. In a beat to wind'ard against a hard gale and tide, the lugger forged ahead better than the lifeboat, being well ballasted and in good sailing trim. Not so the lifeboat; she had to have buoyancy and as little ballast as possible, but in broken water over the sands the advantage lay with her. Seas taken in went out through the freeing valves, whereas the crew of a lugger had to bale furiously to keep afloat.

In the 1880s the schooner *Mizpah* stranded in thick fog, the crew took to their small boat and were picked up in the Gull Stream by the Ramsgate tug *Aid* with the lifeboat in tow. The men could give no idea of the position of the wreck, which had refloated at high water, but she was found by a Broadstairs lugger, and men were put on board to take her into Ramsgate harbour. Vessel and cargo were valued at between £6,000 and £7,000; the salvage award was £350.

Payments of anything up to £50 and more were frequently obtained for a few hours work piloting ships into safety, more if anchors had been lost when riding out a blow in the Downs. Ramsgate and Deal men shared in this work. In 1827 a southerly gale forced a schooner to slip; she was taken into Ramsgate for £65, a sloop into Broadstairs for £25.

Ramsgate, with its fine harbour of refuge, had a big fleet of deep-sea smacks, but here, as elsewhere, the owners of luggers rendered sterling aid, taking out anchors and cables brought down the piers in horse-drawn waggons to be hoisted by crane into the lugger plunging and pitching alongside—a nightmare job with its ever present risk of the swinging weight taking charge, crashing through the bottom of the boat and crushing the men waiting to receive it.

The first lifeboat, *Northumberland*, saved 261 lives between December 1851 and July 1865, when the *Bradford* took her place. She had the invaluable help of a tug, either the *Vulcan* or the *Aid*, always standing by with steam up ready to tow the lifeboat to the scene of a wreck.

What splendid men formed the crew, 150 or more volunteers, the first ten into the boat manning her, with the 1st and 2nd coxswains, twelve in all. In ten years Coxswain Jarman was out 132 times, saving nearly 400 lives; once five times in a week, on another nine times in a fortnight. His successor, Charlie Fish, slept in a hammock in the watch house at the end of the pier, ready to turn out the instant rockets were seen on the Goodwins. Police and coastguards called the crew. In 26 years he was out 353 times, saving 877 lives. His 'finest hour' was 5 and 6 January 1881, when the ship *Indian Chief* was wrecked on the Long Sand. The lifeboat was towed out in the teeth of a freezing NE gale, but on arrival at dusk no trace could be seen of any wreck. The crew decided to lay-to all night, seeking what shelter they could in the bottom of the lifeboat. At daybreak, a mast was sighted about three miles distant, with men lashed in the rigging. The tow was slipped, sail made and the lifeboat, going to windward of the wreck, dropped anchor and veered out cable until under the stern amidst a mass of wreckage; eleven survivors of that terrible night were saved.

Ten years later a call at 3 am saw the lifeboat manned in eight minutes on a pitch-black night, blowing great guns and everything sheeted in ice. The spray froze on the faces of the men as they towed towards the dreaded sands where a barquentine was ashore. Within an ace of getting alongside a huge sea crashed inboard, filling the boat to the thwarts; the bar-tight hawser snapped and the lifeboat was swept away to leeward. Sail was instantly set, but it required ten men on the foresheet before the lug was sheeted home. On reaching the waiting tug the tow rope was taken and the pluck to windward began. Alongside the wreck at last, the lifeboat's crew set about the rescue of the frozen hands in the rigging, lashed by flogging strips of torn sails. All but the captain managed to reach the lee side where the lifeboat was surging beneath the menace of whipping masts and the threat of falling spars. No sooner were the men landed at Ramsgate than a second call came. Without waiting for any warm food the lifeboatmen set out once more to the aid of a boat drifting off the North Foreland with the crew from a sunken collier.

Generally, a salvage award to a lugger was divided into 14 shares; the boat had 3½ shares for the owners, half a share went for provisions supplied by the owners, and one share to each man.

Deal boatmen seldom went fishing and their exploits are given in the next chapter. At times, when huge shoals of sprats appeared off the town, big catches were made, but the financial return was small. In 1879 over 55 tons were sent by rail one Sunday in November, followed by 41 tons on the Thursday; 26 boxes, each containing 1,200 sprats, realised only £3 3s 6d. The cost of carriage was £1 14s 8d, leaving the miserable sum of £1 8s 10d for the men of that particular boat.

Deal men lived dangerous lives. Between 1860 and 1887, 53 boatmen were drowned—26 from luggers, 23 from galley punts —their average age being 31.

At Kingsdown, fishing was on a more extensive scale; in ten days' mackerel fishing in October 1865 over £1,000 was taken, giving a share of some £30 per man. Sharks came right into the Downs after the shoals, but two luggers netted 7,400 fish on Sunday, 13,000 the following day, then 5,800 and 6,000 as the mackerel moved away. Two years later catches worth £80 to £100 a night were made, but in October 1874, while fishing off the sw Goodwin buoy, the lugger *Wild Girl* lost 17 nets which were so heavy with fish that they sank before the men were able to haul them in. Another risk was from passing traffic. A month earlier *Victoria* lost 54 nets, value £110, which were cut by a passing German steamer. In September 1882 the lugger *Pilgrim* lost £100 worth of nets after a heavy haul of mackerel; the ropes broke under the strain, the nets became entangled with the South Sands lightvessel and were lost.

This lugger had been built by J. Bayly at a cost of £400 for mackerel fishing, and launched on 27 August 1872. Four years later she received an award of £450 for putting two anchors and cables on to a Nova Scotian brigantine. (Picture, p 40.)

The forepeak lugger *Lady Rosa*, launched 23 June 1874, was built by Henry Gardner of North Deal. Masts and spars were by E. Bristow, sails and rigging by P. Finnis & Co, and iron-work by Thomas Marsh. Her length was 38 ft 6 in, breadth 12 ft 6 in, depth 6 ft 8 in, and registered tonnage 22. Ten years later she took first prize at the regatta, with *Renown* second and *Pilgrim* third.

When a similar-sized lugger, *Mary*, built by Isaac Hayward, was launched on 8 October 1868, it was stated that she made the fifteenth lugger on Kingsdown beach, and there were no galley punts. The following year the newly built *Staunch* was swamped and sunk getting clear of Admiralty Pier, Dover, and two men drowned; not a happy augury for the new type. On 22 January 1873, the emigrant ship *Northfleet*, while riding at anchor in Dungeness Roads, was run down by a large steamer which proceeded on her way. Panic broke out on board, the night was pitch black and only two boats got away in the fight to get aboard. *Mary* was anchored off Dungeness, and her master, George Pout, saw the distress rockets, hove up and bore down to the rescue, narrowly missing one of the lifeboats, deep laden with 34 people and sinking, no one had thought of putting in the plug. After taking all on board the lugger went on, but found nothing. *Northfleet* had sunk with the loss of 327 lives. Later, the Spanish *Murillo* was identified as the guilty steamship.

Deal, Walmer and Kingsdown lifeboats had no tug to tow them to sea; every trip was made under sail, often in appalling conditions, yet the boatmen never flinched from their voluntary work. Certainly it was not the pay that induced them to risk their lives for those in peril on the sea, the most they received was 10s by day and £1 by night. The 40 or so helpers engaged in launching and hauling up the lifeboat received £3 between them.

At Dover a few galley punts, galleys and punts lay on the steep shingle beach in the harbour. A small fleet of cutters and ketches went trawling on the adjacent grounds, but fishing was not a thriving occupation.

The foresail and mizzen punt *Argonaut*, DR 56, built by Nicholas at North Deal *c* 1880, was still working in 1937 when her lines were taken off by the late P. J. Oke. She was used for lobster and crab fishing in St Margaret's Bay, and for spratting during the season.

The hull, 14 ft 6¾ in overall, beam 5 ft, depth 2 ft 2½ in, was built of elm, cut locally, 13 strakes of planking with ash frames. Inside were three thwarts and side seats extending from the second thwart to the seat at the stern, with three pairs of thole pins each side. Floors had a slight rise amidships, a wide transom and stern sheets on which the helmsman stood, holding a 2 ft 6 in straight tiller.

The foremast, 15 ft long, diameter 3¼ in to 2 in, was stepped in a chock on the floors and secured by an iron collar on the aft

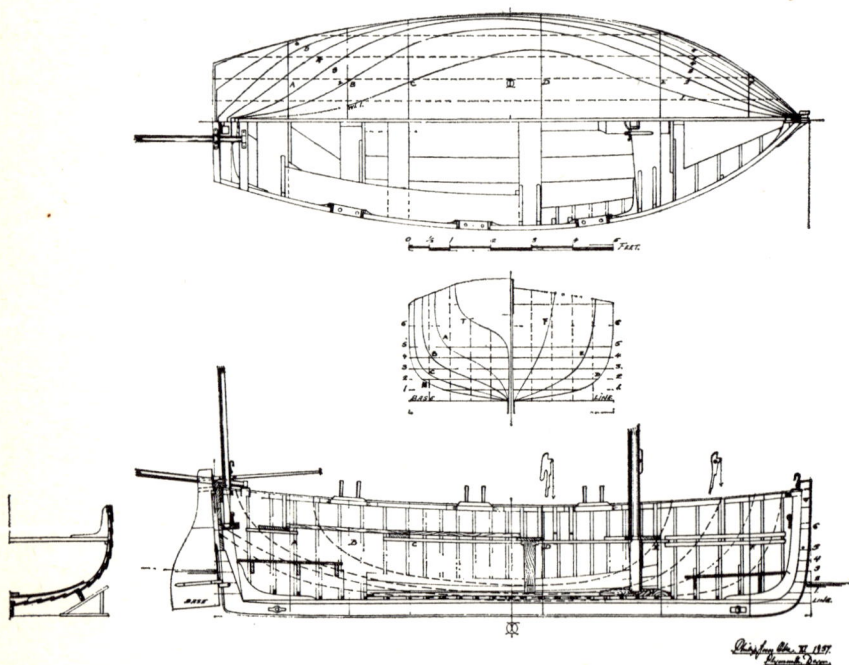

Plans of Dover punt *Argonaut*, DR 56, built at Deal *c* 1880

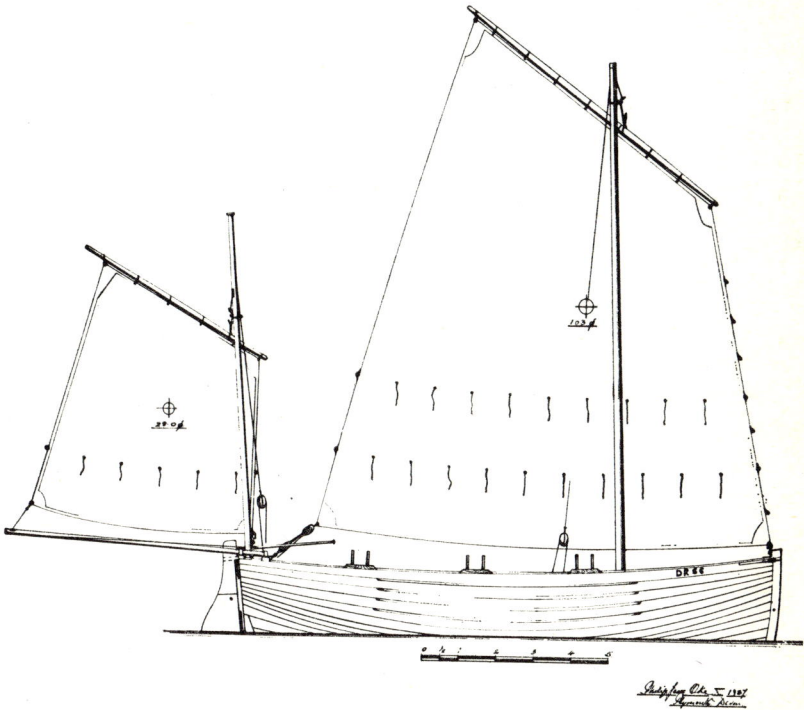

Sail plan of *Argonaut*

side of foremost thwart. On it was set a dipping lug, its head
bent to an 8 ft 4 in yard, with two lines of reef points and seven
cringles on the 'weather'—luff. The tack went to a hook on the
inside of the stemhead; the sheet, two single-block purchases,
hooked right aft; the halyard, with a whip purchase, was
always set up to windward.

The mizzen mast, 9 ft $10\frac{1}{2}$ in long, diameter $2\frac{1}{4}$ in to $1\frac{3}{4}$ in,
was stepped to starboard of the tiller and raked slightly aft.
The standing lug had a yard 5 ft 8 in long, and one line of reef
points. The tack went to a hook at the foot of the mast, the
sheet to the end of a boom 7 ft 1 in long, with its heel through
an iron collar on the transom and another on a 2-in sq beam
across the quarters.

At Folkestone there was quite a sizeable fleet of luggers, many built in Cornwall with the wide transom sterns typical of boats built east of the Lizard. The normal sail plan was a dipping forelug, standing mizzen lug set on a mast raking well for'ard and sheeting to a long steeved-up outrigger, and a small jib on a reeving bowsprit. Boats built at Rye and Hastings had heavier hulls and were similar to those seen in the Sussex ports.

Dogfish and sharks played havoc with the Folkestone fishermen's nets when mackerel were about. In October 1867 Mr Ledger had a 'fox shark', 13 ft 6 in long and weighing 3 cwt 3 qrs, tangled up in his nets; when cut open 27 mackerel were found in the shark's stomach. Another lugger had one 14 ft 10 in long with 19 mackerel and two herrings inside. The piked or common dogfish were abundant and their flesh was known locally as 'Folkestone beef'. Another huge fish caught in a net was a conger eel, 6 ft 4 in long and weighing 50 lb.

Folkestone harbour being tidal, the luggers were kept upright by legs, secured to the sides by long bolts and nuts. Sales of fish were mostly local, Folkestone being a popular and fashionable watering-place; and down to recent times the lofty, tarred sheds were a picturesque if perhaps somewhat smelly feature of the harbour. (Picture, p 37.)

CHAPTER TWO

DEAL BOATS AND BOATMEN

ETWEEN the Forelands, facing east and the dreaded
Goodwin Sands, lies Deal, in the days of which I write a
town literally by and on the sea, for many of the quaint
red brick houses, tarred wooden sheds, sail-lofts and the hetero-
genous collection of buildings always found in a seaport had
their walls washed by the tide at high water. During on-shore
gales the sea seeped through the shingle bank on which they
were built, under the foundations and out into the low-lying
ground beyond. On the beach lay the famous luggers, galleys
and punts owned by the fearless boatmen who earned a living
by pilotage and attending on the needs of shipping passing
through or anchored in the Downs, the roads sheltered by the
treacherous sands which gave such rich opportunities of salvage
from the numerous wrecks.

And what an anchorage! From seaward could be seen the
long, low ridges of houses marking Deal, Walmer and Kingsdown, backed by green meadows and cornfields, church towers
and spires, lines of elm trees, and occasional windmills. To the
south the magnificent sweep up to the white chalk cliffs leading
to St Margaret's Bay and the South Foreland lighthouse; to the
north the ancient town of Sandwich—that Cinque port steeped
in medieval history. Then the rising ground of Thanet, the
town of Ramsgate with its harbour of refuge, the dazzling white
cliffs of Broadstairs and the North Foreland lighthouse. A
pleasant vista to greet the eyes of a homeward-bounder, tired
from long gazing at the ridges and furrows of the oceans of the
world, and one to be remembered with nostalgia by a man outward bound, leaving his homeland perhaps for ever.

Extending for a distance of almost nine miles and parallel to the coast lie the Goodwins, the grave of countless ships. Those treacherous sands have swallowed Phoenician trading vessels, Roman galleys, Viking longships, Norman boats—the list is far too lengthy to enumerate, and still today they claim their toll of steam and motor ships, even when equipped with the latest scientific devices for navigation, radar and echo-sounders. How much more were these sands to be feared in the days of sail, when a skipper might be long without a sight of sun or star, driven by the full force of a gale, or wrapped in dense, dripping fog while his ship was hurried along, helpless in the swift-running tides.

Here indeed is a meeting of the waters where the south-coming tide from the North Sea encounters that swirling up from the Channel through the narrow Straits of Dover. Knowledge of those streams and how best they could be used was innate in the local boatmen whose superb seamanship was acknowledged by every mariner, even if he did not always see eye to eye with the demands made for the use of such services. Between the main banks run swatchways whose depth and position alter frequently; in some places the sands dry out hard and firm around low water, but become 'quick' as the flood tide seeps through the fine, hard grains. This peculiarity invariably means that if a vessel is not refloated promptly she will sink in deeper and deeper. In other areas the sand remains hard and a sunken vessel becomes a menace to lugger and lifeboat. Everywhere the sands are covered at high water by 10 to 25 ft of water. The eastern side is steep-to with depths of 12 to 16 fathoms almost alongside, so that the lead gives no immediate indication of the nearness of danger. Many a vessel was saved from disaster by the vigilance of boatmen cruising around the sands, when their warning shouts caused a hurried alteration of course. For such services no payment was expected or received.

Between the Goodwins and the shore passed an endless line of shipping, the Gull Stream to the nor'ard being the great

Page 57 (*above*) Port Arms station, 1866. *Sappho* and another lugger are seen on their stages. Note four-oared galley, capstan, top of post cut at an angle instead of square as at North End, chain through ruffle, pumps, fore-peakers and great galleys in background; (*below*) the lugger *Pride of the Sea* on her stage at Walmer. Note mast tabernacle with curved timbers, bilge keel, pump and stove funnel from forepeak

Page 58 (*above*) Great galley, also called galley punt, beaching—'knocking up'. Rudder has been unshipped, the mainsheet has a two-single-block purchase and the bow painter has been flung ashore; (*below*) North End station after the great gale of 29 November 1897. The 18-strake lugger has been hauled up as close as possible to her capstan. Note ropes around the sheds to hold them in position

Page 59 (*above*) *Pride of the Sea* wrecked off Shanklin, 30 October 1887. The lugger had then been 20 days at sea, boarding only one pilot, Tom Adams, off St Alban's Head;

(*centre*) lugger *Annie*, DL 14, 1897. Note very rare counter stern, bowsprit lashed to foremast, mizzen staysail and jib on traveller, small mizzen. A topsail can be set on the long pole mast;

(*below*) another view of North End station after the great gale. In the background is *Tiger*, once the biggest lugger on the beach, now smack-rigged and counter stern added. Note great galley with mast stepped amidships, fore and mizzen punt, and differences in capstans

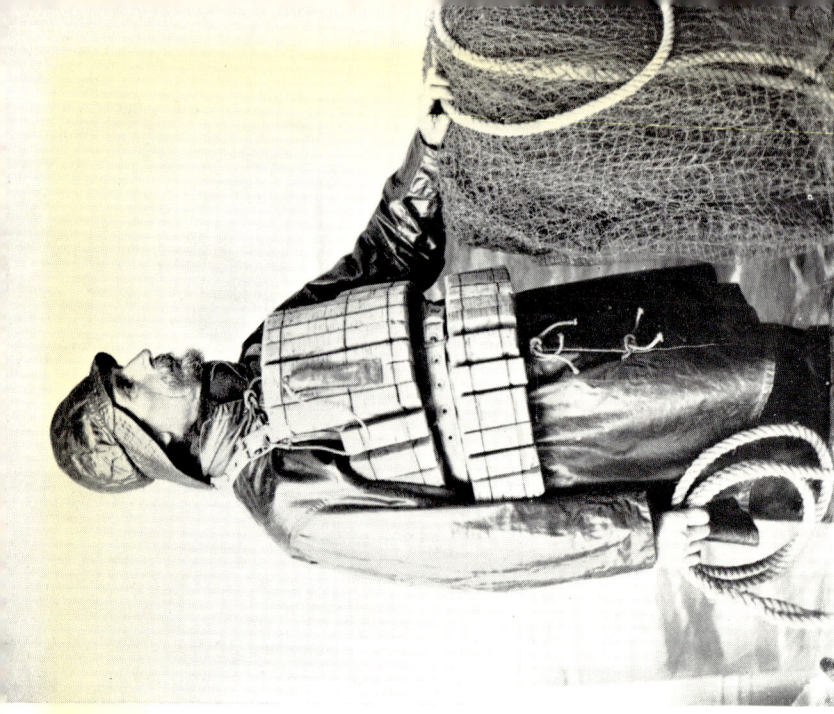

Page 60 (left) Cosmopolite, the last big lugger on the beach, on her stage at Walmer. In December 1909 she was presented to Deal council as a memorial to the famous Deal luggers, by 1916 her timbers were getting beyond repair and in 1925 she was sold by tender for £2 10s; *(right)* Richard Roberts, coxswain of the lifeboat *Mary Somerville*. Note comforter wound round neck, rope lashings to oilskin, cork lifebelts and whistle highway between the Thames Estuary and the Channel. The famed anchorage of the Downs lay between Sandown Castle to the north and Walmer Castle to the south, with depths of from 8 to 10 fathoms; the bottom was mostly chalk, not always affording the best of holding grounds. Here could lie the fleets of the world, sheltered by the mainland from sou'westerly gales, with the Goodwins giving partial protection in easterly winds. Often 400 to 500 sail of ships would be anchored awaiting a favourable slant, and supplying them with fresh provisions, stores and gear brought prosperity to boatmen, tradesmen and others. To the NE of Deal lie the Small Downs where coasters and vessels drawing up to 16 ft found excellent shelter. The bottom was blue clay; in it an anchor would hold firm to the day of judgment, unless the cable parted or the hawsepipes split with the wild plunging of a storm-tossed vessel. The water was shoal, four to five fathoms, and there was less likelihood of being fouled by big ships dragging their anchors.

Although the Downs gave good shelter in certain winds, it provided an uneasy anchorage in others, and when it blew hard from SE, E by N, or ENE, vessels frequently had to slip their cables and run for shelter elsewhere. In westerly breezes the Downs would be crowded with ships which had either dropped down from the London river with a fair wind but had to await a slant before going down Channel, or had run in for shelter. When the wind went easterly it was a wonderfully animated scene as the huge fleet of vessels of every rig and nationality began to weigh anchor. Anyone left ashore hastily made for the beach to hire a boat and be put aboard his ship before she sailed. From seaward came the sound of the clink of the pawls as the capstans slowly turned, manned by sailors stamping out a rousing shanty, the thunder of canvas as topsails were loosed, to fall silent when sheeted home, the squeak of blocks as upper sails and jibs were hoisted, and the slap and gurgle of the tide along a hundred hulls and more. Quick decisions were vital when so many were on the move together, yet serious collisions were rare. Coming in would be the homeward-bounders,

D

rapidly taking in sail preparatory to anchoring, because this change was a foul wind for ships proceeding to many northern and Continental ports. Problem enough in daylight, but a nightmare during the hours of darkness. No skipper worth his salt would hesitate to make full use of every minute of a fair wind for which he might have been waiting for weeks.

Due to its proximity to the Continent, south-east Kent had always been an important place for the arrival and departure of travellers. Julius Caesar landed near Deal and his lack of knowledge of the complex tides brought disaster to many of his galleys. It is interesting to speculate if here is the origin of the name 'galley' given to certain south coast boats.

The Downs was an assembly place for the numerous fleets engaged in the French wars of Plantagenet days, the Cinque ports, with their obligation to provide ships and men for the king, lying close handy. Sandwich was then a thriving port but it began to decline when the river Stour silted up after a wreck had blocked the fairway and defied all efforts at removal; the burghers even tried to cut a by-pass round it. This mishap contributed in no small part to the rise of Deal.

The importance of this splendid anchorage grew as ships increased in size, and Henry VIII, with his zeal for the navy and the safety of his realm, ordered the building of three castles at Sandown, Deal and Walmer. Hundreds of men were employed in these defence works, which were completed in 1540. Until that date the foreshore was a lonely, desolate bank of shingle, separated from the gently sloping mainland by a wide deep valley. The little town of Deal lay about half a mile inland, clustered round the church. Here lived a seafaring population, and as trade improved following the decline of Sandwich it was found very inconvenient to carry goods down to the sea for transhipment to shipping anchored offshore; pilots and seamen also required easier access. Covetous eyes were cast on the shingle bed, which was claimed to belong to the Archbishop of Canterbury, and certain tradesmen erected store sheds, probably without permission.

The castle officers claimed that the buildings interfered with the clear field of fire of their guns, the tenants of the manors that they obstructed their right of access to the shore, and, of course, rent was immediately claimed, even though the shingle was waste on which nothing had ever grown. Petitions and counter petitions were signed and argued over, the lawyers hummed and hawed and the years passed. Appeals were made to influential officers of state, stressing the value of the services now rendered to the navy by the boatmen. Finally, during the reign of Charles I, a naval yard was established on the shingle and a spate of building followed until there was a line of warehouses, offices and store sheds so close to the sea that at spring tides the walls were washed by the waves. The tenants of the archbishop were unable to obtain leases longer than seven years, a state of affairs which prevailed until 1857 when a few men were able to buy their holdings, at just about the time when the importance of Deal was declining.

Deal men had acted as pilots for centuries. In 1242 Henricus de Dele piloted the ship of Charles, son of William, when Henry III invaded France. In 1517 there was trouble about unlawful possession of anchors and the unauthorised exercise of the craft of lodemanship, in other words acting as pilots although not licensed. Returns in 1586 shows 43 vessels belonging to Sandwich, six to Deal and five to Walmer. The owner of one boat of 2 tons, the *Mary*, was Thomas Nicholas. In 1593 another boat, part owner George Rand, helped to refloat a ship ashore on South Sand Head. Payment for such services does not appear to have been in money, but by 'devysion between merchants and them', a practice wide open to abuse, especially when goods concealed by boatmen were stated by them to have been given in settlement of claims.

Medieval ships were unwieldy and anchors frequently had to be slipped, to lie partly embedded for years and ever liable to foul the moorings of vessels anchoring in their vicinity. About the time of the Spanish Armada the boatmen began to sweep for lost anchors which, on recovery, were brought ashore and sold. In 1607 two boatmen, Hudson and Rand, sent a petition to the Lords of the Privy Council asking 'for a small pencyon of £30 yearlie during their lyves' in return for which they would, at their own expense, sweep for lost anchors and cables. This suggestion was approved and the Lord Warden issued certificates of the number recovered. Between 1599 and 1613 this salvage was valued at £1,100. At times, queer objects were swept up, including guns of ancient lineage, but probably the most extraordinary catch comprised the wheels, axles and parts of a phaeton, brought to the surface in 1794.

Deal men have always been of an independent nature. As far back as 1625 it was alleged 'thay change masters when thay plesse', and among the names were Nicholas, Denne and Marsh, descendants of whom were on the beach to the last days of luggers and galleys. Pilots refused to serve in Cromwell's warships, saying the pay was too low; the 30s given to pilot a man-of-war to the Thames was less than the coach fare back to Deal. They could not be pressed, as pilots were exempt from the press gang.

The type of boat then in use is known from an entry in 1674. One was built by a local boatbuilder for £17 10s, very fine and strong, 25 ft long, and of 6 ft 6 in beam. Their number was such that 80 to 100 sailed out to greet King Charles II when he came round the Foreland on 27 June 1675.

Ashore, trade had flourished to such an extent that a charter was obtained at a cost of £337 0s 3½d, authorising a local market; previously everything had had to be purchased at Sandwich, 5 miles away. The urgent need of the market was evident. Three hundred to 400 ships were often at anchor, waiting perhaps a month or more for a fair wind. If they consumed their sea stores it was likely they would be short of food later in the voyage. By day or night, in all weathers, the boatmen were prepared to launch their boats deep laden with stores off that open beach. Pepys mentions this in his diary under date 11 May 1660, when aboard *Naseby*. 'It blew very hard all this night. About eleven at night came the boats from

Deal with great stores of provisions.' Another source of income
was the supplying of beach for ballast, 3d a ton being charged
to Englishmen, 8d to foreigners.

The Downs were now one of the chief stations of the Royal
Navy. Captains of war and merchant ships generally preferred
to make use of Deal boats rather than their own, whose crews
were likely to desert if given half a chance.

In November 1703 a furious gale blew for a fortnight and a
fleet commanded by Sir Cloudesley Shovel rode it out in the
Downs. When the wind took off he sailed for the Thames, but it
came on to blow harder than ever the next day and 160 sail of
ships were soon in dire distress. No canvas would hold, masts
had to be cut away, and several first and second rates were
blown out to sea, including the flagship of Rear-Admiral
Beaumont, which sank after striking the sands. Only one survivor was rescued by a Deal boat the following day. Of all that
brave fleet only 70 rode out the gale, but many were sheer
hulks. The mayor of Deal offered 5s a head for any man saved
and at his instigation the boatmen seized the Custom House
boats after the officers had refused to give any assistance, although men could be seen running about on the Goodwins.
About 200 were rescued, but when the tide rose the remainder
were drowned. The Queen's Agent refusing to accept responsibility, the unfortunate mayor found himself liable for the
maintenance of the survivors and the burial of those who died
from exposure. Finally, he had to pay the coach fares to London
and it was years before he could get any repayment. Yet in face
of this selflessness and the heroism of the boatmen who faced
death to try and rescue strangers, Defoe thought fit to write a
scathing denunciation of the behaviour of all concerned. So
foul was this writing that the Corporation sued for libel.

During the eighteenth century smuggling was rife and an in-
quiry in 1737 revealed that some 200 open boats were running
brandy between the Forelands; wool was smuggled to the Continent. Later, the Government decided to take severe measures
to suppress smuggling. In January 1784 most of the luggers

were hauled up on the beach owing to a long spell of bad weather. An informer drew Pitt's attention to this easy opportunity of destroying the boats and he ordered a regiment to be sent to Deal. Naval cutters lay offshore to prevent any escape to sea, and the soldiers smashed every boat to pieces or destroyed them by fire, leaving the boatmen without any means of earning a living. But years later, when their services were needed in time of war, they seem to have borne no grudge against the authorities.

The charge for landing or boarding a passenger was 7s 6d; in bad weather up to one and a half guineas. The Collector of Customs received £100 a year, the surveyor £60 with ten boatmen; the 'sitter'—a coxswain—of the extra boat had £60 with six boatmen and 13 tidesmen. The 'sitter' of the boat was paid £40 with seven boatmen at £30 a year each.

The outbreak of the French wars brought immediate prosperity to Deal. The town was crowded with troops awaiting embarkation, provisions had to be supplied to the Navy and to the huge fleets of merchantmen waiting for convoy. These provided a temptation to French privateers who were bold enough to board them at anchor, but sometimes the local boatmen recaptured these prizes. A noteworthy case was the boarding of a sloop loaded with 651 barrels of gunpowder for Portsmouth dockyard, a valuable prize to the enemy. Fourteen boatmen saw the incident which took place after dark in February 1793; they launched two boats, rowed alongside and, although unarmed, boarded and recaptured the vessel.

Many and varied were the services rendered. Thousands of pounds worth of specie were brought ashore at considerable risk from ships wrecked on the Goodwins, or landed from HM ships. Tens of thousands of troops were embarked on transports anchored in the Downs, and almost an equal number of sick and wounded landed. The celerity of these operations was astonishing. In 1799 a huge camp was formed on Barham Downs, some miles away on the Canterbury road. The Government offered five guineas a boat load, but the patriotic boatmen

refused it and gave their services for nothing. On 24 August
some 6,000 men of the 1st Division were embarked; a fortnight
later the 3rd Division arrived. Two brigades, 3,300 men,
reached the beach at 5 am and all were on board the transports
by 9 am. The wind was blowing dead on shore with very heavy
surf, but there were no accidents. On 8 September more than
5,000 were taken out, watched by the Duke of Portland and
Lord Cavan from the balcony of the 'Three Kings'. The Duke of
York and William Pitt were at another viewpoint. Having seen
all the men safely on board despite the heavy sea that was running, the Duke of York was put aboard the frigate *Amethyst* and
the fleet sailed for the Texel. Two days later another 2,300 men
were launched in open boats off the beach; the next day 2,565.
Unfortunately the expedition was a complete failure, and in
November the boatmen volunteered to go across to Texel to re-
embark the remnants of this disastrous venture into the Low
Countries. During the preceding two months thousands of sick
and wounded had been landed at Deal.

Throughout all the years of war the boatmen gave their
services, but it is as well to remember that they were free from
the attentions of the press gang. This was an immense privilege
as they were all prime seamen, valuable to the Navy.

During the summer of 1801 Nelson had his headquarters in
the Downs and he frequently came ashore to take his meals at
the 'Three Kings', where Sir William and Lady Hamilton
lodged for three weeks. A Deal smuggler named Yawkins
gained Nelson's attention by volunteering to navigate ships to
bombard French ports and he became choice pilot to the
admiral.

In September 1803 William Pitt reviewed a fleet of 35 large
luggers, armed with 12- or 18-pounders, useful craft to work
into shoal water off the enemy coast. The local boatbuilders
turned out large numbers of flat-bottomed craft as well as their
usual boats. The saddest day was on 16 December 1805 when
Victory rounded the South Foreland with the body of Lord
Nelson on board and lay in the Downs until the 19th.

The year 1807 was a wild one; on 13 January an extraordinary high tide washed over 50 boats off the beach or
smashed them to pieces. The following month a violent NNE
gale blew up suddenly, vessels parted from their anchors and
drove to leeward, 13 coming ashore between Deal Castle and
St Margaret's Bay; in all 23 ships were lost between the Forelands. In September the sea broke through and flooded all the
valley behind the shingle bank, and boatmen rowed far inland
to rescue people marooned in their homes.

The miserable awards given to men who had risked their all
led to such dissatisfaction that in October 1808 the boatmen
refused to put off to ships in distress. An emergency meeting of
the Commissioners was hastily summoned and they agreed to
give certain redress.

Another wonderful feat of embarkation took place on 16 July
1809, when two battalions of the 4th Regiment were put aboard
transports within half an hour. About 100 luggers were employed, each taking some 50 soldiers. Between 700 and 800 ships
lay in the Downs, including over 400 transports. The last vessel
sailed on the 30th and a vast number of craft from all round the
coast as far as Whitstable accompanied the fleet to assist in
landing the troops on Walcheren on what proved to be yet
another disastrous expedition.

The victory at Waterloo brought an end to the Napoleonic
wars and also to the prosperity of Deal. No longer were vast
fleets anchored in the Downs, trade now depended on ships
engaged on less remunerative work and money was tight.
Houses once eagerly sought after by the wives and families of
officers in the Army and Navy were now a drug on the market.
Ruin faced many who had not been prudent during the days of
plenty. Men increasingly turned to smuggling for a living, but
the end of hostilities released naval cutters and crews for preventive duties.

During the long years of war the Government had been apt to
turn a blind eye towards the smugglers, who had an intimate
knowledge of French ports and waters and frequently brought

home valuable information. While in residence at Walmer Castle, Pitt received from a smuggler the first news of the naval victory of Camperdown. Illicit cargoes had often been openly landed on the beach and no action taken.

Special boats, 70 to 80 ft long were built, manned by dozens of hefty young boatmen who thought nothing of rowing across the Channel and returning laden with contraband. In calm weather such craft easily out-manoeuvred the heavy Revenue cutters. Smaller boats from 50 to 60 ft long pulled 10 oars a side. From time to time the Customs people woke up and harried the smugglers, and in 1812 the Government ordered the seizure of all galleys over a certain length. Some prisoners-of-war had escaped in them, paying up to £60 for the passage across, and the continuous running of guineas was causing a drain on the country's gold reserve. The French paid 25s each for these coins. Seventeen galleys were confiscated at Deal, beautiful boats, about 40 ft long, lightly constructed and capable of being rowed over to the French coast in two hours, to quote a contemporary account.

In February 1805 the Revenue cutters *Tartar* and *Lively*, cruising off Dungeness, sighted a large lugger *Diana* making for the shore. On board were found 665 casks of brandy, 118 of rum, 237 of Geneva, several casks of wine, 119 bags of tobacco and 43 bags of tea. Soon after the capture the Customs officers were attacked by armed men and called on the Lancashire Militia, then in Deal barracks, for assistance. In the melee one smuggler was shot and the rest driven off. Nine years later two of the ringleaders were taken, tried and found 'Not Guilty'.

There must have been a lucrative market for such contraband, and considerable financial resources, far beyond the means of boatmen, available for the purchase of such goods abroad.

On another occasion a post-chaise was seized on the Dover Road and found to have 14,000 yd of French lace and 246 pairs of gloves inside, but the boot was on the other foot when another chaise with £10,000 in sovereigns and bullion was stopped and taken triumphantly to the Custom House, the expectation being that it was gold about to be run across to France. To their chagrin, the officers soon discovered that it was consigned to a perfectly respectable banker.

In 1816 the Coast Blockade was established, three frigates being on duty in the Downs, and their fire-eating commander, Capt McCullock, swore that he would make the grass grow in the streets of Deal. Every local boat was watched and followed; immediately one landed, armed men swarmed around to search boat and crew. Soon it was war to the knife. All kinds of cunning ruses and devices were introduced, false keels, hollow masts and spars lined with tin to hold brandy, containers shaped like stones were mixed up in the ballast and ingenious methods adopted to get rid of incriminating kegs the moment trouble was sighted, in the hope that the valuable contents could be recovered later.

Tea and silk goods were frequently taken off Indiamen passing through the Downs, and there was no lack of purchasers when a successful landing was made. One profitable seizure by the Customs realised £1,700 at auction, yielding £150 to each of the boat crews engaged. Such hauls made the preventive men keener than ever to catch the smugglers.

Bonds of up to £250 had to be given before a lugger was allowed to leave the beach, and was forfeited if she was caught more than a few miles out, or found with any dutiable article on board. Fierce fighting at times resulted in blood being shed, men from both sides being killed. Even then few Deal men went fishing, but at Kingsdown it became an increasingly profitable venture.

Efforts were being made to attract visitors and make Deal a popular watering place; and in 1826 the first of the regattas was held; it was to become an annual event for over 60 years and was revived recently.

Every year saw disasters at sea and once again dissatisfaction arose because of the very low awards given by the Salvage Commissioners. In 1831 a deputation of boatmen decided to call on this body and tell the members exactly what they thought of them. One pilot in forceful language told the astonished gentlemen that they were unfit for their job, ignoramuses who knew not the difference between a buoy rope and a cable. One was a farmer, and another a vicar who confessed afterwards that when he joined the board he was told that on no account was an award to be made which gave more than £5 to any man. Little wonder that such miserable sums as £25 to £40 were given for putting anchors aboard, to be divided among 12 to 14 men, as well as the helpers on the beach.

Assistance rendered to Government ships and men-of-war was even worse rewarded. In 1832 HMS *Larne* went ashore on the Goodwins in fog; the captain let go an anchor but unfortunately the warship sat on the flukes, sustaining considerable bottom damage. The second-class lugger *Fox* offered assistance and the captain agreed to take it, as well as engaging two other luggers. Soon one of his officers found fault with the way a boatman was bending a rope to a buoy, and on being answered back, had the man arrested; he was released only after one of the masters had vigorously protested to the captain. After strenuous efforts the ship was refloated, but the famished boatmen were refused any food and were only grudgingly issued with some late at night. The Admiralty were graciously pleased to send £2 to each of the three masters and £1 to every member of the crew.

In November 1836 a gale swept the Channel, driving over 400 vessels to seek the shelter of the Downs. The seas were mountainous, making it impossible to launch any lugger off the beach. When the wind abated, only 150 ships remained at anchor, several had sunk with all hands, nearly a dozen were dismasted, and the remainder were blown clean out of the anchorage and scattered over the North Sea. It is an ill wind that blows no one any good, and incidents such as this provided boatmen with the opportunity of making money.

Even after chain cables had largely replaced hemp rope, it was nothing out of the ordinary for upwards of 100 ships to lose their anchors and chains in a single storm. During sw and nw

gales vessels would drag their anchors and be forced to slip to
avoid fouling ships astern. In a southerly blow with a fierce lee
tide running many a vessel 'would not look at her anchor'
through having too much way on, links would snap through
veering away too quickly and bringing the ship up short and
sharp. A further source of trouble came from wrecks on the sea-
bed; one off Deal Castle was found by divers to have 13 anchors
and chains twisted around it. It was essential to keep the road-
stead as clear of obstructions as possible and during slack times
luggers in pairs swept the bottom with ropes stretched between
them, hoping the bight would catch a fluke standing proud;
grapnels were also used.

Every type of anchor was stored in a field behind Deal
Castle. Here lay huge old-fashioned wooden-stocked anchors
with rings nearly 3 ft in diameter to take the immense hemp
cables—one for a ship of the line weighed 90 to 95 cwt, nearly
5 tons. The more modern anchors with iron stocks weighed 46
cwt and more; chains with every size of link were stacked in
orderly heaps. When ground gear was required the anchor was
slung under a pair of huge wheels and hauled by horses to the
lugger engaged in the 'hovel', the peculiar local name given to
the various jobs performed by Deal boatmen.

In the early nineteenth century a big first-class lugger was 38
ft long, extreme beam 12 ft 3 in, moulded beam 12 ft, with a
depth of 5 ft, and entirely open except for a forepeak about 13
ft long. She carried 6 tons of ballast, the hull weighed $3\frac{1}{2}$ tons,
was clench-built and copper-fastened, the full displacement of
nearly $20\frac{1}{2}$ tons giving a capacity of about 17 tons. The Kingsdown luggers, used chiefly for fishing, could carry five to six
lasts of herring—over 60,000 fish. The maximum draft was
5 ft 6 in, planking $1\frac{1}{2}$ in thick with wales 3 in thick. The normal
crew was seven men and a boy, but 20 to 23 men were frequently on board when man power was needed.

The usual rig was three masts, with dipping lugs on fore and
mainmasts, each stepped in a tabernacle, and a standing lug on
the mizzen. The centre of the foremast was 7 ft 9 in from the

DEAL LUGGER

Forecastle deck

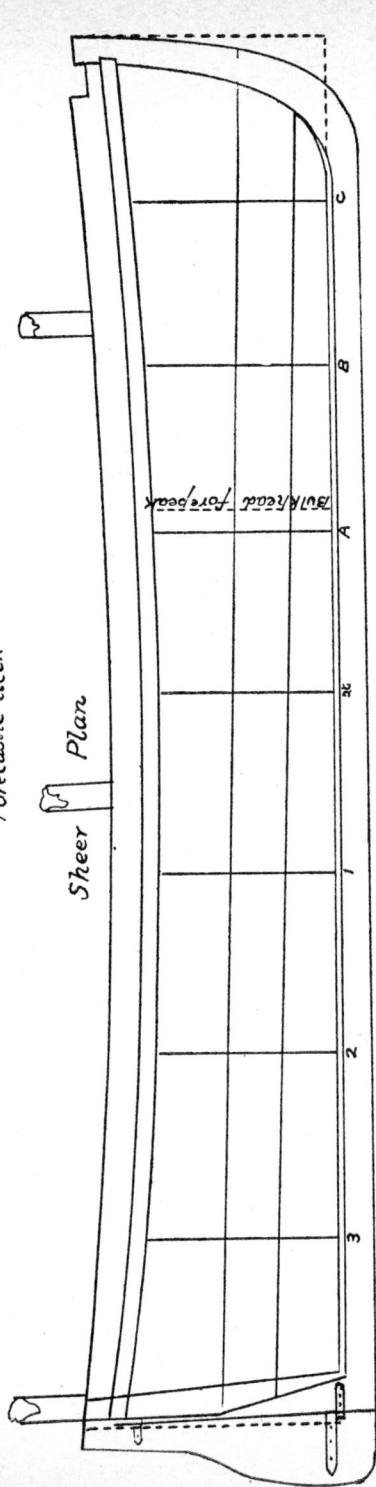

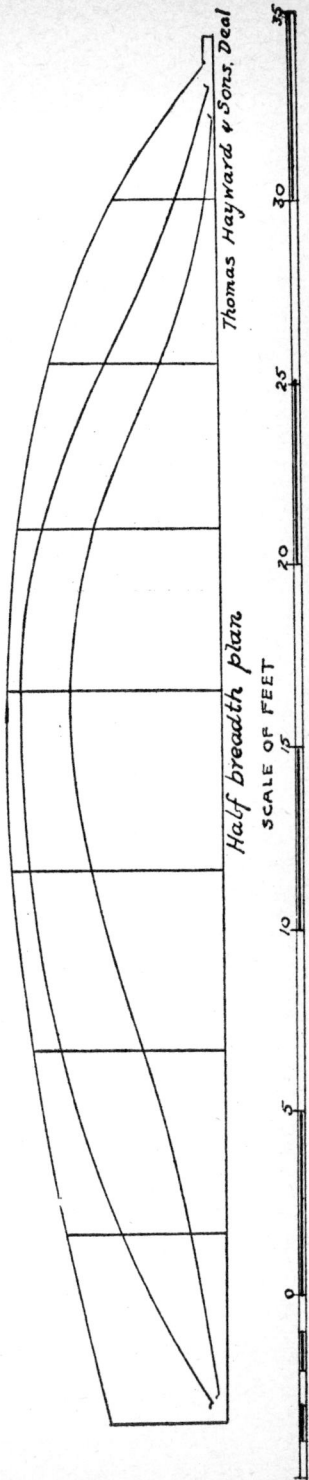

Sheer Plan

Bulkhead forepeak

C B A 2x 2 3

Thomas Hayward & Sons, Deal

Half breadth plan

SCALE OF FEET

0 5 10 15 20 25 30 35

Sheer and half-breadth plans of fore-peaker Deal lugger, 1848

Body Plan

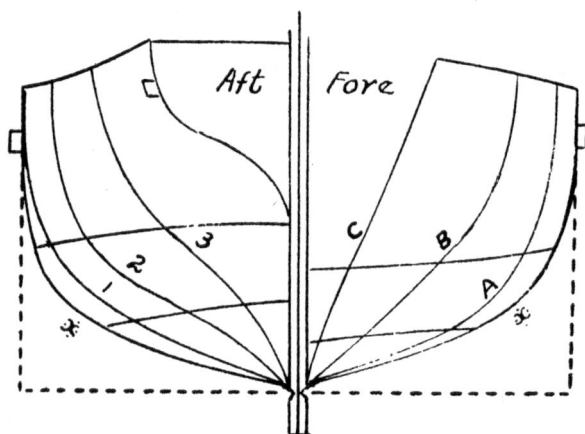

Body plan of Deal fore-peaker

outside of the stem, the mainmast 20 ft 9 in, and the mizzen mast was stepped against a transom 6 ft 6 in wide, off-centred to starboard to clear the tiller port. The mainmast was seldom stepped in winter and never if an anchor was on board; later it was abandoned altogether and fore and mizzen masts only were used. The hull cost £275 with spars and blocks, a double suit of sails £45, or £320 ready for sea.

Strength was essential as a lugger might be launched off and hauled up the beach 50 times in a year, their expected life was 20 years, but this was exceeded in many instances.

The smaller first-class luggers were 34 ft long, 10 ft 4 in to 10 ft 6 in wide, and carried a crew of six in summer, eight to twelve in winter. The hull alone cost around £200, and a further £100 was required to fit her with sails and all gear, a capstan and shed ashore, and all rope. In 1833 there were 21 first-class boats on the beach.

A second-class lugger, sometimes called a 'lasting' boat, was 28 ft long, 8 ft 6 in beam, mostly rigged with two masts and costing £130 to £150. They numbered 15 in 1833.

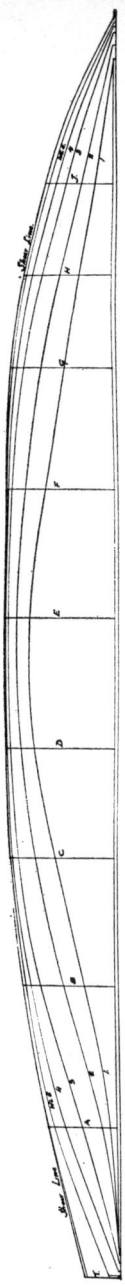

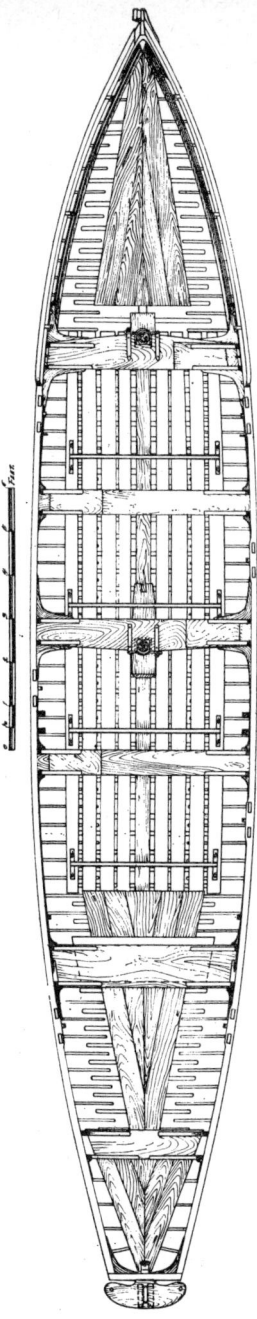

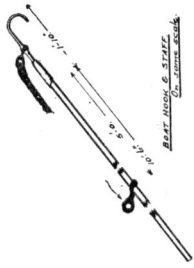

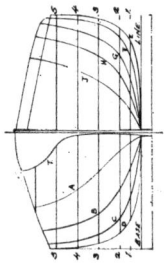

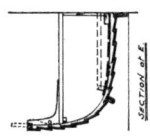

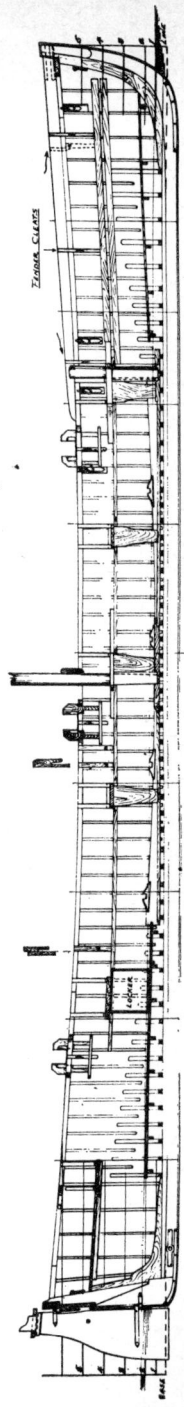

Lines and details of Dover galley *Princess*

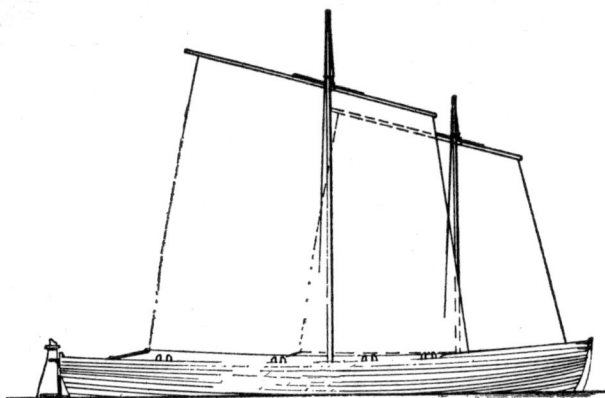

REGATTA RIG. "WING & WING".
Scale ¼" to 1 foot.

The galley *Princess* in regatta rig

Despite the wear and tear of driving head-on to a shingle beach and the arduous work they were called upon to do, many luggers 'lived' for an astonishing time. *Seamen's Glory* took part in a review of luggers in 1803; fifty-six years later she was awarded £94 for services to the brig *Enterprise*. *Lord Paget*, wrecked on the beach on 28 August 1885, was then the oldest at Deal, having been launched 30 years before.

The great galleys were 30 to 36 ft long, beam 6 ft to 7 ft, with one mast amidships carrying a large square-headed lugsail; they were seldom rowed. Planking was up to ¾ in thick, timbers 1½ in square, and about ¾-ton of beach ballast was required. In 1833 only seven were on call; later known as 'galley punts' they increased in numbers as the big luggers declined.

Ordinary galleys were 28 to 32 ft long, pulled four to six oars, and had a mainmast with lugsail. They cost £42 and were generally used for boarding and landing pilots. Fifty were on call in 1833.

The galley *Princess* of Dover, measured up by the late P. J. Oke in 1937, was built by Nicholas at Deal *c* 1880. Her dimen-

Page 77 The lugger *Team*, RX 131, approaching the shore. The flag at the mizzen masthead is the 'bob-wane', the other denotes the intention of the master, Jack Haste, to beach immediately. Note trawl head over starboard bow, small jib and reefed fore lugsail

Page 78 (above left) Stern view of galley *Seaman's Hope*, January 1952; (above right) the lugger *Industry*, RX 94, 28 June 1936. Note clamps, fore iron, chain through strap, oars in raft ropes and (below) lute stern and lantern on mizzen. *Industry* was burnt as a bonfire on 5 November 1949

Page 79 (above left) Lugger about to enter surf breaking on the beach; (above right) Eastbourne lugger *Our Lassie*, built by Tom Sisk at Beach Road, bought by public subscription and given to J. Huggett to replace his boat lost when lobstering; (below) *Team* and other luggers beached. Note lute stern on lugger under sail

Page 80 *Boy Leslie*, RX 23, of Hastings. Note elliptical stern, outrigger to starboard, capstan, the old tan house to right and net sheds to left. This lugger is not in the 1910 register

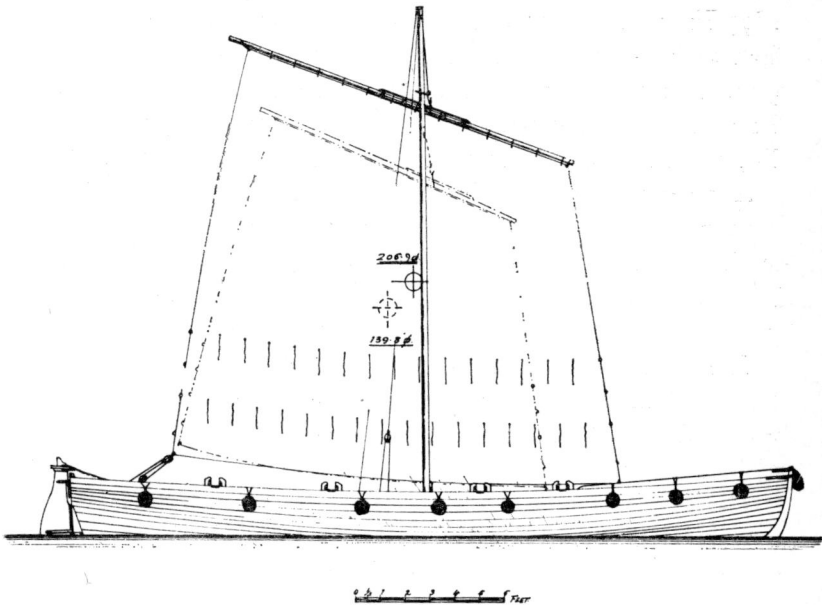

Sail plan of *Princess*

sions were length overall 29 ft $1\frac{1}{2}$ in, beam 5 ft $4\frac{3}{4}$ in, inside
depth 2 ft.

The hull was planked with elm on ash frames, floors were flat
with well-rounded bilges, and the normal crew was three men.
The equipment consisted of five oars, each 14 ft long, a boat
hook 10 ft long with a coir boat rope 45 fathoms long: rope
fenders, Turk's Head pattern at stem and at each thwart, and
for'ard, 17 in all. The flare was an earthenware blacking bottle
filled with turpentine and with a wad pushed down the neck.
Ballast was shingle in bags. The galley was steered with a yoke
and lines, and had oak double thole pins for the oars. A strong
'norman post' was stepped on the floors and secured to the
for'ard thwart by an iron strap. At regattas, or when the need
for speed was paramount, the post was removed and the short
mast stepped and storm sail set—wing and wing.

Oke gives the owner of *Princess* as William Burwell, but in

E

1893 Finnis supplied two small sails to a 'Mr Burvill' of Dover for a galley similar in size. Dimensions of one were: leech 16 ft 3 in, head 10 ft 7 in, weather 11 ft 3 in, and foot 15 ft 8 in. Thirty-four yards of canvas were used and the cost was £4 10s. The second sail of lighter canvas at 1s 8¾d a yard, cost £2 18s.

Another entry in the ledger for the same owner's *Spartan* was for a small sail of 34 yd at £6 0s 6d, and a great sail of 51 yd at £4 10s. In 1892 a great sail cut 18 ft 6 in leech, 12 ft 5 in head, 14 ft weather and 17 ft 3 in foot, cost £4 8s at 1s 10d a yard.

The summer mast measured 20 ft 9 in, diameter 3¼ in to 2 in; yard 14 ft 7½ in, diameter 2 in. The winter, or short mast, was 16 ft 1 in, diameter 3 in to 2 in; yard 11 ft 1 in, diameter 2¼ in to 1½ in.

The smaller galleys measured from 20 to 28 ft in length, rowed four oars and were used when the fee for landing a pilot did not justify launching a bigger boat.

Finally there were the 'punts'. First-class punts, numbering 19, were 18 ft long, 5 ft beam and cost £25. The second-class, about 100 in all, were 14 ft by 4 ft 6 in and cost £12. Generally known as 'paddle punts', they were used for inshore fishing and one was always aboard a big lugger out hovelling or seeking.

All the boats were clench-built of English elm, with small transom sterns; in many the waterlines tended to be hollow, hulls were bright, the pine varnish being put on with long-handled brushes. Rigging was simple, without standing shrouds; the burton was set up as a backstay on the weather side, as were the halyards. The lugsails were very square-headed with many lines of reef points, but some men preferred to set small storm sails instead of shortening down. The tye was a well-greased rope, passing over a dumb sheave in the masthead. Every galley had a strong 'norman post' in the fore thwart for making fast lines when towing, and a large coir rope fender over the bows, with smaller ones along each side.

Nearly all the boatmen were attached to one or other of the many taverns, whose landlord was often the owner of the lugger, but a man was free to go in any boat he chose; hence luggers with a known reputation for speed were never short of a full crew in an emergency. Some 437 able-bodied men belonged to 14 stations and in bad weather they often slept in the taprooms and passages, rather than go home and perhaps miss a call. Each lugger had her own 'stage' and capstan, that for a big lugger had eight to 10 bars, a galley only six, and was made of massive timbers a foot and more square sunk deep in the shingle. The older men helped to man the capstan and were paid sixpence a time, but they received a share of any salvage award. In the palmy days, no member of the crew deigned to do this task. (Pictures, pp 39 and 57.)

What inspiring names the boatmen gave their luggers—*England's Glory, Seaman's Hope, Briton's Pride, Success, Renown, Friend to all Nations*. Their own names were sometimes equally full-flavoured, Luke Jarvis, Absolom Hicks, Jethro Pettit, Jarvist Arnold, to quote only a few. So many had the same surnames that nicknames were invariably used. Perhaps it has been given to us of a later generation to have a better appreciation of the sterling qualities and consummate seamanship of these men, who in their day were frequently neglected. They could be cheated out of their just rewards by crafty lawyers and pompous commissioners, be smeared with the name of 'longshore sharks' and other worse calumies. No doubt they had an eye to the main chance, and who can blame them? Their livelihood depended on their own skill and courage, all they had to sell, so why should it have been considered base for them to drive a hard bargain and get the best terms possible?

Think of those wild winter nights when a shout was scarce heard above the roaring of the gale, the grinding of hulls, the crash of falling spars, and the thunder of slatting canvas as sails, torn from their gaskets, were blown to ribbons. Suddenly the darkness is lit up by the eerie light of blue flares and the dull boom of minute guns is heard from one of the lightships, to be followed soon by a shower of stars as rockets burst in the sky, telling sorely-tried mariners that help is on the way. The wind shrieks and howls, blowing like the wrath of God, rain comes down in torrents, huge breakers are crashing in on the steep beach, grinding, sucking, pushing the shingle in all directions as a dog scatters a flock of sheep, the yeasty foam running back between the pebbles, to be driven in again as the next sea breaks.

What a maelstrom into which to launch an open boat! Yet that was the backcloth against which the Deal boatmen played their noble part in the saving of life and property.

Spray stings the face and reddens the eyes as the men lean against the force of the wind; spume, spindrift and fragments of seaweed drive far inland, up the narrow alleys into the open country where tall elms bend in torment from the lashing they are taking. Groups of men hurry along the beach to make up the crew of lugger or lifeboat, in many a home anxious women hand food and warm clothing to their loved ones, whilst frightened children cling to their skirts, wondering what all the noise and excitement is about, little realising that in years to come they will recall with pride being on the beach when their father's lugger saved an exhausted crew.

The luggers, always ready, lie trigged up on greased woods in front of their capstans, each held back by a chain secured to a firmly anchored post, passed through a hole in the skeg of the keel—the 'ruffle'—and back to a specially shaped hook, stoppered with several turns of yarn which, just before a launch was likely, had replaced the iron ring always there. The rudder is triced up a foot or so to clear the beach. One lugger has a heavy anchor and chain securely stowed amidships, the arms lashed to the thwart in front of the pump, the stock sticking up. Oilskinned figures tumble into her and with orderly speed set about their appropriate duties; some go to the haul-off warp, others man the halyards. At the tiller stands the steersman, watching the incoming fury of the seas, everything depends on his judgment. He is waiting for a 'smooth', and must choose a big sea but one not high enough to overwhelm the boat. It must also be a broad one with a good volume of water, but the lugger must not meet it or she will be overturned in the breaking water, neither must she be tardy in following it or she will strike bottom in the trough and then disaster is certain.

His hand drops as he shouts 'Let go', the man standing by with a sharp knife cuts the stopper, the hook flies open and the chain screams through the ruffle as the heavy boat gathers momentum, slowly at first, then with a roar and a rumble the 20-ton weight rushes down over the ways, the unsheeted mizzen flogging unceasingly with cracks like volleys of artillery. Standing out in the water are a couple of men or more holding on end greased woods. As the lugger rushes towards them they fling the woods down, and she races over them to disappear in a smother of foam with a crash that can be heard half a mile away. From his long experience the helmsman has judged that below froth and bubble there will be solid water enough to support the hull with its living burden and carry it into deeper water. Deluges of spray are flung mast high, drenching the men hanging on to the haul-off warp, fast to an anchor well to seaward. This gives the boat the required cant to pay off on the right tack. The lives of all depend on that slender rope, now tightened to half its size. Hard as an iron bar it bites into the tough Kentish oak. Here is the test the ropemaker had foreseen when he made the warp in his rope-walk back in the town.

A gasp ashore as a huge sea rears up, crests all curving, before it thunders into breaking water. Will the lugger be flung back on to the beach, shattered to matchwood, or will her momentum carry her through? The rudder has already been dropped down on its pintle, the mizzen, now sheeted home to stand hard as a board, falls silent, the close-reefed foresail rises on its mast to flog for a moment before the sheet is hardened in hand over hand. The warp is flung out of its stopper, and, free of the land, the hard-pressed lugger drives to wind'ard, soon to be swallowed up in the darkness of that awful night, into a sea in which it seems utterly impossible for an open boat to live, let alone perform useful work. Like a hound casting on a stale line she beats to and fro, dropping her forelug at every tack. What a sail to handle under such wild conditions! Smoking squalls cut off the tops of the seas so that freezing spray lashes the oil-skinned men struggling with that soaked, iron-hard canvas, the middle of the boat cluttered up with a huge anchor and fathom after fathom of chain, apt to writhe about like a cobra. In the offing, the phosphorescent gleam of the breakers on the sands, hungry monsters eager to seize another victim, to wind'ard the sore-pressed vessel, rolling, pitching, scending, water pouring on her decks as the seas leap up through the empty hawseholes and over her broken bulwarks, her lower yardarms almost dipping into the water on every roll.

Terrifying to come alongside that plunging hull, one moment towering over the boat, threatening to crash down and crush it like an eggshell; the next the lugger is lifted high above the deck and likely to be swept across it were it not for the magnificent seamanship of those gallant men. Time after time might they try to grasp a tackle hanging from a yardarm to pass a hook through the chain, only to see it swing out of reach at the critical second. Then the glorious moment when it went home and willing hands aboard tailed on the fall to bring the chain in through the hawsepipe to be shackled round the mast after being passed several times round the windlass or capstan. Then the inert weight of the anchor had to be lifted out, to plunge down until its broad flukes bit and gradually checked the drifting hull.

Was such a service worth only a fiver a man? Yet that was often the award given by commissioners who sat in judgment weeks after, each drawing a guinea a sitting and begrudging even that meagre payment. And still those humble boatmen went out time after time to assist vessels in distress.

In the spacious days of hovelling, several luggers would launch together and, where stages adjoined, the keenest rivalry existed. Collisions were rare, but when a crash did take place the language was likely to be the only warm thing about! Seconds counted in that wild race to the sands—the prize?—to be first aboard the wreck.

Occasionally a boat missed her launch and fell back athwart the shore; in Deal parlance, a 'dry launch'. Then the risk was that the hull would fall outward towards the seas, fill and be driven along the beach away from her capstan. If possible a man tried to stove in a plank to allow the water inside to run out, but it generally ended in a smashed boat.

It was perhaps even more awe-inspiring to see a big lugger take the beach in heavy weather. She might have been 'seeking' and picked up a vessel in need of an anchor. Terms having been agreed with the captain, the boat cracked on for the shore, nearing which she hoisted a private signal to tell her requirements, and men hurried to the anchor field to select suitable ground gear. Carrying a press of sail, the boat was driven full tilt on to the shingle where a man was standing up to his waist in water, ready to slip the capstan rope or wire through the chain strop at foot of the stem the moment the sea receded. Others dropped greased woods ahead and 20 or 30 men at the capstan bars inched the heavy hull up the steep beach nearly to the capstan; here it was swung round, chocked up and made ready for launching as soon as the anchor was stowed aboard. The next problem was to find the vessel again—no easy job, especially at night, as she might have drifted miles in the meantime.

When a lugger was being hauled up there was the danger that the capstan might take charge. On 6 January 1863 *Albion* went afloat to supply an anchor and chain to a drifting vessel. On returning, as she was being hauled up, the capstan rope broke when the strain was greatest owing to the shelving beach. The lugger ran backwards and the capstan revolved at tremendous speed. 'Unship bars' was the cry, but the last one struck Robert Vickers on the back of the head, killing him instantly.

In January 1862 *Sappho* was being turned round ready for the next launch when the men at the capstan were overpowered. All jumped clear and the lugger ran down the beach. Unfortunately there was not time to unship the last bar which flew out and killed the son of John Files and seriously injured two

other boys. John Files, who died at the age of 90 in March
1915, 'followed the water' from the age of 12 and piloted ships
for over 60 years. A man of fine physique, at an advanced age
he could haul his punt *Jubilee* up the beach by the painter
without assistance, frequently late at night. In November 1848
he was one of the crew of *Prince of Wales* when the crew of 12,
five passengers and 11 Ramsgate boatmen were rescued from
the Bremen ship *Atlantic* ashore on the Goodwins. He often
sailed *Renown* home alone from the Isle of Wight.

Although some luggers were individually owned, the
majority belonged to companies, and a 'set' of boats consisted
of a first- and second-class lugger, a galley, capstans, gear and
tarred wooden sheds on each stage. From a lugger's earnings
the owner took one-third, the crew two-thirds, equally divided.
Seldom was any reward given for saving life alone, even when
men had ignored a chance of salvage to do so. Some ship-
owners, however, realised that to launch a lugger and risk life
and boat called for some payment, but it never amounted to
very much.

I have seen that oft-quoted epitaph of George Philpot in
Deal churchyard. He was on the water from the age of ten and
saved over 100 lives, more than once losing one or two of his
crew. He died in poverty during the 1830s. Contrast this with
the high honours and emoluments showered on men who destroyed life on the battlefield.

The Board of Trade surpassed all, in my opinion, in April
1866 when they awarded the sum of £2 to be shared among 11
men who rescued seven from the French vessel *Ingolf*, wrecked
on the Goodwins in a heavy gale—less than 4s a man. To their
eternal credit, such paltry rewards did not deter the boatmen
from rescue work, and their record over the years is second to
none.

The passing of the Merchant Shipping Act in 1854 brought
considerable improvements, and due consideration was given
to the risk involved in supplying anchors or in salvage work.
The commissioners were abolished and most of the salvage

claims were heard in the Admiralty Court, later presided over
by Mr Justice Phillimore who, having the interests of Deal
boatmen at heart, saw that they received justice.

Share ratios were: in a ten-handed lugger the award was
divided into 14; $3\frac{1}{2}$ shares went to the boat, a half-share for
provisions provided by the owner, but many men preferred to
find their own. In other cases the award was divided into equal
shares, then $1\frac{1}{2}$ went to the boat, 2 if the punt aboard was used
as well.

In normal weather the charge for taking out an anchor and
chain was now £1 per cwt, about its value, and from 10s to
15s a cwt for the cable. One week in January 1863 saw nine
vessels supplied with ground gear; in the first three months of
1866 the total was 25. For the recovery of anchors, the Board
of Trade allowed 1s 6d per cwt, later £2 for every ton of
anchor and chain. From 1866 to 1869 over 600 were swept up
in the Downs and offered for sale at the Lord Warden's depot.
The payments were not so much for their intrinsic value as for
the valuable service rendered in keeping the anchorage clear of
obstructions.

Some boatmen specialised in this work. In March 1873 the
Margate lugger *Secret* landed an anchor and chain weighing
$57\frac{1}{2}$ cwt and, with *Enterprise*, brought ashore 18 tons weight in
under three days.

The improvement in payments was the more welcome because the increasing use of steam tugs had reduced certain
hovels. Big sailing ships no longer anchored in the Downs to
await a fair wind. They towed through to well down Channel;
homeward-bounders took steam for the London river. Carrying
out provisions, stores and passengers had been a certain source
of income, and the Post Office had paid as much as £2,000 a
year for taking out or landing mails; now steamers called at
Southampton or Plymouth. But there was still occasional
money to be earned from salvage.

Even in the earlier days hovelling had been a precarious
livelihood. The late Mr E. C. Pain had a book kept by William

Hubbard from February 1814 to May 1853 in which he re-corded every detail. I am indebted to Mr Pain's executors for permission to quote from this interesting document.

In almost 40 years Hubbard had received £695 as his share of the total of £20,071 10s awarded for the 92 hovelling jobs he was engaged in, sailing in luggers from Deal, Ramsgate, Broadstairs and Margate. Only 12 of the services brought him more than £10, 44 left him with less than £5. One is appalled at the inadequacy of many of the awards, especially when they had to be shared amongst two or three luggers. In his young days, the highest was £750 for a claim settled at Margate for services rendered by the luggers *Fox* and *Queen* to the ship *Apollo*, ashore on Margate Sands on 29 December 1821 and brought safely into Margate Roads. His share came to £15 1s. There was an improvement in the 1840s. On 24 February 1840 an award of £1,536 was given to the lugger *City Queen* for getting the barque *Henry* off the Margate Sand and taking her to Whit-stable, and then London where the claim was settled. Of this sum Hubbard received £50 10s. Even better was the £1,250 awarded to the lugger *Liberty*, which gave him £115.

On the other hand some luggers were exceedingly lucky. In 1850 *Early Bird* launched in a gale with violent snow squalls to go to a brig flying signals of distress. The lugger ran in under her stern, and a man jumped aboard and piloted her safely into Ramsgate harbour. Then a large barque was seen driving, having parted her cables, and another man was put aboard. When beating home *Early Bird* came across a French schooner deserted after collision. Two men were put aboard, slipped the schooner's anchor and ran into Ramsgate. That morning's work earned each man £325—just under half Hubbard's earnings in nearly 40 years!

As pilots the men were frequently shockingly paid consider-ing that they often went seeking down Channel to the Isle of Wight, and even as far as the Start, to try and pick up a vessel bound for a North Sea port. It was a hard life indeed, cruising about in the depth of winter in an open boat with only a tiny forepeak in which to sleep and do such primitive cooking as was possible. Then there was the risk of boarding a ship from the tiny punt and the chance of losing the fee as pilot if a Trinity House cutter put a man aboard at Dungeness, as they had every right to do when The Fellowship of Cinque Port Pilots came to an end in 1853 and licensed men were transferred to the supervision of Trinity House. Many boatmen were now 'not qualified', as they were unable through lack of education to sit for the examination, but they *knew* the Channel waters.

I give but two examples of many. In the spring of 1862 John Williams was put aboard the ship *Royal Charlie*, as she passed through the Downs, to take her to the Isle of Wight. The wind was strong easterly and the captain refused to heave-to off the island and wait for the pilot to transfer to a shore boat. Rather than waste a few minutes of a fair wind he took the luckless pilot 300 miles down the Channel until he met the schooner *Ranshawe* bound for Liverpool. He handed Williams two sovereigns, his fee to the Isle of Wight, and a week or so later he was landed at Liverpool to pay his own train fare back to Deal, or walk if he could not raise the money.

Early in January 1860 the East Indiaman *Earl of Eglinton* left the Downs. A boatman offered to pilot her to the Isle of Wight for £8, but the captain haughtily declined, saying that he had no need for the services of a pilot. A few hours later the ship was wrecked in St Margaret's Bay. Over £100,000 worth of government stores was salved by local boatmen and finally the wreck was sold for £150.

In spite of the fact that steam was gradually ousting sail, the Downs was still a crowded anchorage at times. In 1858 from 31 March to 4 April, 220 sail and five steamers sailed from the roads; 27 April to 4 May, 199 sail and nine steam; 22 to 28 June, 197 sail and seven steam.

The following year, 1859, brought the highest awards yet given, over £10,000 in all. November was an exceptionally wild month; within 12 days 30 anchors and chains were supplied, 17 being taken out on one Sunday. Every large lugger was engaged, but no wreck or loss of life was incurred. *Albion*, staged near the Naval Yard and probably the finest on the beach, received in all £2,022 8s 6d; *Mexborough* £985 10s; *Tiger* £402; the smallest award being £25 to *Sparrow*.

Mary Blane, an old North End boat, earned £260 for supplying ground gear to the ship *Robert Morrison* and piloting her to Margate Roads. *Mary Ann* with *Unity*, received £400 for anchors supplied to the ship *Empress Eugenie*.

The highest awards for the supply of anchors and chains that I can trace are: £550 to the lugger *Fly* for two anchors to *Highland Mary* on 7 December 1870; £700 to *Seaman's Hope* in February 1876 for two anchors to the American ship *Kendrick Fish*. For salvage work, probably the record was £7,000 divided among 62 boatmen for services to the ship *Iron Crown*. Laden with tea, she went ashore on the east side of the sands in a ssw gale on 7 February 1865. John Bailey steered the lugger *England's Glory*, owned by Bill Spears, right across the sands through boiling seas, then fetched to wind'ard, before running down past the wreck. The foresail was dropped as she shot by, six of the crew jumped into the rigging and leapt aboard, to be followed by half-a-dozen lifeboatmen from the new *Van Kook* out on her first rescue mission, her crew all Deal boatmen. Together they swung a kedge anchor clear of the ship from her foreyard; as she drifted it held and the bows came up to the seas. Then the anchors were let go. Tugs were standing by, the tide was rising and *Iron Crown* was refloated within half an hour. The two tugs received £5,000.

This money for salvage work was not automatically given. It had to be claimed and the merits argued in a court of law, far removed from the wild scenes in which the services were performed. If unsuccessful, the boatmen had to pay costs or suffer imprisonment if unable to do so. There was no free legal aid in those days. In 1860 some Broadstairs men were incarcerated in Maidstone gaol and *The Times* published an appeal for £150. So generous was the public response that the amount raised was £100 in excess of the required sum and the men were speedily released.

Walmer and Kingsdown men equalled in skill and courage those of Deal, but their numbers were fewer. In 1850 there were 18 first-class luggers at Walmer and about a dozen on the adjoining beach. Kingsdown men fished more extensively than the others, sending large supplies daily to Billingsgate. No lifeboats were on this 3-mile stretch of coast until the 1860s when three, at times four, were stationed at North Deal, Walmer and Kingsdown, saving hundreds of lives. Even so, luggers landed 270 rescued men between 1858 and 1880. The coxswain generally owned, or had a share in, the finest lugger. Richard Roberts was one of the crew which brought the first North Deal lifeboat from London; he was second coxswain for 22 years, then coxswain until he retired in 1907 to receive as pension £12 per annum—his salary. In his 43 years of service his lifeboat rescued 441 lives. His boat *Early Morn*, one of the swiftest on the strand, was six times winner of the £10 prize at the regattas between 1869 and 1881. (Picture, p 60.)

When the tide was full up it was frequently very difficult, if not impossible, to launch a big lugger—she could not get run enough to clear the breakers. On 2 December 1867 an anchor and chain were put on board *Albion* to take out to the barque *Eena*. Huge seas were breaking on the shingle and the tide was high. The trigger was released and she began her run down the woods, to stop in the wash of the cresting seas. The crew strained their hardest on the haul-off warp but the heavily-laden hull would not budge. Some of the men were washed out, others scrambled over the stern; spars and sails were swept out to sea. Vain efforts were made to haul her up by the capstan, but the weight of over 7 tons was too much and she had to be left until the tide receded. Strained beyond repair *Albion* was later broken up.

Nineteen anchors were taken out on that day, during which a squall capsized the Walmer lifeboat; she righted to go over again on sail being set, and boats from the beach rescued her half-drowned crew. Later in the day *England's Glory* succeeded where *Albion* had failed, but she had to chase the barque to the Isle of Wight before completing her hovel; then she had to beat home against a furious nor'easter.

Nine months later a new lugger 38 ft 6 in long, 12 ft 6 in beam and 6 ft 8 in depth, built by H. & G. Gardener, was christened *Albion II* and her first salvage job earned £400 for putting an anchor aboard *Royal Standard*, ship and cargo being valued at £200,000. Three other luggers shared £800.

During the gale on the night of 16 December 1869 *Renown* was knocked up and swamped but not being heavily laden she sustained little damage. On 19 November 1875, when 450 vessels were sheltering and 50 lost anchors, *Renown* had another dry launch deep laden with chain but was hauled back up the beach and launched again long after darkness had fallen. That winter was terrible, hard frost and snow for weeks, yet ground tackle was supplied to scores of ships without accident, until *Queen of Sheba* was completely wrecked while launching to go to the assistance of a ship in distress. No insurance covered these losses.

Disaster could come in the finest weather. The second-class lugger *Fawn*, a very fast boat, launched on 1 August 1864 to cruise at the back of the sands. The night was calm and very dark, but the lugger was never seen again; it was believed she was run down by a steamer. Three widows and 11 children were left practically destitute.

When boarding a pilot on a sailing ship there was always the risk that the lugger would foul the braces or other gear. The evening was fine on 17 April 1864, when the Kingsdown boat *Nidget* launched with a crew of three to go seeking. Off Folkestone, the East Indiaman *Alfred* was booming up Channel with stun'sails set and burned a blue flare for a pilot. The lugger was put across her course, and as the ship was about to bring up, some ropes on her jibboom caught the mast and the boat instantly capsized. The Indiaman hauled her wind, two lifebuoys were thrown over the side and the starboard lifeboat smartly launched, but although she cruised around for an hour and a half no trace was found of the missing men.

A stiff breeze was blowing with a heavy sea and strong tide running on 30 September 1899, when the galley punt *Conqueror* went off to put a pilot on the barque *Carnmoney*. When about to board, the mast fouled some gear, the boat swung broadside on, sank, and the crew of five were drowned in sight of shore.

It is difficult to believe that shipmasters could be so callous as to leave men to drown, but many such instances are recorded. One must suffice. On 17 October 1874, *Galatea* launched to cruise down Channel with a crew of six. Four days later two men were put aboard ships as pilots, and a barque from St Johns, New Brunswick, bound for Antwerp, was spoken but the master declined assistance. A sou'west gale was rising and later he thought better of his first decision and hailed for a pilot. The punt was lowered with three men aboard; within 50 yd of the barque it capsized. Her yards were immediately squared and she ran off before the wind. The one man left in the lugger was helpless; unable to sail against wind and tide he saw his companions gradually give up the struggle and drown. He was left to sail the boat home alone and report their loss.

Cruising far down Channel was hazardous. Early in March 1878 *Petrel* left Deal with six men aboard, two of whom were shipped as pilots. Last seen off Plymouth when in company with another Deal boat *Pride of the Sea*, the lugger was towed into Brixham on 8 April with all gear missing. No trace was ever found of the missing men. The hull was brought home, refitted and renamed *Walmer Castle*. In March 1892 she again sailed to the west'ard; on the 15th tremendous seas were running off St Catherine's Point and the lugger was seen from Ventnor under a storm jib and reefed mizzen. Soon her crew realised they could not weather Dunnose Head and the foresail was set in an endeavour to beat off a lee shore. Off Horseshoe Bay, Bonchurch, a huge sea struck her, vain efforts were made to launch the punt, and two men could be seen clinging to the bowsprit, only 100 yd from the shore from which no help could be sent. Later the wreck was towed ashore and the bodies of three men were found jammed in the forepeak. This meant that half the crew had turned in or were having a meal, showing how little those on watch had thought of the conditions.

In 1887 *Pride of the Sea* was lost off Shanklin on Sunday, 30 October. It had been a wild night with the southerly gale veering suddenly to nor'west; at dawn the punt was washed ashore and the wreck was seen driving over the rocks, masts and spars snapped off short. Worth £600, her owners had struggled for 11 years to pay off the mortgage, and the hull was not insured. One of her crew, who had been shipped as a pilot, learned of the loss of his five mates when he landed at Deal. (Pictures, pp 57 and 59.)

Many a time a lugger was sailed home from the Isle of Wight by one man, the rest having been boarded as pilots. Charles Pearson, who died in 1915, was one of the last of the Deal pilots. When luggers were finished he would go down to the island in his 14-ft punt and ship as pilot to Continental ports, his tiny boat being hoisted on board. One Christmas Day, about 1910, he took a ship down Channel to the Start but was unable to be landed because the weather was too rough, and was taken on to Australia. The hardships endured on that six months passage seriously undermined his health and he never fully recovered.

A further danger to life followed the erection of the iron pier in the 1860s, in spite of the many protests of boatmen who could plainly see what a menace it would be to boats launching from South End. Soon it claimed victims. Early on the morning of 16 January 1871, a vessel in the Downs sent up a flare which was seen by a watcher on the shore. It was blowing hard from the ssw when the crew of *Reform* were called from their beds and got afloat. At the critical moment the stopper, a small rope used to guide the haul-off warp at the bow, got into a kink and prevented the rope from being flung clear. Instantly the boat flew up head to wind and as the rope slipped through the stopper she

Page 97 (*above*) Old fishermen at Eastbourne: L to R, Harry Boniface ('Uncle'), Henry Mathews ('Dusty'), Jack Mockett, Jack Elms, Alf Boniface, Tom Prodger ('Flummy') and George Prodger; (*below*) sprat punt *Runaway Girl*, NN 54. The removable top strake absent from punt immediately behind, was used in winter for drift fishing

Page 98 (*above*) A Brighton 'hoggie' from a very faded 90-year-old photograph. Note short sprit lowered by tackle from masthead when mainsail was reefed, long reeving bowsprit which went through a ring on the bumpkin, and trawl-beam longer than the boat; (*below*) for sale on Brighton beach, 31 October 1930; *Belinda*, SM 317, and *Elisabeth 11*, SM 237

Page 99 (*above left*) Bow view of Itchen Ferry boat: note sharp floors, round bilges and legs to keep hull upright; (*above right*) Itchen cutter, P 33, laid up at Emsworth, June 1930; (*below*) Itchen Ferry boat at Woolston, January 1937. Note deep heel, rounded forefoot, reeving bowsprit and iron horse across transom

Page 100 (*above*) Poole cutter, PE 122, September 1931;

(*centre*) Portland lerret *Comrades*, July 1937. Note single thole pins, copsea oars and high sternpost;

(*below*) second-class wherry *Bird of Freedom*, Portsmouth. Note lugsail and mast stowed in boat

drove down towards the pier, to strike between the piles. Eleven men were flung out into a wicked sea, few were about at that early hour to render assistance and the men were swept northward by wind and tide. Three managed to cling to spars and were rescued at last by a North End boat, eight were drowned.

At this period when a lugger was wrecked little time was lost in filling the vacant stage, and within six months a new boat was built by Isaac Hayward and named *Galatea*—the largest 'cat' boat on the beach. This was the name then given to hulls with no forepeak; instead they had a small moveable 'caboose' as the only shelter, fitted between and below the fore and main thwarts. It was supposed to be watertight and sleep four men, but a dog in a kennel had more comfortable quarters.

The men invariably wore a thick pilot cloth jacket, trousers, sleeved waistcoat and Wellington boots. Round the neck was a woollen comforter, 3 to 4 yd long; to wind it a man held one end whilst the wearer pivoted round and round half a dozen times, until he was muffled up. Over all went oilskin trousers tied under the armpits, then a long oilskin coat reaching below the knees and tied from top to bottom with rope lashings; buttons were never used. In fine weather a round sealskin cap was worn, in bad, a sou'wester. If a member of the lifeboat crew, a man wore a cumbrous cork belt below a broad leather strap, above was a cork jacket, cut out under the armpits and fastened round the neck.

BOATBUILDERS AND BOATS

The luggers were the production of generations of practical experience and frequently incorporated small improvements ordered by prospective owners. Hulls had to be as light as possible, yet strong enough to carry the deadweight of a big anchor and chain, plus a full crew. Above all they had to have speed. The moulds from which they were built were handed down from father to son; building was a family concern.

F

In 1787 the Navy Office sent a draught to John Burr, a contractor who build boats for the Royal Navy, with instructions to build a 20-ft launch, copper-fastened, in a fortnight for Captain Bligh's ship the *Bounty*. It is interesting to speculate if this was the boat in which he made his famous journey of nearly 4,000 miles.

Burr's charge for a standard 23-ft naval launch was £1 14s per foot and 3s per foot for the wash strake. He also built 20-ft six-oared cutters and 16-ft 'jolly boats'.

The scantlings for a 23-ft launch, breadth 6 ft 9 in and depth 2 ft 9 in were:

Keel	$3\frac{7}{8}$ in amidships
Stem	$3\frac{1}{2}$-in sided
Post, sided at tuck	$3\frac{1}{2}$ in, alow 3 in
Transom	2 in thick
Floors	2-in sided, moulded at heads $2\frac{1}{8}$ in, at throat $3\frac{7}{8}$ in
Futtocks	2-in sided alow, square at heads $1\frac{7}{8}$ in

Just after the close of the Napoleonic wars the North End builders were Thomas Bayly, Michael Bayly, John Harrison, Morris Langley, Richard Mockett, Ratcliff & Allen, and Thomas Stokes; Stephen Brown was at Coppen Street. Thomas Hayward had a shed at South End and boats had to be dragged over greased woods up South Street, payment to casuals being a pint or two. Here had been built 10-oared galleys, and later his 8-oared boats were invincible at local regattas. Thomas died in 1848, Isaac his son in 1887, both aged 80. Isaac Bayley succeeded his father Michael and H. Durban worked for both for 67 years; when 70 he built the galley punt *Cruiser* with help from a boy. James Nicholas started his own business in 1858 and worked in it for 50 years, dying at the age of 83 in 1909. He lived to see the decline of luggers and galley punts and at the end of his long career had built six motor-boats. Gardener was another boat builder; one of his men, Trott, was the last to build galleys and punts.

Every spring the luggers were refitted, repairs being done in the sheds whenever possible; if not, on the beach. The biggest were *Tiger* and *Devastation*, always used when the heaviest anchors, beyond the capacity of the other boats, had to be carried. *Tiger* was afloat for over 40 years; towards the end when her services were seldom required she was sold to James Edgar & Co and re-rigged as a smack to carry produce from their fish factory at North Deal to London. Later she was run down off Dover. *Devastation* was capable of taking 9 tons of ground gear.

The largest lugger ever built was *Alexandra*; Isaac Hayward had to lengthen his shed and dig out 3 to 4 ft of the floor before the keel could be laid. Launched on 17 February 1866, for Ramsgate owners, she cost £700; her length was 46 ft, beam 15 ft 3 in and depth 7 ft 9 in; registered tonnage was 25. Lug-rigged for winter work, in summer she was a cutter and took visitors on pleasure cruises. Her life was short as she struck submerged wreckage on the Goodwins in March 1870, while trying to salvage mahogany logs from a brigantine. Such a boat could not be launched off a beach; Ramsgate had a harbour where she could lie afloat.

In a forepeaker, the foremast was stepped at deck level in a massive tabernacle about 3 ft high and 6 ft long, the side timbers curving down to the deck; the design was similar to the 'feathers' used at Hastings. Below in the forepeak was a heavy pillar to take the downward thrust. The foremast could be lowered back on to a crutch aft when lying to a fleet of herring nets. This was done at Kingsdown, but it is doubtful if it ever was at Deal, unless to ease a boat at sea in heavy weather. First-class boats had 22 strakes a side, the smaller ones 18, planks being up to 1½ in thick. Unfortunately I have been unable to find any record of the scantlings of other timbers. The blacksmith made all the ironwork; the lower pintle on the sternpost was up to 3 ft long to allow the rudder to be lifted clear when launching or beaching. The heel of the sternpost was rounded up to prevent it digging into the shingle.

Masts varied considerably in size, *Pride of the Sea* had a great foremast 30 ft 6 in long, *Petrel* 31 ft 4 in; *Devastation*'s was 28 ft 10 in, and her foreyard 16 ft long. *Princess Royal* had a 22 ft 7 in foremast and a 21 ft 3 in mizzen.

In 1878 a boat 24 ft long, 7 ft 11 in wide and 4 ft deep, built for H. Norris & Co by J. Nicholas, had a 23 ft 6 in foremast, a 12 ft 6 in mizzen with a 10 ft 6 in pole. The bowsprit was 8 ft outboard, foresail yard 13 ft, mizzen yard 8 ft 6 in. Another for W. Hanger was 25 ft 6 in long, 8 ft 9 in wide and 4 ft 6 in deep; her mizzen mast was 12 ft 10 in, the pole 5 ft 9 in. This shows how two men had different ideas for sail plans in almost identical boats. In 1891 a 33-ft boat had a foremast 31 ft from keelson, mizzen mast 19 ft long, bowsprit 16 ft 3 in outboard, outrigger 16 ft 6 in outboard.

In 1896 James Nicholas built the last lugger, not for Deal owners, but for service at Fremantle, Western Australia. He had supplied one in 1877 which was reckoned to be the finest and best built boat in the colony. A repeat order failed to reach him and it was placed in London, but the boat was not satisfactory and Nicholas received the order for the third. Her length was 37 ft 6 in, beam 9 ft 6 in, depth 4 ft, being 5 ft longer than *Early Morn* but with less beam and depth and the forepeak extended to the foremast. The spars were made by H. Bristow, the foremast being 30 ft 8 in long. A double suit of sails was made by G. W. Finnis at a cost of £56 17s 6d and the dimensions of hull and sails are taken from the original ledger.

The great foresail was made from 95 yd of duck; leech 28 ft, head 16 ft 6 in cut down 3½ in a cloth, weather 19 ft 9 in, and foot 25 ft. The storm foresail took 78½ yd of canvas, leech 23 ft 6 in, head 14 ft 6 in, cut down 2½ in a cloth, weather 17 ft 2 in, foot 21 ft 6 in. The great mizzen had 42 yd of ¾ duck, leech 18 ft 9 in, head 11 ft 9 in, cut down 21 in, weather 12 ft 10 in, foot 14 ft 8 in. The small mizzen had a leech 16 ft 6 in, head 10 ft 3 in, cut down 4½ in a cloth, weather 10 ft 5 in, foot 13 ft 2 in.

The keel was Canadian elm, the timbers English elm of seven

years growth, grown locally and fixed in a green state. Planking was English elm ¾ in thick. The only difference from a Deal boat was that the hull was copper-sheathed to the water-line as a protection against the teredo worm found in warmer seas.

A boatbuilder did not work to plans or a half model; three moulds at the most were used, but often only the eye of the master ensured sweet lines. For the smaller boats, elm planks were better and sounder if cut from the clean-grown butt end of a tree about one foot in diameter than from a large trunk, and no more than a year was required for it to season. These trees grew plentifully in the hedgerows and coppices around Deal and the builder always looked for a fine, close-grained bark and a good turn or 'hang' towards the butt. The logs were sawn up in the yard, care being taken that when put over the sawpit they were lined up to utilise the natural hang to the utmost. Planks varied in thickness from ½ in to ¾ in.

Many of the timbers for galleys and punts were bought ready bent or steamed from Faversham, being cut out of straight grown ash saplings, and steamed round a mould; the wood was then almost as hard as bone. The timbers were sent to the boat builder with a curve of rather smaller radius than his mould; he fitted them cold after joggling—or notching to fit over the lands of the planks. This cannot be done with timbers bent round and nailed in place, either cold or hot from the steam trunk. A good builder always gave all planking, thwarts and timber two or three coats of linseed oil before varnishing. Copper fastenings were used throughout.

A galley punt built in 1878 for John Mackin was 29 ft long, 7 ft 2 in wide and 3 ft 7 in deep, with a mainmast 27 ft 10 in, storm mast 24 ft, main yard 17 ft 6 in, storm yard 15 ft. All these boats had three hooks a side to take the tack of the different sized lugsail which was always hooked on the weather side, never at the stemhead.

The third-class galley punt *Happy-go-Lucky* was built by Nicholas in 1883 for Henry Jordan of Walmer. Its main dimensions were: length overall 22 ft 6 in, beam 6 ft 5½ in, depth 2 ft

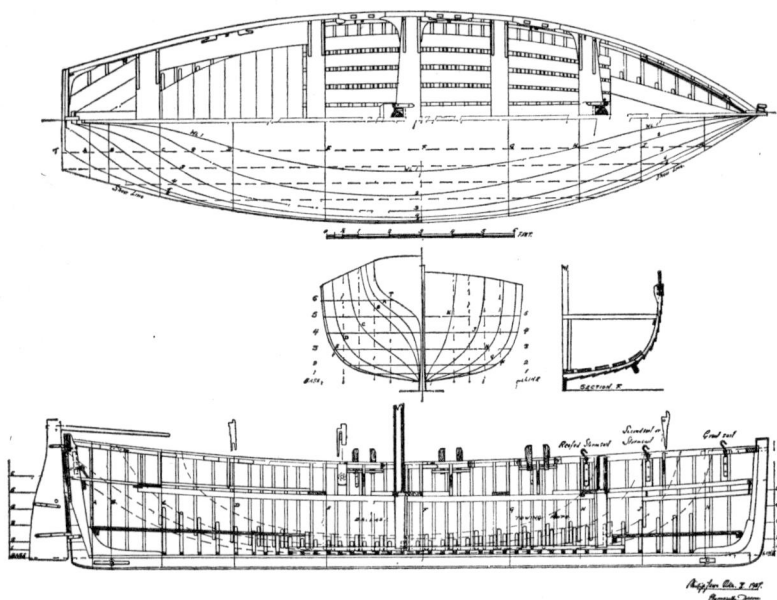

Plans of galley punt *Happy-go-Lucky*

10 in. It was clench-built and copper fastened, with elm planking on ash frames. The floors had a slight rise and went to the
bilge, with clamps for the bilge keels. The great mast was 20 ft
10 in high, diameter 4 in to $2\frac{1}{2}$ in, yard 13 ft 3 in, diameter 3 in
to $1\frac{1}{2}$ in. The small mast was 18 ft 2 in high, diameter $3\frac{1}{2}$ in to
$2\frac{1}{2}$ in, yard 11 ft 4 in, diameter $2\frac{1}{2}$ in to $1\frac{1}{2}$ in.

Finnis cut a suit of sails. The great sail had two lines of reef
points and the head was 'cutt down $3\frac{1}{2}$ in a cloth'. It was made
from 45 yd of 402 canvas, leech 18 ft 6 in, head 12 ft 6 in,
weather 13 ft 10 in, foot 17 ft 6 in.

The small sail had three lines of reef points, tack to mast 8 ft
4 in, 6 ft 4 in when was reefed. 'Head cutt down 17 in.' Made
from 35 yd of 402 canvas, the leech measured 15 ft 3 in, head
10 ft 10 in, weather 11 ft, foot 15 ft 6 in.

When measured up by the late P. J. Oke in October 1937

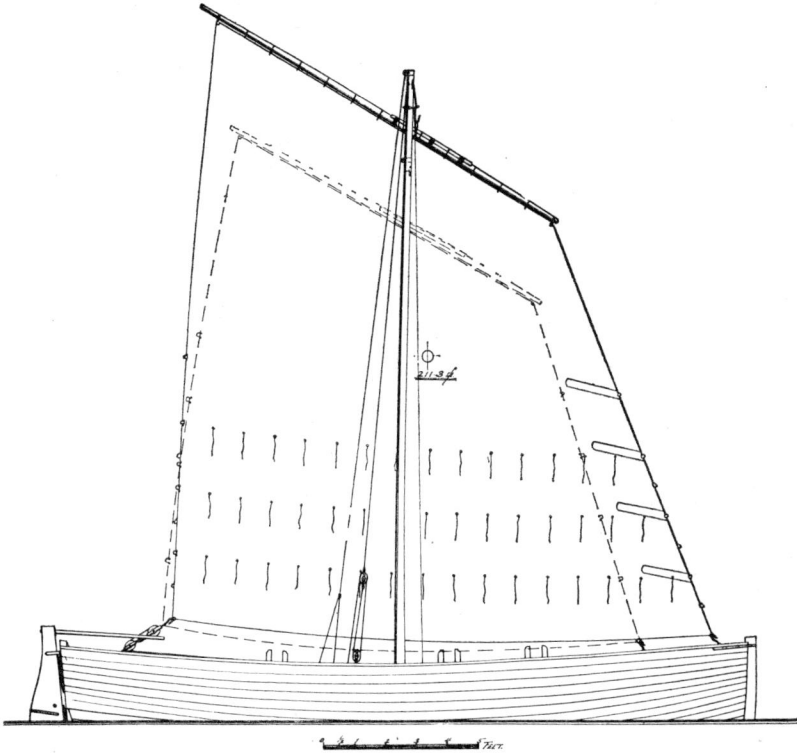

Sail plan of *Happy-go-Lucky*

the hull was in a bad condition but the plans were drawn in accordance with the traditional custom of local builders wherever any reconstruction was necessary.

SAILMAKERS

In the beginning of the nineteenth century there appear to have been two sailmakers in Deal, Philip Finnis at Farrier Street, and Thomas Marlow of Beach Street; Finnis was succeeded by his three sons. Thanks to Mr H. O. Hill, in whose possession they now are, I have been able to study closely three ledgers kept by G. W. Finnis. When the first entry was made in beautiful copperplate writing in March 1870 the talk of the beach was no doubt about the new tea clipper *Cutty Sark*. Would she beat the lovely green-hulled *Thermopylae*? Four years before, the water-front had thrilled to the sight of two superb clippers signalling their numbers on 6 September, *Ariel* at 8 am, *Taeping* 10 minutes later; outside the sands *Serica* was storming along towards the French coast, passing Deal at noon. All had left the Min River together at the end of May, to dock on the same tide 99 days later in the London river, *Taeping* at 9.47 pm, *Ariel* at 10.15 pm, *Serica* at 11.30 pm. A wonderful race.

The sailmakers had only to look seawards to see the results of their labours taking luggers and galleys on their varied missions. Finnis was cutting sails for every class of boat; during the first nine months he made 14 sails for luggers, 17 for galleys and four for punts, 35 in all, using 10 different makes of sailcloth. The following year the total for punts remained the same, luggers were 18 and galleys 23; by 1873 he was cutting 65, those for punts had increased to 15; galleys and luggers were 25 each.

It was still the custom for the majority of owners to order storm sails for luggers every two years; a decade later the interval became longer and longer. *Albert Victor* had four foresails— a great, storm, third and small. Dimensions varied tremendously. *Guiding Star*'s storm foresail took only 7 yd less cloth than *Garland*'s great sail, and she was only a slightly bigger boat. Storm sails were made from 14 in to 16 in wide bolts, great sails up to $27\frac{1}{2}$ in, and 18 to 21 cloths on the foot. Usually a great sail took from 166 to 212 yd of canvas; the largest Finnis made was one for *Florence Nightingale* of Broadstairs which took $253\frac{1}{2}$ yd of 386 Brown and was $26\frac{1}{2}$ cloths on the foot.

Some foresails were high and narrow, others low and wide, much depended on the owner's choice, and often subsequent sails were slightly altered in dimensions. All luggers carried mizzen topsails in the 1870s during the summer months, and a varied assortment of jibs.

Galleys had new sails every second year, sometimes annually. I spent weeks analysing these invaluable records of 27 years, and drawing up scale plans of most of the sails cut. It was a fascinating study. It would appear as if Finnis had either very finicky customers, or that he could not say 'no' to the travellers. In the first five years 30 kinds of cloth are listed in different sizes and weights, 14 in being the narrowest for storm sails, 30 in duck and 36 in cloth for light weather sails. During the next five years he tries another 26 makes, 56 in 10 years; many of the makers are well known, others I had never heard of. From 1880 to 1887 there were 16 more, but evidently times were getting harder as in the last seven years he only had five new makes. What a man, 77 varieties in 27 years.

Each meticulous entry gives the name of the boat and the sail cut, but at times only the name of owner: if a new boat, generally her dimensions, type and builder. It is interesting to note that he keeps to the old names, or just 'boat'; at times 'foresail and mizzen boat' for the small luggers. Nowhere does he mention the word 'galley punt' which was gradually superseding the old name 'great galley'. Always 'cut' is spelled 'cutt' when he gives the gore, either in inches per cloth or the sum total. The finished dimensions are given, next cryptic figures, his secret for the eating in of seams and so on, which ensure a perfectly fitting sail. Then follows the yardage used and generally the size and type of canvas, whether reef, sheet and weather bands were fitted, if the seams were flat or round, the distance of tack from mast; in fact, everything necessary was to hand when another sail was ordered.

A few entries say which cringles had thimbles. Keen boatmen had 'stakens' or half reefs on their sails. Usually there were three lines of reef points, and the cringles on weather and leech had galvanised iron thimbles; above and below were other cringles in the boltropes with no thimbles or corresponding reef points. A man could thus easily tell in the dark which he had in his hand. The plain rope ones were used for fine adjustments in sail area. In use, the next staken was hauled down to tack hook and sheet block and the strip of sail between staken and reef was thus rendered ineffective.

Finnis seems to have slipped up only once. In 1879 he cut a great foresail for *Albert Victor* from 165 yd of 16 in cloth. Five years before he had cut another of almost the same dimensions from 186½ yd of 14 in, 381. Something evidently went wrong, for below his figuring is this sobering entry: 'Had to alter it was to short in the leech. Cutt 8 inches off the foot. Could not sheet the sail. Put 20 inches on the sheet, 19 cloths just.'

Two quaint entries in 1871 and 1873 were for lugsails for two steam tugboats, built by Bayly, one 16 ft long, the other 17 ft 6 in. Were the sails to help the engines along, or to take the tiny tugs to where their services were required? In 1875 he supplied a suit of sails, including a squaresail, to the pilot cutter *Princess*. Cutting sails for lifeboats was his speciality.

There are extraordinary variations in the dimensions of new boats; no two appear to be alike, especially among the galleys and punts. The narrowest galley was *General Havelock*, 28 ft long, 4 ft wide, launched 4 November 1870. Her great sail was cut from 37¾ yd of F, 27¾ in bolts, leech 16 ft 1 in, head 12 ft 6 in, cut down 12 in, weather 13 ft 2 in, foot 17 ft 7 in. The small sail was cut from 24 yd of ¾ cloth. Another galley for Dover was 30 ft long, 4 ft 4 in wide and 1 ft 10 in deep, with a mast 17 ft 3 in long, tack to mast 6 ft 6 in. Others about the same length had a beam of 4 ft 10 in, 4 ft 8 in, 4 ft 5 in. These galleys were used in light weather for landing pilots.

A beam of over 5 ft begins to come within the category of a third-class galley punt, a heavier boat altogether, the bigger ones capable of keeping the sea in really bad weather once they had got off the beach. Many were exceedingly well found; *Lion* had 16 sails in 27 years. Most of them had a set of three sails. *Leader*, 28 ft 6 in long, 6 ft 10½ in beam and 3 ft 4½ in deep, had a mainsail cut from 76½ yd of 402, 28 in bolts, a second sail of 56½ yd of tick, and a third sail of 50¾ yd of the same canvas. The first two were cut down 14 in, the third 13 in.

The length of a mainmast varied from 26 ft to 27 ft 3 in in

first-class galley punts, the storm mast around 23 ft. At sea, it
was usual to have two sails, one either side of the mast. As the
boat came up into the wind one was dropped; the fore part
aback against the mast, acting like a jib, helped to pay the
boat's head round on the other tack. The yard was unhooked
from the traveller, which was smartly rehooked into the eye on
the yard of the lug lying across the thwarts on the opposite side
of the mast. The halyards were manned and this sail hoisted;
the partner lug was left lying in the boat until the next time the
galley punt went about, when the same procedure took place.
This saved perhaps a minute or two in time compared with
'dipping' the lug and the boat lost less way, being that much
less time without the driving power of a sail. This practice was
common in the luggers in the palmy days.

When the men were really in a hurry the norman post was
removed and the storm mast stepped in its place; the small sail
was hoisted, tack to stem and sheet just aft of mast.

The fee for landing a pilot was £1 and as a normal crew was
three to four it did not amount to more than a few shillings a
head, after the boat's share had been taken. Men often sailed
up as far as Gravesend or the Nore to get the job, towing back
astern of the steamer until off Dover where the pilot was
dropped. All hands sat well aft and it was vital to watch the
steering in that seething wake to avoid being sucked into the
propeller.

Hooking-on as a steamship passed was also a dangerous job.
The galley punt had to be sailed at full speed to hold steerage
way, almost stem-on; then the tiller was put hard down and she
shot alongside. Sail was dropped and the bowman reached up
with a 12-ft boathook, to the head of which a coir rope, 45
fathoms long, was attached, and hooked it into anything offer-
ing a hold. A line was caught from the ship just in case the hook
was jerked out. In a seaway, this operation called for cool heads
and skill; many a man lost his life on this service, as it was rare
for the vessel to slow down.

Thomas E. Bingham, master of the big Kingsdown lugger

Pilgrim, was drowned off Dungeness on 21 March 1905, when his galley punt *Gipsy Pride* was dragged under by the Norwegian steamer *Carolus*. He had been connected with Deal as a North Sea and Channel pilot for 40 years, taking vessels as far as Leith and Dundee. He recalled one stormy night when some 400 vessels were sheltering in the Downs; at dawn half were missing, blown from their anchorage. He was on board one which was swept out into the North Sea and driven ashore on the Suffolk coast.

The big galley punts were launched in the same way as the luggers, the smaller ones run down over the shingle, the crew jumping in at the last moment. The boats could tack in heavy seas, even under storm canvas with two or three reefs down. Sheets and halyards were always hitched, never belayed; neglect of this precaution might lead to a capsize and loss of life. Always the boat had to be watched—to avoid being caught aback in puffs in which the wind might shift four points in a few seconds and to ease her over seas by slackening off the main-sheet and hauling it in again, often pressed down to the lee gunwale, yet always rising over a green sea and gliding down the slope. At times a plank might split if a sea was taken badly.

Deal boats all went to wind'ard and 'ratched' better than they ran; being so fast they were liable to overshoot a sea instead of keeping on its back and so driving the bows half-way through the crest. The danger then was a broach-to. To avoid it the sail was hauled down and allowed to drag over the side to act as a drogue and check way; when back on the other side of the sea the sail was hoisted again.

In bad weather on nearing the land the reefs were shaken out to urge the boat at maximum speed, a stern rope was rigged out to hold her from being washed seawards again once she touched the shingle, the bow painter made ready to fling to men ashore. All hands came aft, and the steering had to be closely watched as if a sea were taken on the wrong quarter the boat became unmanageable. Carried in on a big sea the galley punt came in high and dry far up the beach, the men ashore grabbing the bow and stern ropes to hold her up.

When weather conditions allowed, sail was dropped and the boat was brought broadside to the shore opposite her capstan. One of the crew swung himself ashore by the halyards, to hang on and keep the galley punt inclined towards the beach, each sea lifting her in until the capstan rope was hooked in. The pilot sat in the stern sheets and stepped out dry shod when opportunity offered, or else was carried in pick-a-back. As a top hat was part of the stock-in-trade of a pilot in those days, it must have been a curious sight. (Picture, p 58.)

As a galley was run down across the shingle the long, narrow hull would twist appreciably and in time be permanently wringed, but this did not prevent them from giving years of useful service. All Deal boats were launched bows first, except the punts which went off the beach stern-first, the men jumping in over the bows as they came afloat. Many of these small craft lived over 50 years. Usually they were rigged with a dipping lug on the foremast and a spritsail or standing lug on the mizzen. They drifted with nets for sprats, herring or mackerel alongshore within the roads. The season for sprats was from 1 November to 1 April. Starting just before dusk, a boat made one haul and returned. In the 1880s fish factories were established at North End to can some of the surplus fish, as immense landings were sometimes made. In 1892 boats averaged 30,000 sprats a tide, for which perhaps 2s 6d a thousand would be paid; yet three days fishing gave each punt about £11 10s to be shared between three men. The small paddle punts were used for hooking; two men with handlines stood up and fished over the side.

It was drawing towards the end of an age dating back into the dawn of history when a ship disappeared over the rim of the horizon and was not heard of unless spoken by a passing vessel or signalled from a distant shore. Months and years might pass before she was again in home waters. Steamships were now commonplace, soon to be linked to the land by wireless, and Deal was to be left almost a forgotten town as far as hovelling was concerned. Bonding privileges had been withdrawn in

1881 when the port was degraded to a 'creek', and the Customs watch house became a mortuary, for a different kind of spirit.

The seascape is changing. A few brigs, schooners and barges are lying in the Small Downs, and piled up sierras of cloud on the horizon send shimmering reflections across the water in which every detail of hull and rigging is mirrored. Smoke rises lazily from an old clinker-built tug whose paddles churn out yard after yard of creamy lacework on the calm sea. Pools in the wet sand repeat the shape of a few anchors lying around, patient horses stand with chain traces hanging and coupling batts at all angles, looking at the unaccustomed scene, while bowler-hatted carters with corduroy trousers hitched up and strapped below the knee idly gossip or discuss how best to tackle moving an awkward load. A galley punt under big summer mainsail ghosts along, her crew vainly hoping to intercept a steamship whose wisp of smoke rising beyond the chalk cliffs of the North Foreland has betrayed her presence to watchful eyes, ever looking seaward in hopes of a hovel.

The sharp, clear outline of the distant French coast is a sure sign of a 'foxy' day, a weather breeder in truth. An ancient bluff-bowed brig is dropping down with the tide, her sails hanging limp, the breeze too faint to take the creases out of the jibs. Her bows swing round and for a few minutes her pace quickens as the full length of her heavy hull catches the hurrying stream; then she drifts round in an eddy and continues in that undignified movement—stern first. Such a craft is too 'parish rigged' to be worth a second glance. A lad on her fo'c'sle gazes shoreward with interested eyes at the smiling coast, hears again the sounds of cattle lowing, the bark of a dog, even voices, as sounds carry far across water on such a day. Tiny ripples caress the smooth rounded shingle, making every pebble glisten as if newly varnished, gulls wade in search of any morsel left by the tide, or float idly in the shallows. A whiff of shavings is borne by a light air passing a boatbuilder's yard and the 'tap, tap' of his riveting hammer blends with other sounds, the 'ding-din ding' as a ship's bell is struck sharply, followed by an ever diminishing chorus as vessels in the offing likewise mark the passing of time.

Few then gave heed to the thought that just as the sound of those ships' bells vanished without trace, so too would all that seascape pass for ever; luggers, galleys, coasters, brigs, all depart and leave hardly a record to tell of their busy life. A mahogany-faced boatman, dressed in spite of the warm day in thick pilot cloth coat, high-necked guernsey and fearnaught trousers so heavy that they could almost stand erect on their own, knocks the dottle out of his short-stemmed pipe. His keen eye constantly sweeps the Downs; a ship has but to show a wisp of bunting, or be in an unusual position, for immediate action to be taken. Along the strand lie the luggers, always ready for instant launching, varnished planking glinting in the sun and long outriggers stretching back across the road. Beside them the long, low galleys, beautiful examples of the boatbuilder's craft, strakes sweeping fore and aft in unbroken curves, light yet immensely strong. A punt lies upended while the owner gives her a lick and a promise, a knot of hefty fellows lean against the tarred sides of a shed listening to a whiskered old chap laying down the law on how things were done in his young days. One more energetic than the rest smooths down a hump of shingle, nothing must stand in the way of a lugger's run seaward.

A few girls exchange banter with upstanding young boatmen, curly haired, with thin gold earrings in their lobes, held to improve keen eyesight. A grey-haired dame is knitting a jersey, needles flying in and out as she watches her old man pottering about the boat. How much longer will he be able to take his place in the crew, or will he be only fit to earn a sixpence at the capstan bar and eke out an existence in his punt? A few 'toffs' stroll past and comment on what a lazy lot those boatmen are. Appearances are so often deceptive and perhaps within a few hours those same boatmen will be risking their lives on an errand of mercy in the lifeboat. A change is coming. A filminess is slowly spreading over the sky and the westering sun is sinking behind a bank of clouds through which its rays strike fanwise, 'Sun's sett' up 'is backstays,' remarks a weatherwise one, 'us'll 'ave plenty o' wind afore long.' A stately old Blackwaller slowly comes into view round the Foreland, running up Channel before the freshening breeze. As her stern lifts to the sea the sun catches the copper like the flash of a heliograph and the light strikes through her sails, patterning the staysails in deep shadow, glinting on the scrollwork of the trail boards. On the poop stands the helmsman, occasionally giving her a spoke or two. Soon she rounds-to, men run aloft and along the yards, and in a twinkling sails are clewed up or dropped; a splash followed by a rattle of chain tells that she has brought up for the night.

Away at the back of the sands goes a Yankee barque, beating down Channel, the Stars and Stripes thrashing at the peak as she dips her bows into the rising seas. She goes about and instantly her cotton canvas, white as snow, darkens into shadow. A lovely hull, picked out with painted ports, now comes into sight, skysails are furled and the lads are just taking in the royals; the flying jib comes down with a run, anchors are catted over the side and on her lee quarter steams a tug whose tall black funnels belch clouds of smoke. Rusty stains on the hull betoken that the clipper is iron-built, but no profit is likely to accrue to the Deal boatmen with her passing, for she will tow up past the Tongue lightship through the hours of darkness and be in the London river before the expected sou'wester blows up.

This decline is reflected only too clearly in Finnis's sail ledgers. Each year sees a greater number of sails cut for punts, now in demand to supply the fish factory and for pleasure trips in the summer; even the galley punts are not above taking a party out to the Goodwins or across to the French coast. In 1883 out of the 76 sails made, 37 were for the smallest boats and soon they were his mainstay. The last year of the decade sees a total of only 18 sails cut in the loft and the next few years emphasise the decline of the lugger, seldom more than three sails for them made in a year. A slight increase in sails for galley punts just keeps the needles sewing; the entries are still in copperplate, but the letters are more and more shaky as the hand that wrote them was soon to be stilled by death. The last few years in this

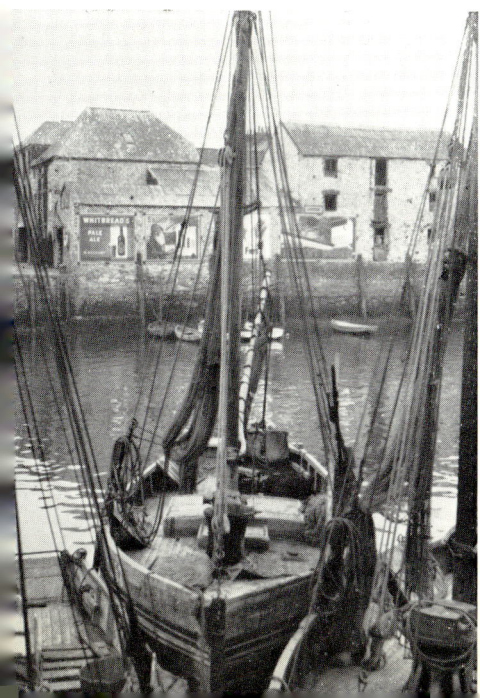

Page 117 (above left) Plymouth hookers. Note high-peaked mainsail hooped to mast, and angle of peak halyards; (above right) *Matilda* of Emsworth, built by Feltham at Portsmouth in 1945; (below) hookers in Sutton Pool, Plymouth. Note capstans on fore decks

Page 118 The
Barbican,
Plymouth. Note
long white mast-
heads on hookers,
short white on
luggers

Page 119 Mylor
Regatta, 1959.
Note jackyard
topsails and big
reaching foresails

Page 120 (above) *Zingueneh*, built at Restronguet, c 1840. Note sharp floors, deep heel and shape of counter; (below) 'long-boomers' in Clovelly harbour. *Teazer*, 218 BD, has more round to her forefoot than 213 BD, an earlier boat

loft must have been grim if all the cash received is entered up, as I believe to be the case. He received between £3 and £4 a week gross; out of this he had to pay his men and supply all materials. A windfall was the £56 17s 6d received for two suits for the West Australian lugger. I like some of the entries: 6s 3d for 'trowsers' but 6s 6d for 'gentleman's trowsers', evidently he put the price up threepence for visitors. Exorbitant! A coat was 8s 3d, sou'wester 1s 4d; if all were purchased together a suit of oilskins cost 15s 6d. A rope tye was 1s 2d to 2s for a galley punt, 3s 6d for a lugger.

I found it an almost impossible task to discover just how he priced his work, because of the enormous varieties of sail cloth used and the fact that the sails were generally cut under the name of the boat; but bills of course were rendered to owners. After literally weeks of tabulating sizes and figures and checking similar items against others for previous years, I eventually worked out that storm sails for galley punts were made for 1s 8¾d to 1s 9¼d a yard, with a few up to 2s 1d, which gave an average price of £2 13s 6d to £2 18s 6d, for identified second-class boats, first-class from £5 6s for storm sails, £6 9s for great sails.

Great sails for luggers were 1s 10½d a yard, storm 2s to 2s 2¾d a yard. The only really detailed entry was 'August 6th, 1885, to Mr Bayly for a boat 38 ft long, 9 ft 6 in wide and 4 ft 9 in deep, fitted with composite thimbles, 2 great foresails, 2 storm foresails, 2 great mizzens, one sett of rigging fitted complete, £55 5s 0d.' This agrees very well with the charge for sails in 1896 for the Australian lugger.

It was much easier to find the price of punt sails. A full suit for a boat 18 ft 6 in long and 6 ft 5 in wide, consisting of mainsail, staysail, mizzen, great jib and small jib for summer use, came to £5 14s 6d. A 26-yd lug foresail was £2 5s, a mizzen 16s, prices per yard for everything working out at from 1s 5d to 2s 0¼d according to cloth used.

One of the entries interested me perhaps more than any other. In 1897 a suit for Mr Case's boat for Westgate, 18 ft long, 6 ft

G

wide and 3 ft deep. This was none other than *Enchantress*, a herring punt in which I sailed several times before the 1914–18 war. On the death of her owners, she was sold for conversion to a yacht, after 50 years of work.

Some of the large punts were entirely spritsail-rigged; a 16-footer had a 13 ft mast with a 12 ft 6 in sprit, a 7 ft 6 in mizzen with an outrigger 6 ft 6 in outboard.

For lifeboat work a great foresail, storm foresail and mizzen for Walmer were priced at £20, for Broadstairs £21 15s, an average of 2s per yard, the great foresail costing £7 16s 3d, storm foresail and mizzen £13 8s 1d.

From 1892 to 1897, when the entries cease for ever, Finnis made 347 sails at a total cost of £1,318 9s 2d, giving an average of just under £4 a sail.

The great gale of November 1897 wrecked many capstans and some luggers; store houses which had survived gales for 60 and more years were moved bodily, and tremendous damage was done. (Pictures, pp 58 and 59.) In addition to this loss over 50 capstan grounds had been acquired by the Corporation for road and promenade improvements. By the turn of the century the fate of the luggers had been sealed and anchors were no longer available, even if urgently required. The barque *Lord Elgin* lost hers in the Downs in January 1900, and new ground tackle had to be obtained from London. In May, the Walmer forepeaker *Cosmopolite* took out a London anchor to a German barque.

Before leaving Thanet in 1952 I paid a last visit to Deal. Four galleys lay on the beach, twisted and wrung with long years of exposure and work, now only used at regattas. One was *Seaman's Hope*, named after the old lugger. I talked with her owner, Thomas Upton, for whom she had been built by Nicholas 45 years before, four men taking 6 weeks to build her 'with other jobs.' Her cost was £38, a sovereign less than the usual charge. The big lug cost £5, the small one £2 10s, altogether with oars and gear she cost between £50 and £60 ready for sea. The elm came from Lord Northbourne's estate, the timber being the estate men's perquisite; the trees cost 10s to

£1 each. After felling they lay in a dyke for six months before being taken to the sawpit and cut up into planks. She pulled eight oars and was chiefly engaged on pilotage work and salvage from the Goodwins, when two years old being employed at the wreck of ss *Mahratta*, landing 40 cases of tea. How that took me back. It seemed but yesterday when my late brother and I cycled over to Deal and saw the beach piled high with chests and salvage; in the offing every boat that could float was plying to and from the sands. (Picture, p 78.)

The galley would make six to seven knots; all her original timbers, the $\frac{1}{2}$-in iron keel and the copper fastenings were still good, but a new piece had been scarphed into the heel of the sternpost—little enough in major repairs. I roughly measured her up. Length 29 ft, beam 6 ft, depth of keel to garboard $3\frac{3}{4}$ in, stem to plank $2\frac{7}{8}$ in. Heel sternpost $6\frac{5}{8}$ in, thickness $1\frac{1}{4}$ in, head $2\frac{7}{8}$ in. Plank 5/16 in thick, frames and floors $\frac{3}{4}$ in sq, space between timbers $4\frac{1}{4}$ in, floors $1\frac{3}{4}$ in. Stringer $1\frac{3}{8}$ in × $\frac{1}{2}$ in, gunwale $\frac{3}{4}$ in wide. Thwarts $\frac{3}{4}$ in thick, some 7 in, others $8\frac{1}{4}$ in wide, six in all. The galley was steered by a yoke and tiller lines.

Not a lugger remained by 1952, the last of them, *Cosmopolite* (picture, p 60), had fallen to pieces from neglect on Walmer beach nearly 30 years before. The old virile life of the beach had altogether vanished.

CHAPTER THREE

THE SUSSEX COAST

RYE and Hastings, two towns of the Cinque Ports, have
a history dating back for centuries, but unfortunately
fishing boats were far too humble and common to merit
the attention of medieval chroniclers who were more concerned
with charters, wars and the like. Rye declined in importance,
but is still the registration port for the fishing boats, although
the Hastings men were 'the principal fishermen of England' in
Saxon times, according to Manship, writing of the Yarmouth
fisheries in 1619. For many years before the Norman Conquest
the creek harbour had been used by galleys passing to and from
Normandy, carrying men preparing for the eventual invasion.

The earliest known record of the type of boat is found in a
charter granted between 1140 and 1149 by the Abbot of Fé-
camp who held the overlordship of much land around Hastings.
His shares in the catches from the fishermen of Rye were defined,
two shares and a half in a boat of 26 oars, one in a boat of under
14 oars, suggesting the use of vessels similar to the longships,
and at times setting a single square sail on a mast amidships.

In these open boats Kent and Sussex men sought the herring
on far distant grounds, setting up their rude huts on the dunes
at the mouth of the Yare in Norfolk; there they beached their
boats, landed and salted catches, and dried their nets, claiming
the right of 'dene and strand'. They also acquired property in
the town of Yarmouth and the right to administer justice, much
to the annoyance of the local inhabitants who, however, could
do little about it. The Cinque Ports men had many privileges,
granted by royal decree, in return for the furnishing of vessels
of war for the defence of the English Channel and the transport

of troops to the French wars. All these privileges have gone, except one, the right to carry the canopy at a coronation.

Their arrogance led finally to a pitched battle in 1297 when 17 Yarmouth ships were burned, 12 looted and over 160 men killed. The prosperity of Hastings as a fishing port began to decline as other towns nearer the fishing grounds came into prominence. Then the French landed and practically destroyed the town in 1377; the loss of all our French possessions removed the need for troop transports. Finally a tremendous gale destroyed the harbour during the reign of Queen Elizabeth I, ruining the town as a port and thenceforward all vessels using the landing place had to be beached for unloading, a condition still prevailing. Photographs in my collection show brigs landing coal into carts alongside, a hazardous situation when the wind increased to a gale, driving ships broadside on to the beach and wrecking many a collier.

Probably the loss of the harbour brought about the change from the sharp-bottomed Viking-type boats, to heavy, well-built flat-bottomed craft capable of being launched off and beached on the steeply-shelving pebble strand.

At the beginning of the nineteenth century it was stated that:

> herrings commonly appear on the coast about the beginning of November and the season for them usually continues for six weeks. So immense is the number sometimes caught here that £900 worth have been brought to land in a single day. Soles, skate, mackerel, gurnet, whiting etc are also taken in great abundance. There are many hands constantly employed in building boats and in this occupation the inhabitants of Hastings have acquired considerable celebrity. Landing place is called 'The Stade', vessels 50 to 100 tons burthen are worked up to it by means of a capstan with surprising facility and expedition.

In March 1833 four Hastings boats took 10,800 mackerel, the next day two boats 7,000, a year later for a night's fishing one boat netted £100 worth. These catches were sent to London by swift cutters or to the nearest market available, often being forwarded to Billingsgate by horse vans driven at a gallop with a change of team every 10 miles in order to make the 5 am market.

The 1849 Report states:

The fisheries at Hastings were formerly conducted by boats of an inferior class, from 25 to 30 ft in length, some of which are open, others but half-decked, but from the frequent loss of life, the many difficulties they had to contend with, and the want of a harbour or other means of shelter, it was rendered necessary to enlarge and improve them.

The boats of the present day are of very superior shape and construction, some are 35, 40 and 48 ft in length, rigged with three masts and lugsails, crew consisting of nine persons and carry about 140 mackerel and 110 herring nets in their respective seasons. There are two seasons, one to the North Foreland for herrings, the other to the Land's End for mackerel, where the good qualities of the boats and skilfulness of their crews are soon called into effect to overcome the many difficulties they have to encounter. . . . A large space is allotted for their cabin, which is fitted in a very comfortable manner, they contain eight bed-berths, beside ample convenience for stowage of provisions and fuel in cupboards and lockers, they possess also a fireplace which gives them an air of comfort so highly necessary to their existence and presenting a striking contrast to lying on deck, or sleeping on wet ropes and sails, as in boats of a former period. There being no harbour to run into, the fish are landed by means of ferry boats, which are launched through the heaviest surge to land their cargoes of fish, but not without sometimes capsizing and losing the whole.

The fishing seems to be very lucrative, some boats after a voyage share £40 a man, besides his provisions, the master sometimes receiving thrice that sum, as the boat generally belongs to him and is supplied by him with nets etc.

A typical lugger, built by T. D. Thwaites, had a keel 38 ft long, breadth 14 ft 11 in, depth 6 ft 3 in; weight of hull $17\frac{1}{2}$ tons, ballast 10 tons; cost of hull and spars £250, clench-built and copper-fastened, three lugsails, topsail and jib. Crew eight men and a boy.

In those days the planking was of oak grown in the Sussex Weald; later elm was more generally used, with oak frames. The smaller luggers were two-masted, often with a spritsail instead of a lug on the mizzen. It is probable that the lug rig was introduced during the Napoleonic wars; it was always a favourite rig in France and familiar to Hastings men who frequented French harbours on smuggling expeditions.

On Christmas Eve 1842 it came on to blow hard from the south'ard when four vessels were on the beach discharging cargo, three stranding and becoming total wrecks. In the evening a lugger beached from France with a cargo of turkeys. On 12 October 1846, the lugger *Albion* was lost with all hands in the North Sea, and 2 June 1860 was remembered for a furious sw gale in which the big lugger *Endeavour* foundered with her crew of eight men and a boy, and several luggers lost men overboard. In October there was a tremendous 'swim' of herrings on a calm Sunday morning, five boats catching 5, 6½, 7, 7½ and 8 'last'—a nominal 10,000 fish, but as counted actually 13,200. During the month of October 1884 catches were usual until the end of the month; on the 29th herrings were selling at £27 and £28 per last. The next day so heavy were the landings that the price dropped to £4 to £5, and those boats unable to sell had to accept £2 10s per last for 'overdays'.

The mackerel voyages to the west'ard took their toll. On 9 March 1862 the lugger *Crystal Palace* was wrecked with all hands on Plymouth breakwater and two others lost men overboard. In October 1877 mackerel were plentiful; Stephen Foord had 14,000 prime fish, sold for 7s 3d per 100, and about three last caught in 'kettle nets', two being transferred to another boat for sale in Brighton. Lawes had 9,000 and two last, at Eastbourne five and eight last. These enormous landings swamped the market and the following day prices dropped to 3s 6d to 4s 6d per 100, but a day later J. Bumstead had over 4,000 in his drift nets and was lucky enough to get 7s 6d per 100. He had a new lugger built, named *Favorite*, and she was afloat for the first time in September 1878.

In September 1896 it began to blow hard and six luggers had to beach at Eastbourne, another got into Newhaven. The gale continued to harden and during the following days two other luggers had to beach at Eastbourne; 56 RX tried to ride out the storm, but the cable snapped and the rudder was lost, so that, helpless to make headway, she was driven ashore near Pevensey.

The rise of Hastings as a holiday resort with the coming of the railway had brought a change in conditions; the three-masted lugger was found unhandy for trawling for soles in Rye Bay and within a decade or so disappeared in favour of the small fore and mizzen boat with a keel length around 30 ft. Fitted out for trawling, they cost about £200 ready for sea, with herring and mackerel nets £350; lining—'hooking'—was also carried on.

According to their size, the boats were known as 'luggers', the largest, fully decked, being 27 to 30 ft in keel length, and ranging between 7 and 16 tons. The next—the 'bogs'—were similar in design but ranging between 4 and 7 tons; then came the 'punts', all open boats, some with a small foredeck and under 4 tons measurement. Instead of the mizzen lug they often carried a spritsail; leeboards were in common use until the introduction of a metal centreboard about 1885, which was liable to buckle when a boat was rolling heavily or if she touched bottom.

The luggers carried a fore and mizzen lug, jib, mizzen stay-sail and topsail, occasionally a fore topsail with its luff laced to a yard—the 'quant'—and hoisted with halyard through a hole at the masthead. The sheet went to the after end of the lug yard, a heel rope rove through a hole in the heel of the quant and was given two or three turns round the mast before belaying to the luff hook. The topsail sheet belayed to the snatch knee of the mast case. When tacking, the sheet and halyard were shifted over to leeward. The sail was always set a'weather.

Hull construction followed normal practice; each floor timber was shaped on its under side to fit over the lands, the ribs—here called 'futtocks' or 'futtock timbers'—were fitted midway between two floors, and in the early days they, too, were notched, later practice was to omit this for the sake of

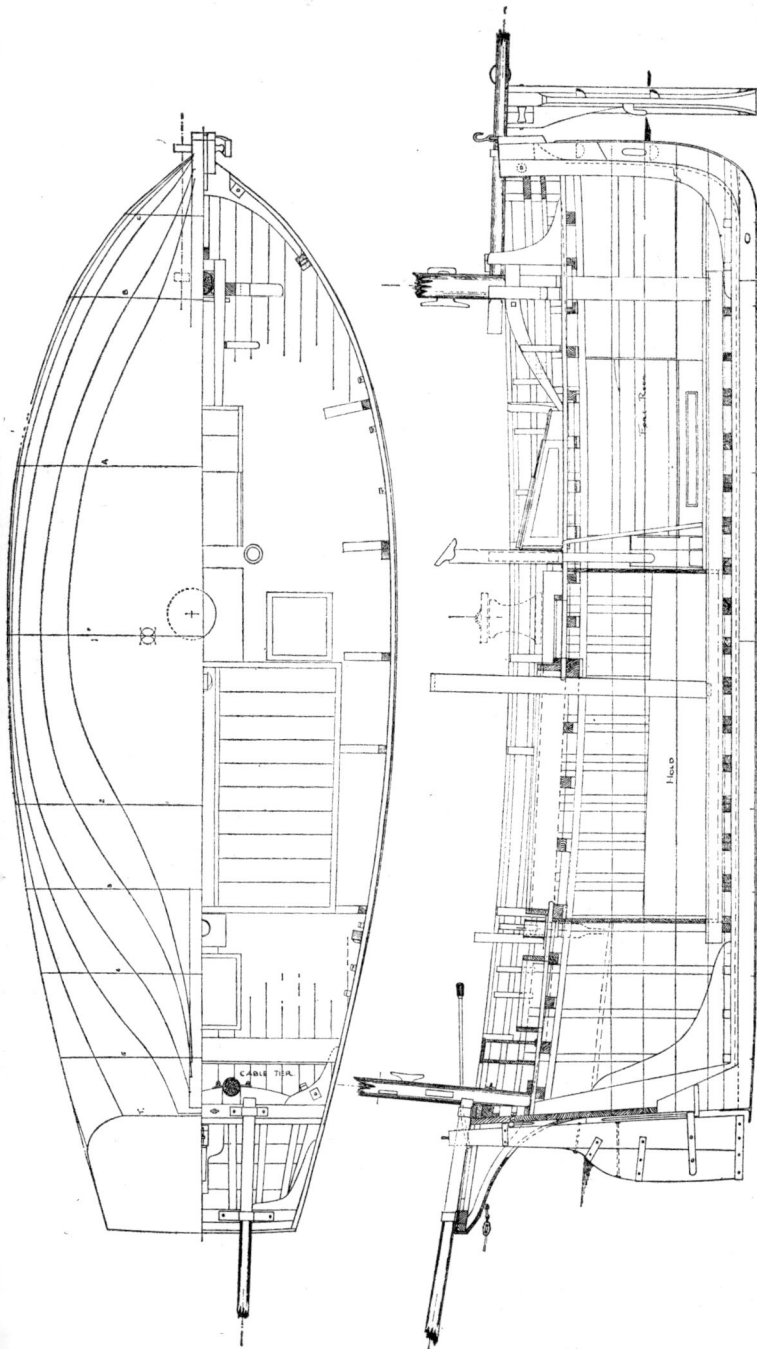

THE *INDUSTRY* OF HASTINGS: BUILT 1780: OVERALL LENGTH 32′ 8″, BEAM 4′ 9″. LINES TAKEN OFF BY P. J. OKE (S.N.R.)

Lines of Hastings lugger *Industry*, taken off by the late P. J. Oke for the
Coastal Craft Sub-committee of the Society for Nautical Research

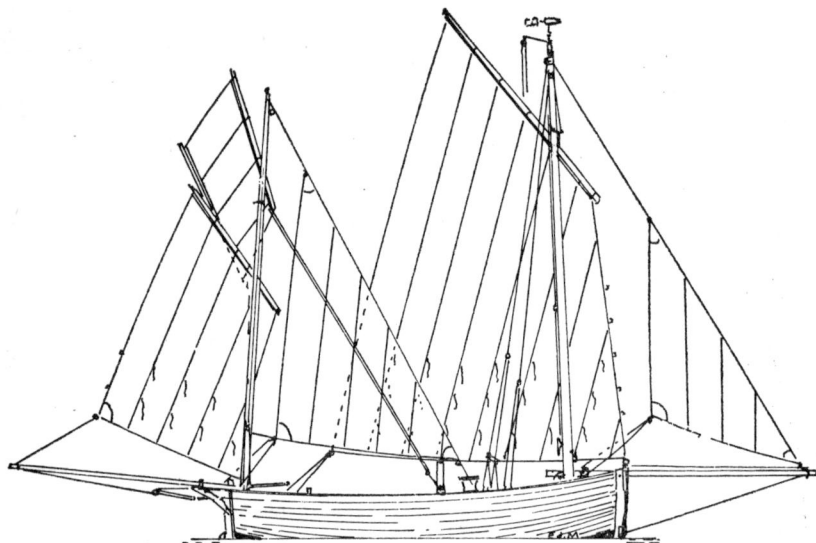

FORE MAST 32'- 6" dia, 8"-4".   YARD 18' dia 5½'- 3"   BOWSPRIT 20' outboard 14'-3", 4½'-3"
MIZZEN MAST 30', dia 6'-3½"   YARD 12' dia 4"- 2½'   TOPSAIL YARD 11' dia. 2½'- 2"
OUTRIGGER 18'-4" outboard 14' 4"sq to 3" dia

Sail plan of *Industry*

extra strength. They extended downwards to two and a half or
three strakes below the floor head. At the turn of the bilge the
outer edge of three or four planks was 'browed'—bevelled—for
about an inch to make the overlap neater. Bottoms were broad
and flat with a well-rounded bilge, usually fitted with a deep
bilge keel. When on the beach a few short thick planks, called
'blockings', under the bilge keels held the boat upright.

Keel and bilge keels were shod with iron; that on the keel
continued up the stem and over the stemhead where it was
formed into an eye to take the luff hook; to starboard was the
stem horse with an iron sheave, to port the gammon iron—
local name 'fore iron'—to take the bowsprit, here called a 'jibboom'. On each side of the forefoot was a 2-ft iron plate with
the 'strap stem chain hole', through which a reeving line was
always kept rove, its ends brought up on each side of the stem

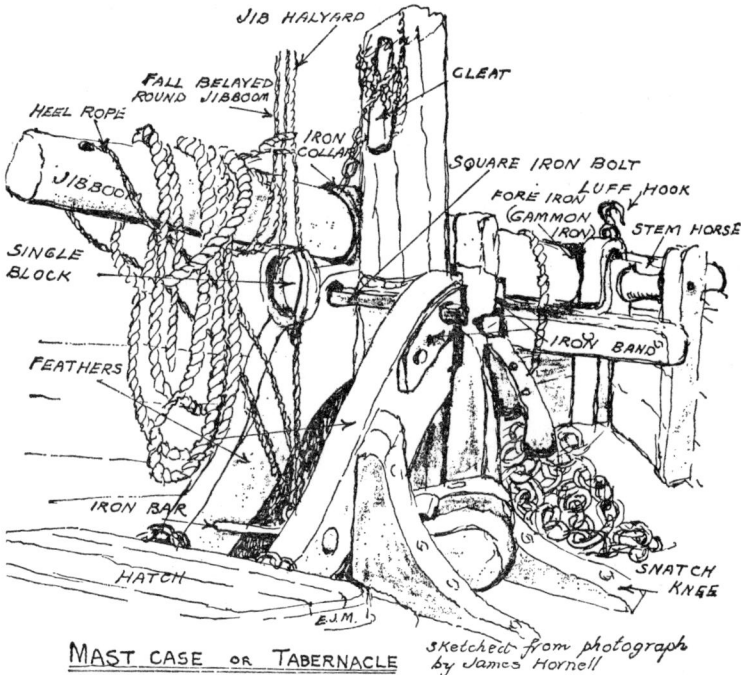

JIB HALYARD

FALL BELAYED
ROUND JIBBOOM

CLEAT

HEEL ROPE

IRON
COLLAR

JIBBOOM

SQUARE IRON BOLT

FORE IRON LUFF HOOK
GAMMON
(IRON)

STEM HORSE

SINGLE
BLOCK

FEATHERS

IRON BAND

IRON BAR

HATCH

SNATCH
KNEE

E.J.M.

MAST CASE OR TABERNACLE

Sketched from photograph
by James Hornell

Sketch of mast case or tabernacle

and bent together abaft the stemhead. On the port side of the
stem were two heavy cleats—the 'clamps'—fixed about 2 ft
apart, to enable a man to climb aboard. On the starboard side
was a down-turned cleat used as a lead for the jib tack.

The shape of the stern differed considerably, originally the
transom was square but later a counter was built on, curving
outward from the old transom which now formed the after
partition of the cable tier. This 'lute' stern was considered to
give increased lift in a following sea. Then came the fashion of
closing in part of the space under the lute by continuing the
run of the upper strakes until they met those on the opposite
side—the 'elliptical stern'—but many fishermen did not consider it lifted so well. With this stern an iron or steel rudder was
fitted, allowing only a narrow slot for the trunk; rudders were

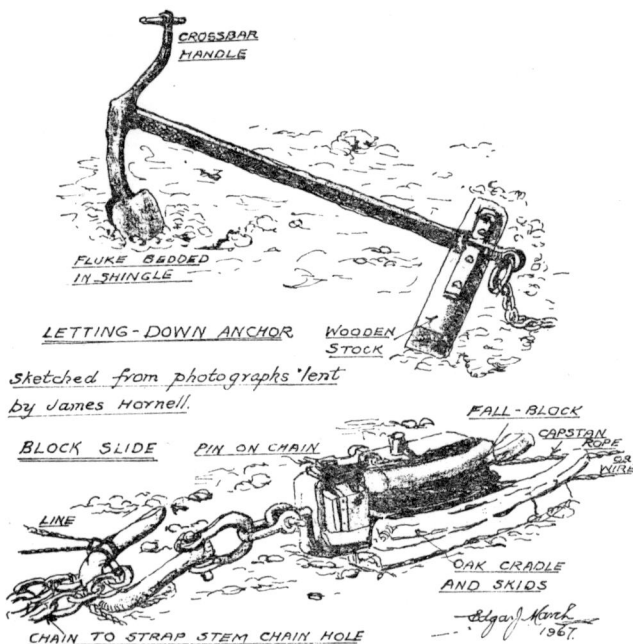

CROSSBAR HANDLE

FLUKE BEDDED IN SHINGLE

LETTING - DOWN ANCHOR   WOODEN STOCK

Sketched from photographs lent by James Hornell.

FALL - BLOCK

BLOCK SLIDE   PIN ON CHAIN

CAPSTAN ROPE OR WIRE

LINE

OAK CRADLE AND SKIDS

CHAIN TO STRAP STEM CHAIN HOLE

Sketch of letting-down anchor and block slide

invariably hoisted up a foot or two when the lugger had to be beached. Individual builders stamped their personality on their sterns, making it easy to tell the yard where a boat was built.

The hull was divided into four compartments separated by three bulkheads, first the 'fore room', then the 'middle room', next the 'chay', and finally the 'pat' or 'after place'.

The fore room was the cabin, with lockers and bunks, an iron stove and coal locker, as well as a food cupboard. The middle room was the fish and rope room, divided fore and aft on either side for stowage of fish, the central part for the net ropes. Overhead was a large central hatch with coamings—local name 'covings'—with a 'scudding hole' cut in a deck plank through which herring and mackerel were transferred to the hold below; some 9 to 10 in in length these holes were closed by a block of wood tightly wedged in.

The chay was the largest room; here the nets were stowed, and at the fore end of the hatch stood the 'veer-away post' or 'tow post'. Originally it rested in a tabernacle, being the lower part of the main mast when three lugsails were set. A platform of pine boards covered the bottom of the chay to a point above the bilge strake where a longitudinal board—the 'spurkin'—closed the space between the platform and skin planking. Ballast was shingle, called 'beach'.

At the stern was the pat, used as a sail locker and store. On deck, between the middle-room hatch and the fore-room companion, was a wooden hand capstan, worked by two men turning handles. A 'scud pole' was lashed fore and aft between the foremast and the veer-away post when hauling drift nets, which were shaken before being passed down into the chay. Later practice was to bundle nets and fish all together into the chay and scud the fish on the beach.

In lute-sterned boats (picture, p 78) the anchor, cable and gear were stowed in the 'cable tier'. The lower pintle was long to allow the rudder to be raised without coming free. When this was done the mizzen burton purchase was disengaged and the hook passed into an eyebolt in the rudder head, raising it through the trunk. The tiller was wood, later iron, with a return loop to clear the mizzen mast.

The foremast was stepped well forward, about 4 ft from the stem, its heel resting in a tabernacle—the 'mast case'—made up of three vertical planks forming a box with the after side open. It extended to about 18 in above the deck, and was morticed to the keelson together with the 'samson post', the squared timber inside the case taking the weight of the mast. (See sketch, p 131.)

On deck, the forward ends of two massive curved timbers—the 'feathers'—were let into the top of the mast case, port and starboard, and further secured by an iron bond passed round with a thick, square iron bolt passing through the feathers abaft the mast. A lighter bar passing through the after ends of the feathers was used for making fast ropes and purchases. At deck level there was another iron band, and the fore ends of the mast case were supported by three very stout oak knees, with smaller ones at the after end of feathers, forming an exceedingly massive support for the mast. The fore knee—the 'knighthead'—had the jib outhaul made fast to it; the starboard knee—'snatch knee'—had a downturned cleat to catch the cable when required.

The inboard end of the reeving bowsprit—local name 'jib-boom'—went to port of the mast case through outer and inner iron collars. The mizzen mast was stepped to starboard, its heel resting at deck level in a mast case fitted either in a recess cut out of the fore side of the 'square', or thwart, or between two strong cleats nailed against it. It was held in place either by a straight strap or by a half collar according to the depth of the recess. Below deck was a small samsom post, bolted to the side of the sternpost.

A mast crutch—the 'match'—was stepped in a hole cut in the square in lute-sterned boats; in those of elliptical build it was stepped in the mast thwart, between the mast and the port bulwark. A weather vane—the 'bob-wane'—usually in the form of a fish, boat or cock, was fitted at the mizzen masthead. The outrigger went out over the stern a little to starboard of the mast, the inboard end squared and secured by two collars, one on the rail, the other on the square. It generally had a slight steeve upwards.

The jib halyard purchase consisted of two single blocks—known in Hastings as a 'single fall'—the fall belaying to the heel of the bowsprit; the tack went to an iron traveller with an outhaul leading through a hole in end of bowsprit and, in the days before trawling became common, down under a cleat on the starboard side of stem, and belaying around the foremast case knee. Each of the two jib sheets passed inboard through holes in the bulwarks just for'ard of the foremast.

The rigging of the foremast consisted of the lug halyards, the forestay and the light halyards. The forestay was called the 'fore burden', a corruption of burton, the general name, the purchase being a Spanish burton. Halyards and forestay had luff tackle purchases—a double block above a single one. The purchase was always set up to windward, hooking into an eye on the end of an iron chainplate just under the bulwark, abaft the mast. The burton hooked about 2 ft further aft, the falls belaying round cleats abaft the purchases. The iron traveller on the mast to which the foreyard was hooked was here the 'parrel', derived no doubt from the old-fashioned bead parrel of bygone days. To strengthen the yard to take the strain, a long oak bar —the 'fishing'—was nailed to the yard, and the sail was bent by rovings—'knittles'—the tack going to the hook on the stem-head. Three rows of reef points were usual. The sheet rove through two single blocks, each with a hook, one going to the clew, the other into an eye at the fore end of the 'fore sheet strap' bolted obliquely on the outside of the bulwark, abreast the cable tier. The fall belayed to a bulwark cleat for'ard of the purchase.

The light halyards rove through an eye at the outer end of a curved iron arm—the 'lamp-iron'—projecting on the after side from an iron strop round the masthead. This had to be removed when the foremast was lowered while the lugger rode to her nets, the light then being shown on the gunwale on the side on which an approaching vessel would pass.

The mizzen having a standing lug, the halyard purchase went to starboard, the burton to port, the falls belaying on vertical cleats near the end of the square. The sheet rove through a hole in the end of the outrigger to a luff tackle purchase, the fall from the double block reeving through a cleat on the starboard side of mast to belay round a cleat near the foot of the fore side. The tack hooked on to a 'luff-hook' to port of the mast. In later years the lantern was carried on the mizzen. (Picture, p 78.)

The stay—the 'Tommy Hunter'—was generally set up to give the mast a forward rake, the luff tackle purchase being hooked to an eye in the upper collar of the veer-away post, or to an eyebolt in the deck, and the fall belaying round a cleat on the fore side of the mast. The sail had two lines of reef points. When a mizzen staysail was set, a spar—the 'manacle boom'— was used to boom out the foot when running free.

The mizzen topsail had two yards, one on the head; the other, a shorter one, was bent on the after part of the foot of the sail, the sheet being bent to the yard, and belaying to the luff hook. Sheaves were generally 'dumb', the rope passing through being well greased; later sheaves were adopted.

When the nets were down, a round basket was hoisted on the light halyards. A flag hoisted on either mast when nearing the shore indicated the intention to beach without delay.

The foremast was lowered by the burton, then hooked to the stem, and rested on the 'match' near the stern; to raise it, the mizzen burton was hooked near the head of mast, and when it had been raised to a sufficient height, the weight was taken by the fore burton.

Generally speaking, these arrangements were universal in luggers, with slight modifications to suit local conditions or a skipper's choice, and the variation in nomenclature is interesting. Although both at Deal and Hastings there were steep pebble beaches the conditions for launching and landing differed considerably.

When coming ashore, especially when the ebb was well advanced, it was usual for a lugger to drop her anchor some way off the beach, to be used as a haul-off warp, the chain being taken to the deck capstan. By means of the reeving line at the stem a chain was hauled through the hole in the forefoot and the ends shackled together, a line was thrown ashore and the bight of the chain hauled in and passed over the hook of the 'fall-block' carried on a small wooden cradle—the 'block slide'. Through this block ran the capstan rope, or later wire, its free end made fast to a chain shackled to an anchor or other purchase buried in the beach, shoreward of the block slide.

When all was ready men tramped round and round the capstan, slowly hauling the hull up the slope, assisted by the greased wooden blocks—the 'trows'—placed under the keel as required. A horse was harnessed to a long pole when a heavy lugger came ashore. The risk of being pooped by a big sea was always present. Then the boat would fill with water, slew

Page 137 (*above left*) The only known print of a 3-masted lugger under sail, *Beatrice Annie*, *c* 1910. Note tack of fore lug hooked to end of iron bumpkin, fore girt stretching weather leech of fore lug, and oar hole. The light masts are bending to the strain of the big lugs;

(*centre*) Restronguet oyster dredger. One reef down, second pendant rove. Note dredge over port rail;

(*bottom right*) Falmouth Quay punt, laying-to, April 1926. Note reef in staysail and diagonal reef in mainsail to give a clear view all round, the leg-of-mutton mizzen and short iron bumpkin at stem

Page 138 (above) Gig *Slippen*, built *c* 1830, leaving to collect the dead from wreck of the 7-masted schooner *Thomas W Lawson* and bring them to St Agnes for burial, December 1907; (below) Scilly Isles Regatta, 1903; from top: *Lily*, St Martins; *Dolly Varden* and *Lloyds*, St Mary's; *Bonnet*, Tresco; *Leo*, St Mary's; *Cetewayo*, St Agnes

Page 139 (above) *Czar* of Bryher, a 7-oared gig with two bullocks a side and tow ropes round their horns, salved from ss *Minnehaha*, wrecked April 1910. *Czar* is passing west side of Bryher, Heathy Point, the rock is called 'Droppy Nose'. Land in distance is North Hill of Samson;

(centre) gig *Dolly Varden* outside Frank Watt's carpenter's shop at St Mary's;

(below) Frank Peters of St Mawes, descendant of builder of *Newquay* in 1812, presents the gig's original moulds to Tommy Prior, chairman of Newquay Rowing Club, 1954

Page 140 (above) The gig Shah on arrival at Brabyn's yard, Padstow, for refit in December 1954; (below) Shah refitted. Mr Brabyn and his workmen

broadside on and be battered to pieces unless prompt action was taken, this usually consisting of stoving in a plank with a heavy maul to allow the water to run out and lighten the boat. Pooping was a serious danger with an open boat, but the big, fully-decked hulls were immune. (Pictures, pp 77 to 80.)

The boat lay stern towards the sea and launching was not a wild rush down as at Deal. A 'skid-chain' had replaced the hauling-up chain through the hole in the forefoot and passed over the hook of the fall block in which the capstan wire ran The hull rested on trows, and others were laid down farther seaward as the boat was pushed slowly down. Half the men leaned their backs against the bows, moving the boat foot by foot until she rode over the edge of the shingle bank. The skid chain was then freed and away the boat went down the slope, sliding over the last few trows laid out in the water. If necessary, the crew manned the deck capstan and hauled off by means of the chain to the anchor which had been dropped before the boat was beached. In the old days a single-fluke 'hauling-off anchor' was used and left permanently embedded. A 'letting down' anchor, with the fluke of one arm made into a cross-bar handle, was used from early times, the fluke being bedded into the shingle and the end of the skid chain shackled to its ring. One man moved it down the beach as required to check the lugger, while a fresh trow was placed in position or to prevent too rapid progress. (See sketch, p 132.)

The small open boats went drift-netting for sprats during the first three months of the year, then a change was made to larger meshed nets for mackerel. Some men preferred lining— or 'hooking' to use the local name—until well into the autumn, when the herring nets were put aboard, finishing up around Christmas. Ring-net seining for mackerel was practised at one time. (Picture, p 97.)

The men worked on the share system. If drifting, the crew numbered six men and a boy. After the general expenses had been deducted—food, net repairs and incidentals—the number of shares, 14, was divided; one to the boat, six to the nets, one

H

to each hand, a half share to the boy. The skipper had an extra quarter share over his one, and another quarter went to the boat attendant on shore.

The beach presented an animated scene 70 and more years ago. A big catch, landed an hour or so back, lies on the pebbles with a half circle of buyers assessing its worth to them; some whiskered old men with stovepipe hats or billycocks stand beside younger fellows in caps, most with hands in pockets and a nonchalant air as the auctioneer starts the sale. A mystic sign, probably unknown to the fishermen standing nearby, tells who is bidding for their night's work.

Close by are lines of hawkers' flat carts, the horses quietly munching in nosebags, and dozens of hand carts belonging to less affluent cadgers and a smart van or two owned by the leading fishmongers. Drawn up on the shingle are luggers and punts, a few with very meagre catches on display. In the background the tall, tarred net sheds and the Fishermen's Church, and on the skyline the ruins of Hastings Castle. Men from one lugger are hurriedly shaking their nets over the bulwark, hoping that prices will not fall before the buyers reach them. Other boats lie bows-on to the beach, men hastening with baskets of choice fish, trusting to catch the eye of a manager from one of the big hotels out betimes to secure prime quality fish for his visitors.

In the offing are a few late arrivals cracking-on, while early comers are making sail, outward bound. A smoky haze from many a household fire lies over the town and a few early risers are 'walking up' an appetite for breakfast, or stand watching the scene on The Strade where a brig is unloading coal by 'jumpers' into carts alongside.

A few hours later the scene has changed. Farther along the promenade a band is playing lively music; the curious little bathing machines, painted in bright stripes, with their high gig wheels, are lined along the water's edge, kiddies shout and jump about while mamas or nannies, in long skirts sweeping the ground, see they do not get into mischief. A Punch and Judy show has attracted a small crowd of excited children, a few 'mashers' swinging canes stroll along, ogling any attractive girl; a smart punt has a pleasure party aboard, and other boatmen tout for custom.

Towering over all are the two big pleasure 'yachts', *Albertine* and *New Albertine*, with all sail set ready to push off the moment a full load of passengers is aboard. Years later those yachts were sold to Newhaven buyers for conversion to 'boulder boats'. *Albertine* had her clinker planking levelled with wedge-shaped boards, then doubled with carvel planking. For some reason or another her sister was never used, having been broken up in Sleeper's Hole, Newhaven, as was *Albertine* in later years.

'Bouldering' used to be a great industry in Sussex. Boats were put ashore under the cliffs on an ebbing tide with an anchor out astern. A gang of men picked up the blue flint boulders into baskets, ran up a plank on to the boat and tipped the contents into the hold. Sailing ships later took the flints away for use in the Potteries, where they were ground up and used to put a gloss on china.

Motors, first introduced in 1912, rapidly came into favour, and after the 1914–18 war sail soon was auxiliary. Seeking the herring shoals off Margate ceased, the men waiting until the fish appeared off Hastings; trawling for soles in Rye Bay was more profitable. By the 1930s the Corporation provided horses and kept the capstans in repair. Owners paid a heaving-up fee of 4s 6d to 6s every time the capstan was used, also 'stade-dues' of 24s for a berth on the foreshore.

So many tides have ebbed and flowed at Eastbourne since there was any intensive fishing there that it has proved impossible to obtain much first-hand information. The late Bob Hunt who was most assiduous in seeking data, wrote me early in the 1950s:

> I went to Eastbourne to see old Mr Fred Hurd, the last of the Eastbourne big-boatmen. He is 86 and his memory very bad and is inclined to wander in his reminiscences. What I did get was that he went to sea fishing at the age of 13 years, at 14 he went for three years running to the South of Ireland, mackerel catching

out of the ports of Kinsale and Baltimore. This was in Eastbourne boats owned by Mr Popham, a wealthy man who went in for fishing. He bought several local luggers, one being the *Little Florence*, built and owned by George Gausden at Eastbourne.

Popham had her lengthened and dandy-rigged. He also had some built, the first one being the *Queen of Sussex*; she was built with a centre board which was taken out later. Mr Hurd could give me no dimensions, except that the *Queen of Sussex* was about 50 ft long.

Popham had a big racing yacht built at Eastbourne called the *White Slave*, first rigged as a 'schooner lugger', that is lug-rigged with the biggest mast aft, later at Cowes she was changed to a cutter. He also had a yacht called the *Paradox*, a steam auxiliary lugger.

Other fishing craft owned by Popham were the *Happy Thought*, *Bird of Freedom*, *Nick of Time*, *Free Will* and *Fred Archer*, which was bought from Plymouth, also two steam carriers called *Romulus* and *Remus* which used to bring the mackerel from Ireland to England.

I got the names of a few of the 'shinermen' of Eastbourne which were half-open luggers 27 to 28 ft long . . . *Band of Hope*, *Crystal Spring*, *Star of Hope*, etc. . . . There were big decked luggers owned at Worthing and Dungeness.

In an 1892 issue of *The Yachtsmen*, there was a paragraph to the effect that the lugger-yacht had returned from the Mediterranean, also that *White Slave* was classed as a '40-rater', and that in the spring the *Queen of Sussex* had been purchased at Eastbourne by Mr Collingwood Hughes of Hamble; 'he has since been fishing and shooting in her on the coast of Holland'. Bob unearthed many faded photographs, and in other letters wrote: 'I wish I could get you more dates and details, but it just can't be done. I've left this too late. When I was a young man I knew Tom Sisk very well, he was George Gausden's foreman boatbuilder. . . . I remember old Laddie Simpson telling me, years ago, he had a lugger built at Porthleven for £100 . . . it's too late, worse luck.'

Whilst on the subject of lug-rigged yachts mention should also be made of the big three-masted lugger *New Moon*, 136 ft overall, 220 tons burden, OM, built at Hastings in 1859.

Bob's photographs show typical clinker-built hulls. *Little*

Florence had quite a graceful counter stern, an enormous mizzen lug and jib; when dandy-rigged a 'jacky' topsail was set on the mizzen, and the mainsail was loose-footed. As at Hastings, the oars, boathook and spare spars were carried outboard over the port rail in rope 'rafts', although some luggers used 'lumber irons'. All had foremasts close to the stem.

The sprat punt *Pet* was built of timber left over from Popham's yacht *Paradox*. These small fore and mizzen boats had a moveable top strake—'washstrake'—fitted in winter to give increased freeboard when drift-net fishing. All Eastbourne fishing boats were registered at Newhaven. (Pictures, pp 79 and 97.)

Brighton, now world-renowed as a holiday resort, was once a prosperous fishing port called Brighthelmstone, despite having no harbour and only an open shingle beach as at Hastings. As a result of two raids by the French in 1514 and 1545, official attention was drawn to the ease with which hostile landings could be effected only a short distance from London. The defences were strengthened, but much of their cost fell on the fishermen who then outnumbered landsmen by about four to one. The fair apportionment led to continual disputes, and four commissioners were set up 'to enquire into Petetion 1579 to Privy Council'; the fishermen were ordered to meet and 'sett down in wrytinge their auncient customs and orders'.

A square space in the midst of the houses, known as the 'Hempshares', was laid out in plots for the growing of hemp for making nets. During the thirteenth century, settlement had been made between the lay rector and the vicar regarding small tithes from fishing.

The fleet of about 80 vessels was divided roughly into two classes:

1. Smaller boats working local waters.

Fare	Burthen	Fish	Season
a. Tucknet	3 tons	Plaice	February to April
b. Drawnet	3 ,,	Mackerel	May to June
c. Harbour	8 ,,	Conger	Summer
d. Cok	2–6 ,,	Herring	October to December

2. Larger boats going farther afield.

Fare	Burthen	Fish	Season
a. Shotnett	6–26 tons	Mackerel	April to June
b. Skarborow	18–40 ,,	Cod	June to September
c. Yarmouth	15–40 ,,	Herring	September to November
d. Flew	8–20 ,,	Herring	November to December

Nets	Length	Depth
Nor'ward (boats 30 tons and upwards)	20 yards	5 ranns
do in smaller boats	20 ,,	4 ,,
Flew (alias heake)	28 ,,	4 ,,
Shotnett	28 ,,	2 ,,
Cocks heake	28 ,,	2 ,,

The 'Orders' state the minimum length of nets, but the 'Fares' give an average considerably longer. The Orders required a minimum of 28 yd for a shotnet, but the Fare gives a length between 30 and 24 fathoms, the average 54 yd.

In Middle English 'rann' means a hank of string. Sussex mackerel nets had 26 'crossings'—meshes—to the yard, herring nets 32. At Hastings in 1604, Corporal ordered that 'no fishermen of the towne should fish with any trawl net whereof the moak holdeth not five inches size throughout'. In the Brighton dialect 'moak' became 'mox', with 50 moxes to the rann.

'Each voyage a speculative venture for the men, as shares not wages, each man at least one share for his bodye', and in addition another share or part share according to the nets and lines he took to sea. Tucknet fare was:

Eight men at one share	8
Boats and nets	4
Vicar	$\frac{1}{2}$
Master	$\frac{1}{4}$
Churchwardens	$\frac{1}{4}$
	13

Say a catch of £13, then each share was worth £1. The vicar

received 10s, master 5s, and churchwardens 5s towards the maintenance of the church and the defence of the town. The proceeds of the four shares for boat and nets were divided between the owner of the boat and the men who took nets or lines.

A tithe book for 1758 gave the vicar's share as 'mackerel fare £3 17s 4d, herring fare £9 14s 5½d', churchwardens' as £1 18s 8d and £4 17s 2¾d respectively.

In 1580 the commissioners estimated that Brighton had 80 fishing boats, 400 able mariners and 10,000 nets. In 1618 the landsmen's share was agreed at one-half of the sum raised by the fishermen. In the early eighteenth century the fishing 'decayed' and the Council of Twelve disappeared. The town then developed as a health resort and an Act of 1772 set up 64 town commissioners; these remained until 1854 when Brighton became a borough with a mayor, 12 aldermen, and 36 councillors.

To return to 'The Auncient Customes', Tucknett Fare was 'betwene Ffebruarye and Aprill yerelye certeine smale boats called Tuckers to goe to Sea uppon the Coaste for Playce of the burden of three ton or thereaboute'. Every boat had eight or nine men and two nets.

Shotnett Fare: 'Yerelye tyme out of mynde from Aprill to June used to go to sea for Mackrell, other boates called Shotters of diverse burthens between six tonn and twentye-six tonne.' (Every boat from six to 10 tons used to take two shares, above 10 and under 18 tons 2½ shares, from 18 to the biggest three shares, every man having above four nets ½ share 'for his bodye' and not above. . . .) 'The nets in lengthe betweene thirtye and twentie-fower fathom and in deepness two ranns every rann fyftye moxes deep whereof everye fower netts have used to take a share so THAT everye boate in this voyage takinge two shares and a halfe havinge tenn men takinge a share a man and havinge fower score netts maketh thirtye-three shares and a halfe, v.z. for fower score netts twentye shares for tenn men tenn shares for the boate two shares and a halfe for the Viccar the Towne and the master one share.'

Skarborow Fare: June to September boats between 18 and 40

tons used to 'voyage to Skarborowe to fish for codd (begining about fortye yeares agorn) . . . every man in biggest boats a lyne a leade fower lynees of hookes and two noward netts contayninge twentye-fower yeardes in length or thereabouts . . . for his bodye and the necessaries aforesaide one share . . . in the smaleste sorte everye man bringinge with him two lynes two leades and one heake conteyninge twentye-eight yardes in length and fyve ranns in deepness $1\frac{1}{2}$ shares. . . .'

Yarmoth Fare: '15 to 24 tonn boate 3 shares, 24 to 30 $3\frac{1}{2}$ shares, over 30 4 shares. Man for his bodye $\frac{1}{2}$ share.' The boats used two sorts of nets, one called 'flewes al heakes' had '30 to 24 fadom length, 4 ranns deep, every rann 50 moxes deep, every three of these nets took one share.' The other sort, called 'norwarde netts', were 'between 15 and 10 fadom in length, 5 ranns deep, every rann 50 moxes and every four nets took a share.'

Cok Fare: 'Cockes 2 to 6 tons . . . every boate havinge a master and a sayle took $1\frac{1}{2}$ shares . . . two sorts of netts, one called cockes heakes of 30 to 24 fadom in length 2 ranns deep, the other called flewes the lengthe aforesaide and 3 rannes in deepness. . . .'

Flew Fare: Boats called 'flewars', '. . . one sorte of netts called flewes 33 and 24 fadom in length 3 ranns deep . . . so that every boate takinge 3 shares havinge 8 men at halfe share and 39 nets maketh 21 shares. . . .'

Harbour Fare: 'In somertyme with harbour hookes for conger . . . every man with 4 lines of hookes each 50 fadom one share and 12 lines withoute a man 1 share . . . boate with 12 men and 12 lines without men had 16 shares. . . .'

Drawnett Fare: 'Small cocks 3 tonn to drawe mackrell by the shoare. . . .'

Quarter share: This was employed for the building of forts and walls towards the sea for the defence of the town and the provision of shot and powder.

Then follow further Orders giving sizes of nets:

After 1st Auguste 1581 forfeit for every nett so found 10s . . . the Conestable the Churchwardens being seafaringe menn or anye two of them shall fower tymes the yeare yf they shall thinke it needefill searche view and measure the lengthe and deepness of an mann's netts in Brighelmston . . . no man shall hier any person for wages except Skarborowe voyage, penalty 10s, or to go in any other boate 20s.

Hookes. Every line of small hookes to contain 9 score yards and not above if so forfeit 20s and no mann to have more than fower such lynes every man shall pay the seventh fish to the boate of three of his lynes except the master and the young men called Tacheners master to have all the fishing of his fower lynes without payinge any duetye to the boate the Tacheners shall have for the keeping of the boate the fishing of every their fourth line without paying any duetye to boate Penalty 20s.

If a man lost any small hooks at sea:

For every line lost 2s to be maid him by ye company in equal portions . . . if fower or more lost the whole catch except boates part to be equally divided among company and every man losing hookes to have 2s . . . if man lose any heake norward or shotnett to have 10s for heake 10s for norward fower shillings for shotnett . . . no inhabitant of towne to dryve for herrings between Shore-haven and Beachi on any Saturday night or Sunday untill evening prayer bee done, forfeit foe every time 20s . . . if dryve with any tucknet before sunrise or after sunset 10s . . . if go to sea with tucknet to fish for playce before Shrove Tuesday 10s for every time . . . the churchwardens to have in some convenient place at all tymes 4 barrels of powder, 40 round shot, 10 chain shot for every great piece.

Complaints were made that the scarcity of timber was increasing the cost of maintenance of boats.

Of late years because of iron furnaces placed near Downe risen from 3s 4d a ton to 13s 4d, wood from 2s 6d a load to 7s, load of coal from 6s 8d to 14s, billet or tallwoodd from 2s 6d the hundred to 8s and shipp boorde from 16s the hundred to 50s.

Two books of parchment were written . . .

one with Earl of Arundell and Lord Buckherst, the other in a chest locked with 3 locks in some convenient place in Brighelm-ston, keys kept by Viccar or curate, constable and churchwardens . . . to be read openly yearly in presence of fishermen and other parishioners . . . officials and 20 ancient inhabitants can make alterations if needed with prior consent of Arundell & Buckherst.

All signed or put their marks, 90 in all; only seven could write their names, one having the outlandish name of Xpofar Ingelard; Deryk Carver, adds Mr, and Steven Pyper, precedes his signature with 'by me'. One can imagine with what smirks and pride these worthies took up the quill pen and carefully wrote their name on the parchment, whilst others could only make their mark—and what a variety they are! John Eston drew a perfect heart, John Coly an inverted triangle, double like an hour glass, William Body a crude arrow, John Anstye a crooked cross, the swastika. Joe W. Wood used a rather suitable mark, three parallel lines crossing three others to form a diamond-shaped mesh. A circle with six spokes was chosen by Nicholas Goodd; perhaps he was a wheelwright; Edmond Lock and John Cheasernan repeated the hour-glass symbol.

I wonder if those unlettered fishermen had much knowledge of the imposing document to which they appended their marks —those many lines of thick black script without any punctuation, all those 'in primes', the 'aforesaide' and other legal phraseology which was 'solemnly signed on the XXIIIth daye of Julye in ye yeare of ye Raigne of our Soveraigne Lady Elizabethe ye XXIIth by ye Right Honorable the Lorde Buckherst and Richard Shelly Esquier at Brighthelmesto aforsaide in ye presence of the saide fishermen redd ratified and confirmed'.

This 'Booke of all the Auncient Customs 1580' is still preserved, and all those men, long dead, are not forgotten.

In 1626 a petition to Parliament stated that whereas from 26 to 30 boats formerly went to the North Sea each year for ling, cod and herring, by reason of the dangerous times that had come upon the country the number had been reduced to eight. By the end of the century over 50 boats were working. When Brighton became a fashionable resort, due largely to the patronage of the Prince Regent, fishing began a renewed era of prosperity. In 1793, records show 45 boats engaged in the mackerel fishery and 25 fishing with trawls. Fantastic prices were realised for the first mackerel caught. In May 1807 40 guineas a hundred was paid at Billingsgate, or 7s each fish at six score to the 100. The next load fetched 13 guineas a hundred; the following year the price at Dover had fallen to 1s for 60 fish.

The type of boat peculiar to Brighton was the 'hoggie' or hog-boat, sprit-rigged, the larger stepping two masts, the smaller, one only. (Picture, p 98.) Hulls were short and beamy, apple-bowed and immensely strong. From a contemporary model, *c* 1794, the length was well under twice the beam, and the craft was flat-bottomed and clinker-built, with a transom stern, curved forefoot and slightly raking stem. Fully decked, the hull was divided into three sections, all at different levels. A small hatch in the middle of the foredeck gave access to the cuddy, the only warmth coming from a fire bucket. There was a long hatch amidships and a smaller one aft. The mainmast, rather longer than the length of the hull, was stepped in a three-sided tabernacle with two shrouds a side and a forestay to the end of a curious spar, the bumpkin, actually a broad flat spar slotted over the stemhead, with the heel secured to a beam across the deck. On the fore side of the mast was a hand windlass for hoisting the sprit.

The mainmast carried a large spritsail with its luff laced round the mast and head extended by a light sprit. Its heel rested in a rope—the 'snotter'—and a purchase hoisted it, with its fall to the windlass. The foresail had three lines of reef points, its luff being laced to the fore stay and its head to the masthead. A short mizzen mast passed through a hole in a cross thwart and the heel rested on deck; the spritsail sheet rove through a hole in a long outrigger.

The 'hoggies' made excessive leeway and, to counter this leeboards were fitted; when let down the leeboard rested against a heavy chock—the 'clump'—bolted to a strake close to the waterline. These beamy craft are well depicted in Cooke's engravings, which show the bumpkin well bowsed down, the wooden beach capstan and an anchor with a broad board stock for bedding into the shingle. They sit upright on their bilge keels, no blocks being required.

About the middle of the nineteenth century the two-masted lugger became popular and the design of the 'hoggie' changed, the hull being lengthened and a long reeving bowsprit fitted.

This ran out through a ring on the fore end of the bumpkin, and on it a jib was set, hauled out on a traveller. Two sweeps were carried, worked on the quarters in a rowlock cleat nailed to the gunwale. By 1886 only three survived and these went soon after, one being burnt on a Guy Fawkes bonfire. Another, broken up, yielded 100 lb of copper nails worth about £5.

The luggers had vertical stems and sterns, full lines for'ard to give buoyancy when beaching, and most were fully decked with high bulwarks. As on the Hastings craft, the square transom was replaced by a 'beaching counter' corresponding to the lute stern. As late as 1910 leeboards were carried, similar to those used in the 'hoggies', but many luggers had centreboards, about 4 ft in length, and raised by a tackle from the foremast head. The majority were built locally and at Shoreham, the port of registry, but in later years a number of Cornish luggers were bought.

Hulls were built of oak for keel, stem and stern posts, but ash for timbers and strake planking. Decks were of pine and elm was seldom used except for the transom. In general, the Brighton luggers were similar to those at Hastings.

Great changes had taken place on the beach. Up to the beginning of the nineteenth century it shelved gently to low-water line and beyond and was sandy; hence boats returning from a fishing trip came in on the top of the tide, to be left high and dry as it ebbed. A capstan was only used to haul a boat high up under the cliffs for repairs, or in very bad weather. Then the problem of erosion arose and, fearing for the safety of the land, the authorities built heavy timber groynes out seawards to impede the erosive effects of onshore winds and the up-Channel current. This brought in shingle and pebbles on the west'ard side, increasing year after year until a steep slope resulted. Boats had to be beached and hauled up by a capstan.

Three luggers finally lay on the beach for years, *Elisabeth II* built at Hastings in 1910, *Belinda* and *Victory*, gradually falling to pieces. Although motors had been fitted, no one wanted these heavy old craft, and in July 1940 the Admiralty ordered their

destruction as they were considered an undesirable obstruction
at a time when invasion threatened, following the evacuation
from Dunkirk. Bob Hunt told me that John Plugh built *Belinda*
and *Victory* at Brighton, the sails being made by Basset. (Picture,
p 98.)

A good lobster ground lay about 12 miles from Littlehampton
in the vicinity of the Owers lightvessel, and the Selsey men used
small clench-built cutters with a length of 24 to 26 ft, deep
draught and good underwater lines. A fair average length for
spars was: polemast 37 ft, gaff 16 ft, boom and bowsprit 22 ft
6 in. In light weather, a big yard topsail was set.

In Chichester harbour the Bosham boats had deep keels, a
hull length from 16 ft upwards, nine strakes of planking, a short
foredeck at gunwale level and a fish tray aft below rail level, a
transom stern, and oars working against thole pins. A single
mast, stepped well for'ard, carried a very high, narrow-cut
lugsail; some had centreboards which improved their ability to
windward.

The Emsworth and Langstone luggers were also clench-built,
average length about 15 ft. Their very pronounced V sections
made them rather crank as no centreboards were fitted. False
keels of wood, or wood and iron, fitted below the structural
keel, gave a draught of about 18 in. Hulls were decked for'ard
with a fish tray aft, each had two sets of thole pins, and as many
boats were slow in stays an oar would be used to help them
round. (Picture, p 117.)

The rig was a long-luffed, square-headed lugsail, tanned almost black and dipped every time the boat went about. The
sails stood well but the fishermen seldom attempted to sail hard
on a wind, preferring to down lug and row. The lug was tacked
down to weather on the foredeck, sheet to each quarter, with
two shrouds and a forestay as standing rigging. Small beam
trawls or oyster dredges were worked, and the men fished for
mackerel outside the harbour if good catches were being taken.

There were two main oyster companies in Chichester harbour,
one at Emsworth, the other being the Bosham-Chichester com-

pany. These two had the main leases with the Emsworth Channel Company and the leases went from Copperas Point, south of Dell Quay, to East Head, part of Bosham Channel and the best part of Itchenor other than where the sailing coasters used to anchor. The other oyster concerns used Thorney creek and Snow Mill, West Wittering, where good beds existed in the seventies.

At the turn of the century several Shoreham smacks were sold to Bosham, including the ketch *Gem*, but after the collapse of the fishing she was sold to the Hamble and much of the fishing activity went there as well.

Between the wars, the hulls of old coasters and 'scallopers' lay derelict and forlorn with frayed ropes flapping in the breeze. Among them was *Echo*, a 96-ft ketch built at Emsworth in 1900, once owned by Fosters and fishing out of Newhaven. Her clipper bow had a very pronounced rake aft, the forefoot joining the keel just for'ard of the foremast, and a 14 hp steam engine drove a propeller. Another lay with broken back at the foot of the slipway from which she was unsuccessfully launched, and a large timber structure, all weed-covered and rapidly falling to pieces, told of an industry gone for ever.

CHAPTER FOUR

THE HAMPSHIRE AND DORSET COASTS

IN the Solent area, the typical boat out working in all weathers was the Spithead wherry, a type practically unchanged from the 'bumboats' known to Nelson and very similar to eighteenth-century ships' boats. They plied for hire from the hards at Portsmouth and Southampton, seeking passengers requiring passage to the Isle of Wight, and even carrying livestock at times. In July 1822 the authorised scale of charges, drawn up by Act of Parliament, was approved by the justices at Winchester. For passengers to or from Portsmouth and Ryde 'wherry with one man 5s, two or more 7s'; from Southampton to Cowes 'a wherry or rowboat with two men 12s 6d, with four men £1 1s'.

Similar boats attended on shipping and naval vessels anchored in Spithead, taking out stores, fresh vegetables and provisions, collecting and delivering officers' laundry and similar services. These wherries were built to go through the tumble of broken water and the short, steep seas kicked up by an east wind on an ebb tide. In really bad weather they would cruise round the Fleet on the lookout for custom when a ship's boats were kept hoisted. The charge for daily hire at Portsmouth was 12s 6d with two men, £1 1s with four. The fare for a single passenger was 1s, a horse 1s 6d, for a man and a horse 2s 8d, with a shipping and landing charge of 3d.

The double-ended, clench-built hulls were constructed of oak, copper-fastened, and were remarkable for longevity, remaining in the service of families until it seems but little of the original boat could have remained, so numerous were the repairs and refits carried out over the years.

The first-class wherries were about 30 ft overall and half-decked for'ard, with locker berths on each side of the cuddy and a small stove against the bulkhead. The rest of the boat was open and fitted with side benches and a wide thwart aft.

The rig was a short mast on which was set a foresail fitted with brails, its head extended by a long sprit. This could be quickly lowered when coming alongside a ship-of-war, the low mast then clearing yards, braces and booms. At anchor, the sail was brailed in to the mast; two or three sprits of different lengths were carried to suit the weather. The staysail had its tack hooked to the stemhead and, like the foresail, had double sheets and one line of reef points. The mizzen mast, stepped well inboard, had a small spritsail sheeted to the top of the sternpost. Steering was by yoke and lines, enabling the helmsman to go for'ard. In light weather the boat rowed easily, there being three oak rowlocks a side above the gunwale. In dirty weather a washboard was fitted to protect the passengers sitting just for'ard of the mizzen, but in winter they must have been blue with cold and soaked with spray.

The greatest beam was aft of amidships; rising floors with well-rounded bilges gave an almost semi-circular section. Ballast consisted of 3 to 4 tons of iron stowed under the platform and about 20 $\frac{1}{2}$-cwt pigs with handles stowed in the 'lodge', about 1 ft wide and 10 ft long on the floors from the mizzen mast to the third thwart. In blowy weather these were stowed in an open locker under the weather bench and shifted over whenever the boat tacked.

Turkish Knight was 34 ft 6 in overall with a beam of 9 ft, draught for'ard 3 ft, aft 3 ft 11 in. The length of the foredeck was 14 ft 9 in, with a depth from the top of the keelson of 5 ft 6 in. The sheer, slack aft, swept up for'ard. The mast, stepped 12 ft 3 in from the foreside of the stem, had two shrouds each side and a forestay.

Woodham measured 27 ft overall, beam 8 ft 3 in, depth 4 ft 9 in.

Page 157 The gaffer *Two Sisters* in Polperro harbour. The first boat is fitted with an iron horse, the next is a double-sheeter. Note mainsail is laced to the mast, the timmanoggy—the tack rope from topsail pole through a sheave block on the gaff down to the deck

Page 158 (above left) Bristol
Channel pilot skiff No 19 racing
Note cross-cut mainsail, big jackyard topsail, angulated jib and jib
topsail, reaching foresail;
(above right) Falmouth pilot boat
No 8; (below) Gloucester pilot
boat No 3, Berkeley Castle, built
c 1885

Page 160
Swansea harbour, 1843. Note how the flat-bottomed, deep hulls sit up-right in the mud, and the clench-built paddle tugs with tall funnels. The white skiff alongside the cutter in the background is probably a pilot boat

The foremast, stepped on the floors 7 ft from the stem, was 19 ft 6 in long, the sprit 17 ft, mizzen mast 15 ft, sprit 10 ft 6 in, and boom 7 ft.

The second-class wherries were much smaller, open, pulling and sailing boats, chiefly used in Portsmouth harbour and setting a small lug at times. (Picture, p 100.)

Robert Gomes of Gosport was the first sailing master when the Kaiser bought the *America's* Cup challenger *Thistle*, renamed *Meteor*, and he chose as crew many local and Portsmouth fishermen.

Cowes and Ryde watermen used a transom-sterned boat about 15 ft in length, 4 ft 8 in beam and 1 ft 10 in depth. It was rigged with a staysail, sprit foresail and a mizzen mast stepped against the transom, the sail sheeting to a short bumpkin.

In winter the men went fishing in the Solent, using handlines or seine nets. In summer they took trippers round the warships lying in Spithead, or the yachts anchored in fleets during regattas. Dozens of the finest steam yachts in the world lay off Cowes during the famous Week, while cutters, swinging main booms 90 and more feet in length, raced daily among graceful schooners and smaller craft of every class. In hard blows topmasts were housed, mainsails reefed, then with lee rails awash skilled hands on the long tillers and split-second judgment were needed to just clear an anchored vessel, or to go about in a thunder of slatting canvas with a score of men hauling in the main sheet. These men came from Essex and the Itchen and Hamble rivers; in winter humble fishermen, but in summer captains in command, whose word was law, even to owners.

Boats of the Itchen Ferry type were to be found in practically every creek along the north shore of the Isle of Wight and around Southampton Water. At Fishbourne a few smacks, some built locally, sailed out of Wootton Creek, stowboating or oyster-dredging in the winter months, but usually laid up in summer. Others were working from Newton Creek where prolific oyster beds gave considerable employment, and vessels up to 500 tons could lie in the harbour. One or two sailed from

I

SPITHEAD WHERRY "WOODHAM"

LENGTH 27'-0"
BEAM   8'-3"
DEPTH   4'-9"

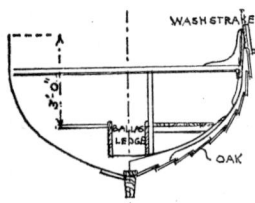

Washstrake

L.W.L.

WASH STRAKE

OAK

MIDSHIP SECTION

BALLAST LEDGES

L.W.L.   GUNWALE

Drawn by W. M. Blake 1-4-36
Coastal Craft Sub-Committee
Society for Nautical Research

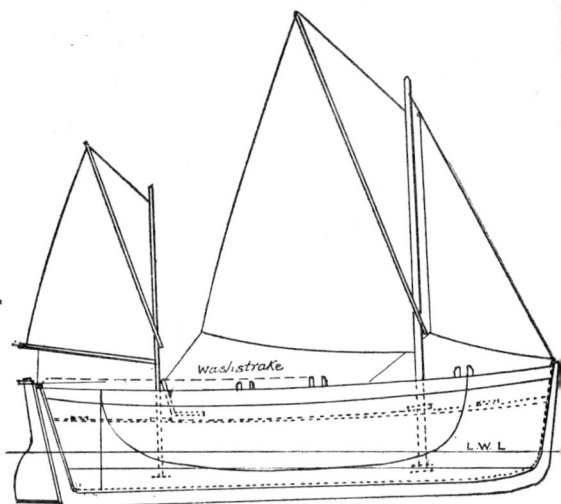

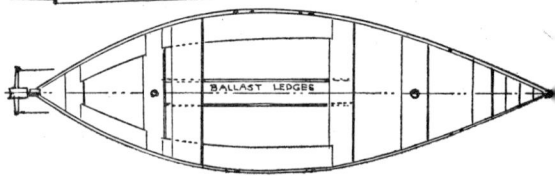

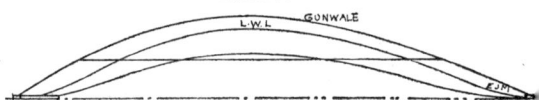

Plans of the Spithead wherry *Woodham*, drawn by W. M. Blake

Eling, and Fawley on the west side of Southampton Water, but the principal fishing was from the Hamble and Itchen rivers.

For information concerning the Hamble River fisheries I am indebted to John Leather who wrote me:

> The Hamble river smacks, other than Itchen-type boats, seem always to have been a very mixed lot. Many of them were old Essex cutter smacks sold away, others were bought from Chichester Harbour, some were converted yachts and pilot boats.
>
> In 1890, 22 smacks and 80 men were spratting, by 1920 there were only two or three smacks left in the trade. One of them was the *Racer* which was originally owned by my great-uncle, Capt Turner Barnard of Rowhedge, Essex. Other spratters were the *Albion*; *Secret* built at Rowhedge by Harris in 1864, 21 tons, and owned at Hamble by Robert Scovell; *Ariel* owned at Bursledon

in 1920 and built as a clench-built Bembridge pilot boat. Her skin was replaced by carvel planking at Moody's yard in about 1870. The old Colne cutter smack *Gipsy Queen* also ended her days owned in the Hamble.

Some of the smacks dredged oysters in the North Sea a hundred years ago, including the *Jane*, built at Hamble village in the yard then owned by Scovell. She was copper-fastened. *Laurel* foundered in the North Sea through her chain plates carrying away but her crew was saved by a steamer. The *Star* was built at Brightlingsea in 1868, 62 tons and broken up at Southampton. Other local smacks included the *Welfare*, 21 tons, built at Brightlingsea in 1865, *Jemna* built by Harris at Rowhedge in 1852. *Martha*, 17 tons, built at Wivenhoe in 1802, was owned by Hiram Dimmick of Warsash in 1890. *Result* 25 tons, built at Harwich in 1870, was owned by John Scovell in 1890. Some smacks were built at Hamble such as *Pearl*, 17 tons, launched there in 1863.

One of the largest oyster and shellfish fishing firms in the area was the Scovells Hamble Fisheries Co Ltd, who owned many smacks and had a building yard at Hamble.

Albion, when not fishing, was sometimes employed in bringing cider from Totnes or potatoes from France to Southampton and the Hamble.

The crab and lobster trade seems to have been established about 1860, Norway and Brittany were originally suppliers, later almost exclusively Devon, Cornwall and Ireland. Hamble lost its direct interest in the trade, which became concentrated at Warsash. *Peri*, built as a fruit schooner by John Harvey at Wivenhoe

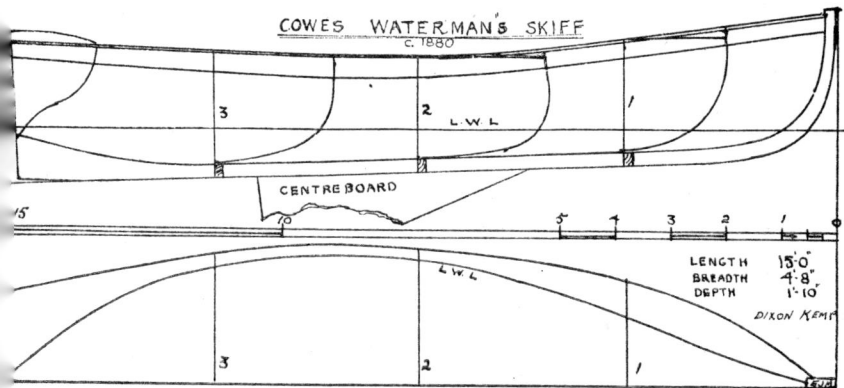

Lines of a Cowes waterman's skiff

in the 1850s, was one of the early crab carriers, making many voyages to Concarneau, from whence she brought some of the first crabs to Warsash, probably in the 1870s. She was both raised and lengthened during her career and was the largest craft in the crab trade, at one time rigged as a two-masted schooner, later as a three-master. She was hulked at Hamble about 1880.

The trade between the Hamble and France declined in about 1885, but a brisk trade with South Ireland and the West Country flourished. The *Ellen* was one employed in this trade and she once made the passage from the Fastnet to the Hamble in 49 hours, though other boats are credited with doing it in 40 hours. She was lengthened at Hamble about 1880.

The *Jubilee* was a schooner yacht, formerly the *Lotus*, built at Lymington about 1887. She was bought for crab carrying and had a well built into her and all her yacht panelling removed. This work was done at Warsash. The *Cupid* was an Isle of Wight pilot boat with a fish well installed at Warsash. The schooner *Imogene* was lost with all hands in the North Sea on a carrying voyage from Norway about 1890. The old yacht *Stella*, once a noted Clyde racer, ended her days as a crab ketch and was broken up about 1912.

In 1920–22 only four ketches remained in the crab trade, the *Gem*, *Ceres*, *Macfisher* and the *Mary Leek*. They brought crabs, lobsters and crayfish from Devon, Cornwall and Ireland; auxiliary motors were installed just after the war. The *Ceres*, SU 2, was about 40 tons, launched at Poole in 1869. She was intended for the grain trade which then flourished between Poole and the Channel Islands. On her maiden voyage the *Ceres* grounded on the Kimmeridge Ledge off St Albans Head and was badly holed, but salvaged by a crew from Hamble and fitted with a crab well. Sometimes she made 20 round trips in a summer, once two voyages in 11 weeks to the North Sea for oysters. In some winters she dredged scallops in Caen Bay in company with the Essex fleet. For 35 years she was skippered by Capt Robert Williams of Hamble, who kept her up like a yacht, and when she was laid up on the mud for the last time he often gave her a jog out with the pump 'just for old times sake', After 1914 her last skipper was from Hallsands, in Devon.

A typical trip was from Hamble to Ivycove near Hallsands; the *Ceres* lay anchored off with the red ensign hoisted to the peak meaning 'bring off your crabs'. The local crabbers put out with their boats loaded to the thwarts, the cock crabs were, of course, the most valuable, but inevitably the catches contained more 'shes' than cocks. About four boats usually unloaded the contents of the Hallsands kegs or store pots. The crabs were tallied and any lobsters or crayfish were put into net bags and suspended in the well, packed so tightly that they could not move a claw. The crab fishermen were quite unconcerned at walking over the boatload of crabs with loud scrunching noises. The catches were transferred in bushel baskets to the *Ceres'* deck. The four boats would unload a typical 2,560 she crabs 378 he crabs, 336 lobsters and 46 crayfish. The *Ceres* then moved to lie off Hallsands itself and the crabbers from there and Beesands brought off their catch. The total tally in the well was 6,300 shes, 650 he crabs, 500 lobsters, 54 crayfish.

At that time the village of Hallsands was becoming derelict due to the dreadful mistake of suction-dredging ballast from the foreshore to be used in the construction of the Old Keyhaven docks project some years previously. The inhabitants guessed the outcome of the dredging and rallied to fight it. When the dredger moorings were laid they grappled them and dragged them ashore, with all the population laying on the rope shouting 'We'll all go to prison together'. But, of course, official views prevailed and a community was destroyed.

To discharge the crabs, the ketches always went on the Hard at high water and the crabs were passed into the tarred wooden cages called 'carbs', which were hauled alongside. The lobsters and crayfish were carried up to the stock pond to be supplied as required for London hotels and restaurants and to the passenger ships from Southampton.

A good number of men from Hamble and Warsash were employed in sorting and packing. The 'carbs' were usually moored in fours, some along the Hamble foreshore where the old mooring stakes can still be seen in the mud. Horses and carts cluttered the hards when despatch was in progress.

Mr James Saunders of Hamble (now Senior Yacht Surveyor of Lloyds Register of Shipping) recalls the following: 'Most Itchen-type fishing boats in the district were built cheaply for yacht skippers by the yards which laid up their yachts in winter. They were usually planked in red pine on oak and the interior of the hulls received a coat of coal tar when new as a preservative. Many of the fastest were designed and built by Arthur Payne, of Summers & Payne. The *Nellie* of Hythe was a noted fast boat.'

Mr Saunders' father, like many of the Hamble river population at the turn of the century, came originally from the West Country. He owned the Itchen boat *Rosalie*, 18 ft 0 in × 8 ft 6 in × 4 ft draught, built at Itchen and owned originally at Eling. He was captain of several moderate-sized racing yachts, including the 12-metre *Cyra* and the 15-metre *Dorina*. In winter he fished with the *Rosalie*, principally trawling.

A profitable bed of oysters was found off Lee-on-Solent and for a time a small fleet of Itchen boats worked there dredging an average of 300 a day at 4s 6d a hundred. Each boat would work three dredges. The *Rosalie* always raced in her class during the regattas, when a long tiller was often needed to keep her off the wind. The *Oyster*, Capt Bevis, was a noted fast boat from the Hamble.

Up until about 1930 twelve to fourteen Itchen-type boats worked from the Hamble under sail alone. Motors were introduced during the 1930s, two of the type still work from Warsash. Most of the owners were skippers of the 8 and 6-metre yachts of pre-war days. . . .

During the nineteenth century and in the early years of the twentieth regattas were held at Itchen and Hamble, sometimes at Bursledon. Everyone took a holiday, bands played lively tunes, and bunting fluttered on a colourful, peaceful scene. The local smacks, yacht gigs, dinghies and coastguard galleys sailed keenly contested races; there were even ladies' sculling matches. I have an amusing photograph of a lovely lady at the helm of quite a sizeable yacht, grasping the tiller in her left hand and holding a parasol in the other.

The principal events were for fishing boats, divided into two classes, 30-footers and 22 ft 6 in boats. All lay at anchor with sails lowered, and the moment the starting gun fired anchors were weighed, sails hoisted and sheeted home in two shakes of a jib sheet. Many owners were famous yacht skippers who handled their humble fishing craft equally skilfully and were as keen to win the first prize of £3 as a Queen's Cup at Cowes. Often, in addition, a new mainsail was given by Ratsey & Lapthorne, and at the Itchen Ferry Regatta in 1901 the prize was a suit of sails from the same famous firm. Many boats bore yacht names, one was *Windfall* owned by G. Bevis who, in later years, skippered the 23-metre *White Heather*, *Florence* by J.

Diaper; A. Diaper owned *Ileen*, and later he skippered the huge racing schooner *Westward*.

A time allowance of two minutes a foot was given to the smaller boats, and in 1898 at the Hamble River Regatta a race was staged 'for old class boats, but over 100 years of age not allowed to compete'. Nine boats started.

In a copy of *The Yachtsman* for 1892 I came across the following tribute to these fishermen-yacht skippers. 'The brothers Parker are typical Itchen yachtsmen and in their cleverness at the tiller prove that yacht skippers are born, not made.'

A century and more ago Itchen Ferry was a picturesque village of red-brick houses and cottages, a jumble of tarred sail lofts, and boatyards around which clung the scent of newly sawn wood as sawyers cut out the planks from the round. On the hard lay shrimpers and trawlers; across the river plied the ferry punts, while up and down Southampton Water passed a constant procession of sailing vessels of every nationality and rig. There was an occasional steamer too, but even she was fully rigged with masts and yards to help the engines in fair winds, or to bring her into port in the event of a breakdown. As soon as a boy was able to scramble about he made himself useful in his father's boat; soon he was afloat and out in open water. Stowboating and spratting in winter bred a hardy race. Rivalry between different owners led to improvements in design, as speed was paramount to get the early market. Such men were naturally in great demand as yacht hands, and the names of famous captains, Diaper, Parker, and many another, soon became household words wherever yachts and yachting were discussed in pub or club and along a water-front. Ashore, men like the Paynes and Hatchers built splendid craft, both for working and pleasure, ever seeking that elusive 'something' which made a boat faster than all others although in outward appearances they looked alike.

I can best describe this by quoting from a letter from Edwin Paskins, then 87, written to my friend Bruce Jones in April 1947, aobut the Itchen Ferry smacks *Star* and *Fanny*.

To talk and tell of our old boats takes me back many, many years and re-awakens old memories. Shall I speak of the *Star* first, because the *Fanny* was her offspring? The *Star* was built in a spirit of pique at Itchen Ferry. When Father started life he wanted a new boat built and a man living in Itchen Ferry heard this and he came to Father and asked him to let him build one for him. He had been chaffed and told that he didn't know how to build a boat and so he begged Father to let him build his and he would let them see whether he couldn't build a boat.

Well, he built the *Star* and truly built, for he built her with red pinewood throughout and oak bearings and proved his power and worth to build. During all the years that Father lived at Itchen Ferry and Southampton he entered her every year in the regatta races and she was never beaten. Every year first prizes. Then when we came to live at Cowes she makes quite a stir amongst the yachtsmen, for again she won every prize.

Then Mr Grant, Secretary R.Y.S., came to Father and asked him to allow John Samuel White to haul the *Star* up on the slips at East Cowes to take the moulds of the *Star*, so that they could build a yacht for him on the exact lines. That was the birth of the dear old *Dolly Varden*, built 1872, and how proud they were of her. When the race began, Mr Grant came to Father and begged him to take charge of the *Dolly* in all her races. Year after year he steered her to victory.

Then I came along and grew old enough to want a boat to work and it was decided to have one built on the lines of the *Star*, only a little more beam and one foot longer. *Star* was 21 ft, *Fanny* 22 ft. Our old home had a very long back, ran right through into the next street and so Father decided to have a large shed built, big and roomy enough to build the *Fanny* and he gave Mr John Watts the job to build both shed and boat. In the building I don't suppose any boat had been built with such care and all under Father's supervision. I was kept home to be with Mr Watts and my principal work was to give everything two coats of linseed oil before being placed in position. All the oak beams first, as they were placed in position, then as each plank was planed, two coats of oil before being nailed up. It's that that has kept the *Fanny* in such lasting condition. I was very proud of my little cabin, the ceiling was all beaded and had two coats of white enamel. When she was ready to launch, the end of the shed was taken down and the high brick wall leading into the street was pulled down, giving us plenty of room to turn into the road.

What a splendid boat she proved to be. The first year we entered them both in the Cowes Regatta and we beat the *Star*, but only by a few lengths and that was because it blew half a gale from the west . . . how I long to feel my hand steering them to victory again.

Star was broken up at Southampton *c* 1923, *Fanny* is still afloat and won the 'Old Gaffers' race at Cowes in 1969.

Henry Parker was appointed mate of the *Arrow* in 1851, the year in which she sailed for the Queen's Cup, won by the *America*, unfortunately going ashore at the back of the Wight. Clinker-built at Lymington by Inman in 1821, *Arrow* was one of the most famous cutters in yachting history, having a racing record of some 57 years against old and new yachts of all classes, always holding her own. In 1845 she had been bought by Mr T. Chamberlyne for £100 when lying derelict at Southampton waiting to be broken up for her copper bolts. Parker was appointed her captain in 1860 and the following year *Arrow* was lengthened and carvel planked. Her successes continued, and in her last season she took 11 prizes in 16 starts. Captain Parker retired when the yacht was put out of commission, but was retained on the establishment until his death at the age of 72 in 1892. *Arrow* was broken up about 1907.

Ben Parker, who owned the fishing smack *Annasona*, was sailing master of the Kaiser's yawl *Meteor* II before bringing the big schooner of the same name from America, where she was built for the Emperor in 1902.

Tommy Diaper owned *Eileen*, and many a close contest was sailed at Itchen regattas between these two racing skippers. In 1872 Dan Hatcher built the 40-ton cutter *Norman* and against such cracks as *Bloodhound*, built by Fife, and *Myosotis*, built by M. Ratsey, Diaper sailed her to win 66 prizes in eight seasons. In 1890 he had *Valkyrie* I, the 77-ton cutter built for Lord Dunraven the previous year, and he acted as pilot to the big American cutter *Navahoe* when she raced in English waters the following season.

In 1870 when the Marquis of Ailsa brought his 35-ton cutter

Foxhound to the Solent he found his Scots skipper and crew were outsailed, having secured only two prizes in the first 13 races. He therefore engaged Ben Harris, who had successfully sailed the 60-ton *Vanguard*, and *Foxhound* won twelve prizes in 21 starts, including a Queen's Cup, the smallest yacht to win this trophy in 18 years.

The Marquis now ordered a yacht from Fife to compete in the new 40-ton class, the renowed *Bloodhound*, and placed her in charge of Ben Harris, winning 72 prizes in 149 starts in six seasons, crewed by Itchen men. Subsequently *Bloodhound* continued her successful career flying the racing flag of another owner.

During the months when many of the men were away yachting their smacks were laid up in the mud, but so easily handled were they that often a lad of 15 or 16 would manage his father's boat alone, having learned to work the trawl and smack under every varying condition of tide and wind. Considerable skill was called for when driving at night through a fleet of craft at anchor with a strong tide running. Hauling-in meant several minutes' hard work before the cod was lifted inboard.

Usually the crew of a 3- to 4-ton boat consisted of one man, or a man and a boy. Trawling was carried on by day and night, the dark hours being best for soles and plaice; being quick movers they were apt to dodge the ground rope in clear water or daylight. In a strong tide if the trawl became 'fast' on an old anchor, wreckage or rocks a heavy strain was thrown on the warp and the boat had to be brought head towards net immediately. The warp was so arranged that this could be done quickly, the headsheets were let fly, foresail lowered and the warp hauled in hand over hand for'ard. If this failed, the boat was sailed over the net against the tide to try and clear the ground rope. At times the net became full of sand, weed and rubbish; then the mast halyards were used as a crane, the fall being taken to the winch. Or the bowsprit would be run in and used to form the barrel of a 'Spanish windlass'; with such a purchase even heavy baulks of waterlogged timber could be lifted.

When trawling, a length of net, warp and smack of about 300 ft was out and foresight was required to keep clear of anchored ships, sandbanks and moving traffic. Bringing the warp well aft kept the boat off the wind, amidships caused her to luff. If driving across the Solent in westerly winds, the foresail was dropped and a small jib set with its traveller well in on the bowsprit, the peak of the mainsail was lowered just below the horizontal and the foot triced up, the loose foot arching away from the boom.

A favourite ground for spratting was Christchurch Bay; although open to the prevailing winds it was possible to run for shelter. In some years the shoals came right inside the Needles and even as far up as Southampton Water.

The upper and lower beams of the stownet were about 30 ft long, meshes about ½ in knot to knot. A long-stocked anchor and plenty of stout rope and cable held the boat against the strong tides. The upper beam was some 30 ft above the lower which was weighted with iron; hence the mouth of the net was approximately square, the 'gape' being about 900 sq ft. 'Hip ropes' fast to the ends of the upper beam passed up to either side of the forward rail; the rope was fast to the lower beam. Before hauling began the net was closed by a rope starting from the middle of the lower beam, through a ring on the upper beam to a block on the bowsprit.

Spratters dreaded getting a net full of fish, especially if the weather was blowy and rough; the net floated as long as there was life in the fish, but should it sink it was often impossible to raise it again. To prevent this, a full net would be cut in several places to start the fish out of it; better to lose a few bushels if net and catch could then be brought alongside.

London dealers had rail trucks full of empty barrels waiting. It was the usual custom to sell to larger merchants who quickly cleared the stowboat, which immediately returned to the fishing ground. Price varied from 4d to 5s a bushel, and the catch was sold and resold by the first buyer to the smaller dealers. Fresh from the sea, sprats are iridescent with shades of green and pink, but they soon dull to silvery; after three days the heads and gills turn crimson which passes off a day later; by then the fish has long since lost its delicate flavour.

At one time there was an extensive crab and lobster trade with France, but it declined around the 1880s when about 22 boats were spratting from the Hamble river alone. *Racer*, built in Guernsey in 1858, was one of the last spratters fishing after the first world war.

There were two classes of spratters. One was the punt, an open boat 13 to 14 ft long, straight-stemmed and transom-sterned, full-bodied with a beam of 5 ft and depth of 2 ft 6 in. These were very weatherly, the rig being a sprit mainsail and two headsails. Match sailing had been popular since late in the eighteenth century and, after shipping as yacht hands, many men made alterations to improve the sailing qualities of their boats, adding a lead keel and sometimes a false deadwood. Designers had their own ideas but generally beam remained about one-third of the length; clinker build was never adopted.

The other class were the boats 21 to 25 ft in length, always carvel-built, half-decked for'ard with a small cabin below, and wide waterways. There was a fish tray about 10 in below the gunwale at the stern, into which the fish were emptied when the beam trawl was hauled.

The rig has undergone many changes. In the early years of the nineteenth century the foresail tack went to the stemhead, a long mast on which was set a boomless mainsail with a short gaff. Both sails worked on iron horses. Such a rig was lacking in head canvas and in the 1850s the tack of the foresail was taken to a short iron bumpkin about 1 ft outside the stem. Next came the adoption of boomed mainsails, bowsprits, fidded topmasts and even huge jackyard topsails, but the more usual rig was a pole mast, the vertical yard of the topsail extending some 5 ft above the masthead. Sails were usually tanned and set well, as might be expected with owners well versed in yacht practice; some left their sails white, others used red ochre.

Many of the hulls had raking midship sections, ie the

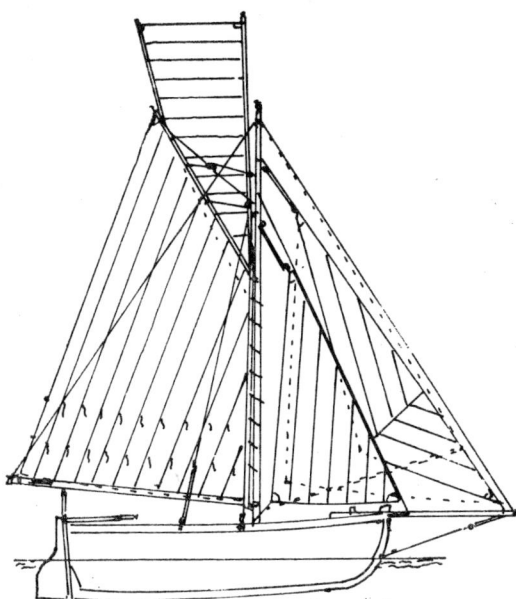

ITCHEN FERRY PUNT "NELLIE"

Sail plan of Ferry punt *Nellie*

broadest width of each succeeding waterline was progressively
farther forward from the waterline downwards. Keels had little
siding, the weight of iron was small; reliance was placed on
loose ballast inside the hull. This, combined with considerable
beam, was considered sufficient for stability, but when pressed
down in a squall there was a tendency to capsize. In the 1890s
lead keels became the vogue and beam tended to be reduced;
many hulls had 'wine glass' midship sections and rockered
keels. On regatta days, spinnakers and balloon jibs made an
appearance. Some boats retained the short iron bumpkin and
set the jib on a reeving bowsprit. (Pictures, p 99.)

The boats were smartly kept, mast and spars were nearly
always varnished with a touch of white at end of boom and
bowsprit, topsides grey, white or blue with a black top strake,
bottoms red, black or dark green. Name and registry numbers
were in black or white according to the colour of the top strake.

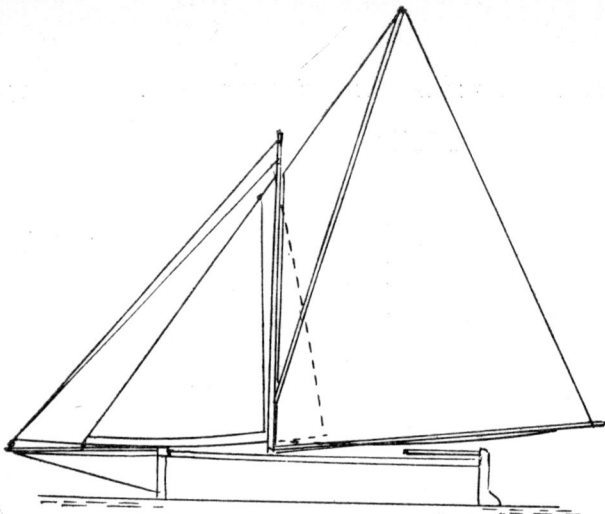

ITCHEN "PUNT"
C 1880

ITCHEN BOAT
Summer rig

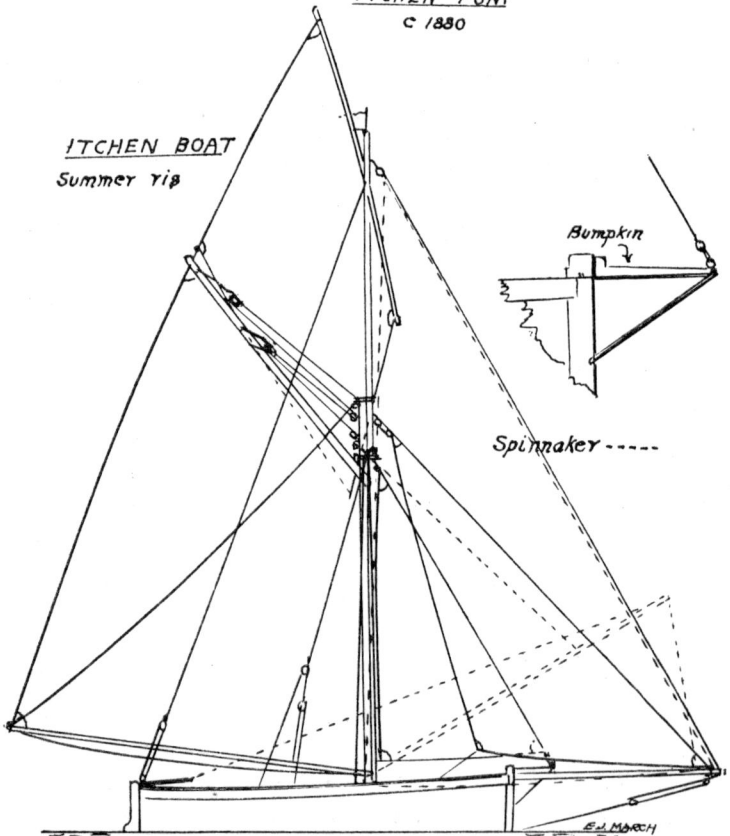

Bumpkin

Spinnaker - - - - -

E.J.MARCH

NOTE At regattas some skippers - yacht sailing masters - set spinnakers

Sail plans of Itchen boats

In the later boats hulls were increased in length to 26 to 27 ft. Many of these boats were very long lived. John Leather writes me:

> The *Nellie* was built by Hatcher in about 1862 at the Belvedere yard for Giles of Itchen, later at Cowes. About 1877 she was bought by Mr Banks of Hythe and was then in a derelict condition. She was refitted by Charles Payne at the West Quay boatyard. In 1886 she was partly burned out forward when fishing at Rye, and was then reconditioned and lengthened about 20 inches by H. Luke, Oak Bank Yard, Itchen.
>
> She was used for shrimping in her early life and had the old boomless rig. Her boom was added in 1921 or 22. She is still afloat and sailing in the Southampton area, but was recently re-rigged as a Bermudian sloop.

Another old-timer is *Wonder*, designed and built by Dan Hatcher at Northam in 1860 and now owned by E. F. Nicoray and kept at Eling. Her lines were taken off by J. W. Holness in 1966 and he kindly sent me a draught. (See plans on p 303.)

The length overall is 19 ft, waterline length 18 ft 9 in, beam 8·1 ft, draught 3·5 ft, depth 4·2 ft. Sail area 375 sq ft.

CONSTRUCTION

Floors were variously contrived. Sometimes a hogging piece or keelson of wood or iron was worked on top of the keel, its siding being about one half; this formed a stepping rabbet for the heels of the frames which rested on top of the main keel and were spiked to the hog, the whole being strengthened in some boats by iron floor knees, bolted through frame and plank. Aft, a stepping line to take the heels of the frames was cut in the deadwood; in crack boats the space between plank floor and keelson was filled with cement and boiler punchings, smoothed off level with the top of the keelson.

In the 21-ft class no keelson was worked. A typical boat, *Nellie*, built by Dan Hatcher, was 21 ft 9 in overall, 7 ft 10 in beam, and depth 3 ft 9 in. The lower waterlines were hollow for'ard, the straight keel was 3-in sided, 7 in deep to rabbet; 15

grown oak frames, 3 in × 2½ in at heel, 2½ in moulded at heads, were spaced 16 in centre to centre; between were steamed frames 1 in × ¾ in, beams oak 2½ in × 2¼ in, deck planking 6 in × ¾ in, side planking 1 in thick, deadwood knee 4 in thick, apron 5 in.

Mast, 27 ft deck to truck, gaff 12 ft 7 in, boom 16 ft 8 in, bowsprit to port of stem, 15 ft 7 in, iron bumpkin 1 ft on stem-head.

The loose-footed mainsail had eight hoops, cloths 16 in wide, jackyard topsail pole 11 ft 2 in on an 18-ft luff, and a yard 9 ft 5 in on a 19-ft leech, head 7 ft. When reefed down, the boats were usually sailed without a jib; many set a jib-headed top-sail in lieu of a jackyarder. The rudder, 2 ft 3 in wide and 1½ in thick was fitted with a tiller 5 ft 9 in overall, socketed into a 5 in × 4 in post.

The size of the rudder obviated the use of too much weather helm and kept the boat on a straight course when left to herself. If being sailed single-handed this allowed the man to attend to trawl and sails without difficulty; it was also handy for checking speed when put hard over quickly in opposite directions. In a fresh beam wind speeds of up to 6½–7 knots were common. The most favourable winds up and down Southampton water are NE and SW, both 'soldier's winds', but with wind SE it was a dead beat down to Calshot, NW to Southampton. Just how to make the fullest possible use of wind and tide was innate knowledge to the Itchen men.

Farther along the coast at Poole the early boats were clench-built, 14 to 20 ft long, and rigged with a boomless mainsail, a small jacky topsail, a jib, and sprit mizzen set on a mast stepped against the transom and sheeting to the end of an outrigger. Later came the change to cutter rig, very similar to that of the Itchen craft, but the hull had more powerful bow sections in-stead of hollow lines. Carvel build soon replaced clinker and the size increased to 25 ft, floors were flatter, the forefoot rounded, and iron ballast was carried inside in addition to a heavy iron band on the keel. (Picture, p 100.)

Page 177 Bristol Channel pilot skiff No 3, *Gwen*, on the slip at Pill. In centre is William Russell, then a westerman; to right of ladder is Joseph Adams, pilot and owner

Page 178 (above) Liverpool pilot schooner No 9 escorting the Royal cutter yacht *Britannia* up the Mersey. Note boom on fore staysail and canvas dodgers aft;

(below) Mumbles oyster skiff *Emmeline* in 1922

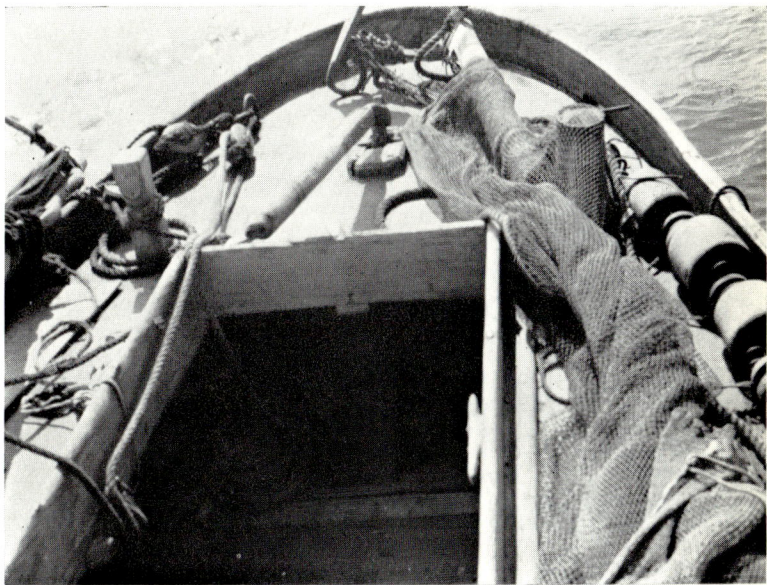

Page 179 (*above*) Morecambe Bay prawner, *Alice Allen*, trawling in heavy weather;

(*centre*) stern view of Morecambe Bay prawner showing bobbins on chain, tiller, square posts— 'knogs'—and anchor store under deck;

(*below*) prawner at Pwllheli, *c* 1910

Page 180 (above) fitting a new transom, Polperro; (below) model of cod yawl *King Orry*, RY 75

At the turn of the century there was a further increase in size to 30 ft keel, beam 11 to 12 ft, and centreboards made the boats faster and handier under sail. One or two built with a length of 35 ft, proved to be too much for two men to handle comfortably and they were converted to yachts.

John Leather writes:

> About 30 boats worked from Poole in 1908, mooring up near the town. They trawled for fish in season, working off Christchurch Ledge and in Bournemouth Bay. Leaving at dusk, they trawled all night and returned at dawn. Some of them dredged oysters in the harbour. At that time a few of the old clench-built boats were in use and a 50-year old boat was fishing in 1912. The boats built 60 years ago resembled the Southampton and Solent fishing cutters in form and rig. They were decked to just aft of the mast and side decks with coamings extended to the transom. Side benches extended from the cuddy bulkhead aft, usually with removeable boards in the front of the seat. Behind these boards and under the side decks was the fish stowage. No thwarts were fitted.
>
> The rig was a pole-masted cutter with a long-luffed mainsail and a foresail set on a bumpkin. Until about 1906 the boats averaged 20 ft or less, gradually they increased in size to 27 ft by 9 ft 8 in, with a draught of 4 ft.
>
> Ashton and Kilner were noted builders 60 years ago and the lines of one of their typical boats have the following dimensions. L.O.A. 28 ft 6 in, beam 9 ft 9 in, depth 7 ft 6 in to bottom of ballast keel. Draught 5 ft 2 in. The *Sunbeam*, built in 1912, is supposed to have been larger.
>
> Motors were first fitted during the 1914–18 war, but a certain amount of sail was carried for the next twenty years, proving useful when caught out in a blow and the motor broke down. In the 1950s one boat, *Sunshine* built in 1892, was still fishing.
>
> During the 'thirties the fleet numbered around 27 all with motors fitted in the cuddy for'ard.
>
> When spratting was carried out a 14-ft beam trawl having a net seven fathoms long of the usual fine mesh was worked. The beam was raised about four feet above the iron trawl heads by steel supports which bolted to them; the net had pockets. Sprats were trawled from early November and for the following three to four months, occasionally for five months. A very good catch was 250 bushels in one day. In 1931 they fetched only 3d to 4d a bushel

K

during a glut, but about 3s if scarce. The fleet worked from Swanage to the Needles.

Another type of craft peculiar to Poole Harbour was the flat punt. Scores were in use in 1908, the average size being 15 ft long 8 in deep, with whaleback decking over the hull like a gun punt. They were used for duck shooting and odd fishing in sheltered waters. Some had centreboards and a sprit rig under which they could, and did, tow a dredge for oysters.

THE DORSET COAST

The type of open boat used at Portland for launching off and landing on Chesil beach was a heavily-built, double-ended craft, eminently suitable for the purpose, with a history dating back for centuries. The 1849 Report states:

There are two sizes, the largest, 20 ft overall, used for mackerel fishing, and the smaller, 17 ft overall, in which they go out with their crab pots. They are sharp at both ends, very flat floored, pulling generally six oars, double-banked, that is three each side, the oars being, as it is called here, 'copsea', that is a large piece of wood or lug attached to the loom, having a hole in it for the thowl pin, which is soon fitted to the boat. They are all rigged with a lug, foresail and sprit mizzen, steered with a rudder and have in the keel, just before the scarf of the sternpost, a hole, through which is rove what they call a 'start-rope' used for hauling the boat up stern foremost, so that she is always launched bow to sea, with two or more hands forward at the oars to keep her to when once on the water. They are beautiful seaboats, never capsizing from their great beam and flat floor, and live in any surf.

When HM steamer *Sphynx* got on shore at the back of the Isle of Wight, the Admiralty directed me to procure two and send them up from Portland with their own crews for the purpose of assisting in laying out anchors etc, and they proved most useful there.

In pulling, they never keep stroke, but each side gets on as best it can. I send a sketch by one of the principal boat-builders, Mr Talbot of Weymouth, indeed, I may say, the only builder of the Portland lerret.

(*Signed*) Robert Kerr
Commander RN.

The particulars given were: length overall 20 ft, keel 17 ft, breadth extreme 7 ft 2 in, moulded 7 ft, depth 2 ft, ballast ¼ ton, light draught 7 in, load draught 2 ft fore and aft. Burthen in tons OM 4. Crew 7. Cost ready for sea £22.

Questions were raised as to the meaning of the name 'lerret' and its origin, and the Commander replied:

> I annex a note just received from Captain Manning, Deputy Governor of Portland Castle. 'Many years since I was particularly anxious to discover, if possible, the meaning and origin of the term "lerret", as applied to the boats here, and after much research, which occupied some considerable period, I obtained the following information from a very respectable old man named Pearce, who died about 18 years since, and who for many years had commanded merchant vessels trading between the port of London and different places in the Mediterranean. One day, while in conversation with Pearce, he was giving me an account of his having been caught in a heavy squall in the Gulf of Venice, and, being compelled to put into Ancona, his vessel much disabled. During the progress of spinning his long yarn and talking of Ancona, he said "I conclude you are aware why our Portland boats are called lerrets", and on my expressing my ignorance, but at the same time wishing to obtain information on the subject, he proceeded as follows:
> ' "Upwards of 100 years since, as I have been informed, a Portland man was master of a vessel trading to Ancona, and while there was induced to pay a visit to the far-famed "Lady of Loreto, or Loretto": the gorgeous finery of which made such an impression on his mind, that after his retirement from the toils and troubles of a maritime life, he came to reside in his native village—Chesil—and had a particularly fine boat built, which was a great improvement on the boats then in use here and to which he gave the name "Lady of Loretto" and, Pearce went on to say that at some future date he would show me a paper to convince me there was some foundation for the tale he had related. Accordingly, about three weeks afterwards Pearce, who was at the time alluded to about 80 years of age and a great martyr to rheumatism, sent a message to me to the effect that if I would call upon him he had something to show me. On my proceeding to his residence, he produced a curious old document, called a "Church gift" (a certain description of conveyance of real and personal property where the Law of Gavelkind is in

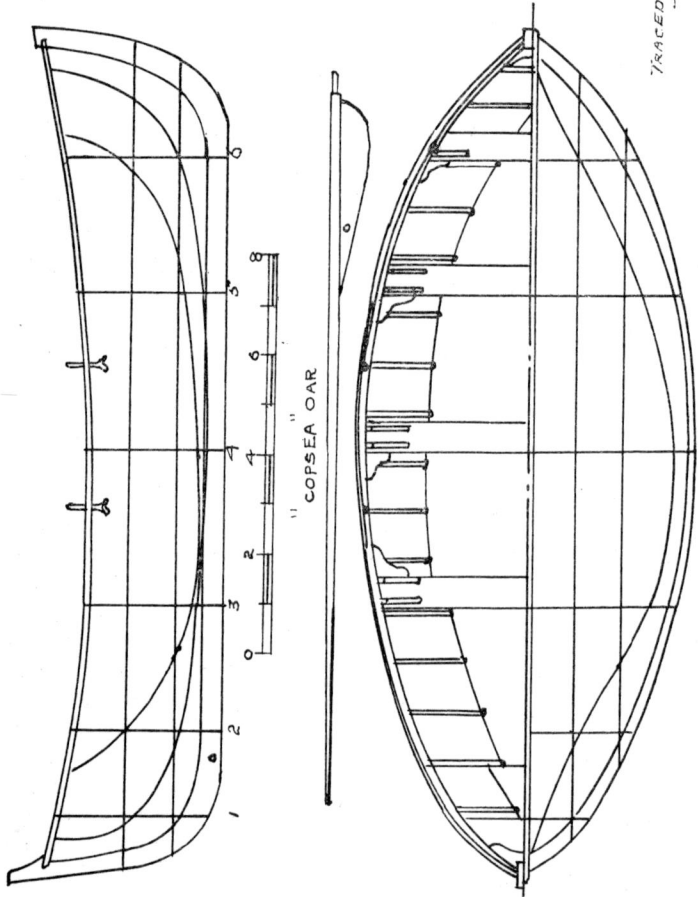

PORTLAND LERRET

"PUSSYFOOT"

L.O.A 17'2" BEAM 7'-0"

LINES TAKEN OFF BY W.M.M.

NOVEMBER 1935

COASTAL CRAFT SUB-COMMITTEE
SOCIETY FOR NAUTICAL RESEARCH

TRACED

"COPSEA OAR"

Lines of the Portland lerret *Pussyfoot*

operation, as is the case in this island) dated as far back, if my memory does not fail me, as 1682, and amongst other property mentioned in the said deed of conveyance was the following:

'I also give to my son John my boat, with all her gear, called "The Lady of Loretto". I have not the slightest doubt but that the term "lerret" as applied to the boats here, is a corruption of the word Loretto, taken in connection with the circumstances I have related.'

(*Signed*) Charles Augustus Manning

In the 1930s, several lerrets were still in use. I have photographs of two, *Comrades* (picture, p 100), and *Pussyfoot*; the sternpost is carried up above the gunwale and forms a useful handhold when the boat is being pushed into the water. In 1953 I had a reply to my letter to Miss Dorothy Arnold who wrote that the lerret was still being built in Weymouth, and that the boats 'we use here are rowed by four men and one to throw out the net or seines. . . . Mr Huddy has one called the *Queen Mary* which is now about 20 years old and has another 30 years old . . . it has no sails whatever; the older boats of years ago, I have been told, were much bigger and heavier, being rowed by six or eight men.'

A small snap was enclosed of *Queen Mary* getting afloat with the start rope coiled round the head of the sternpost and four men each pulling an oar.

The lines of *Pussyfoot*, taken off in November 1935, show a marked similarity to many of the early Scottish open boats and it is interesting to speculate if the *Lady of Loretto* was built to the form seen by the shipmaster when in Scottish waters.

When a lerret is beached, it is hauled up the steep slope on greased oars, but is run down by men pushing at the sides and stern.

CHAPTER FIVE

THE DEVON AND CORNWALL
COASTS

O N the South Devon coast the steep shingle beaches at Beer Head and Sidmouth were similar to those on the Sussex shores, fully exposed to every onshore wind. In the mid-eighteenth century eight to ten luggers lay at Beer, three-masted with high-peaked lugs and long yards. The main tack hooked to the weather side, the fore to an iron bumpkin projecting downward at an angle of about 45 degrees. A curious feature was the wooden spar bowline—the 'fore-girt' (pronounced locally 'fore-good')—used to stretch out the weather edge and corresponding to the Cornish 'vargord'. This spar fitted into a cringle in the luff of the fore or main lug, the heel being lashed round the mast by a rope about 3 ft long permanently rove through a hole in the butt. Some boats used a rope bowline on the main instead of a spar.

The mizzen was a standing lug with two lines of reef points; fore and main had three rows, but here again opinions differed. Some men preferred to have no reef points and carried a hard-weather sail, the 'fore mizzen', with three lines of points, its tack hooking to the inner hook on the bumpkin. Halyards and a burton set up to windward were the only rigging.

A little aft of the foremast was an oar port on either side through which the oars—here known as 'paddles'—were worked in calms. The boats always left the beach with only two masts up, the main being stepped when out at sea; the spars, being light, tended to take a pronounced curve in a breeze.

Hulls were rather sharp-bottomed, undecked and clench-built, ballast being bags of shingle. Their cost was about £29.

One of these old-fashioned boats, *Beatrice Annie*, E 80, was still fishing in 1917, but was broken up in the following year. The length overall was 28 ft, beam 11 ft 6 in, depth 5 ft, with a vertical transom stern. (Picture, p 137.) The majority of the boats had long discarded the mainmast.

In landing, the boat was sheered broadside on, being then pressed against the steep bank of shingle, sails were laid aback and the ballast thrown ashore; then the boat was hauled up by her capstan.

Little Jim, built by Lavers at Exmouth in 1916, was 23 ft overall, keel 21 ft 1 in, beam 8 ft 6 in, depth 4 ft 2 in, draught 1 ft 9 in for'ard, 3 ft 3 in aft, flat floored with rounded bilges, three bilge pieces, decked to mast, four thwarts and one aft 15 in wide. The foremast was 29 ft 4 in, yard 12 ft 6 in, mizzen mast 13 ft 3 in, yard 8 ft 3 in, outrigger 11 ft 1 in. There was an iron bumpkin 1 ft below the stemhead, 3 ft 6 in, with two hooks.

At Sidmouth, 14-ft fore and mizzen boats were used for crab and lobster fishing; the larger luggers went after mackerel and herring. Hulls had to be strong to stand up to the heavy strains of launching and beaching in all weathers, yet light enough to be hauled up a steep beach.

When launching, the boat was pushed down over greased woods and out into enough water to float her; then the last man jumped in over the stern. Launching in bad weather under oars, the boatman at the tiller worked it with one hand and had an oar in the other, standing in the stern sheets 'sheaving'— shoving—and, watching the seas, he could direct the other men to pull hard or easy according to the height and character of the surf. The boat was run down on woods into the white wash of surf, and bow and midship oars were manned. Then they would wait for a smooth, and the final push out might well see the man almost waist high in water before tumbling into the boat. The first under-tow of a wave carried the boat forward to meet the crest of the next sea, but the shallow froth gave little grip for the oars and it was more a case of working in sand and shingle. This first sea had to be taken at speed, and as the boat

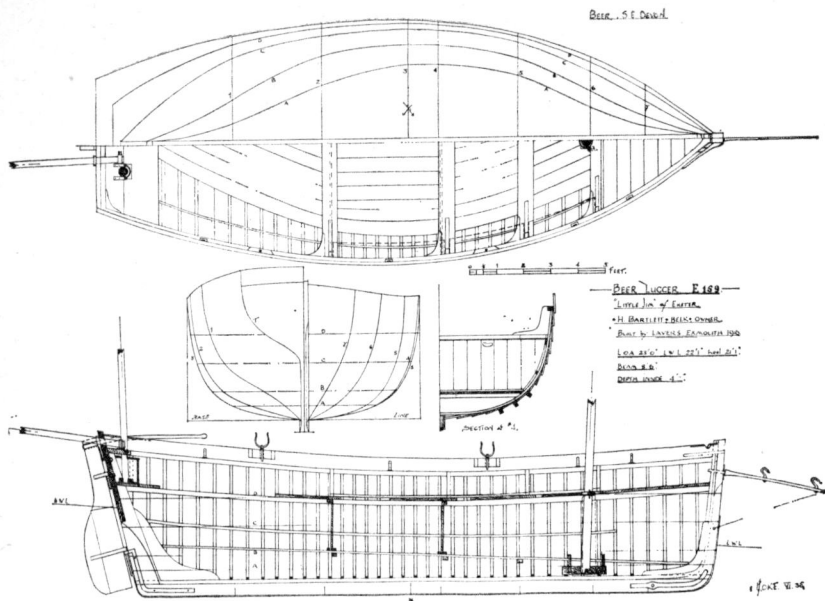

Lines of the Beer lugger *Little Jim*

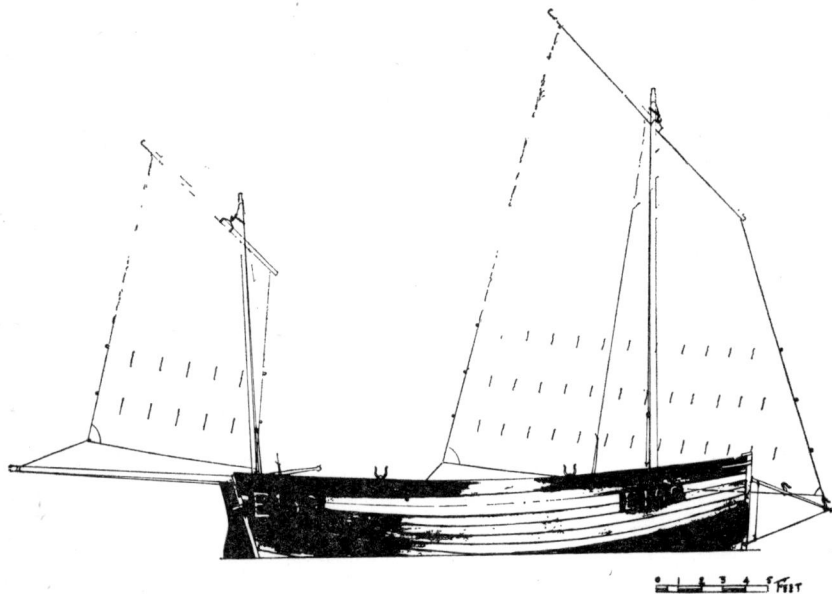

Sail plan of *Little Jim* measured up by the late P. J. Oke, June 1935

crashed through the crest, spray fell high over everything; but by pulling hard headway was made, the interval between each breaker becoming longer.

If mackerel fishing, the lines were out as soon as the boat was well clear of the surf. First went the 'bobber', a line with a lighter lead than the others in order to tow nearer the surface and made fast to the mizzen stay. Then two lines weighted according to the strength of the wind with 2- to 3-lb leads, made fast on either side amidships; a fourth line was sometimes towed from the stern opposite the bobber. If it was obtainable the best bait was the sand eel, kept alive in a bottle and hooked by the head, or a slip off a mackerel's tail pickled in salt and water; once the fish started biting the finest bait was a fresh-cut piece from under the tail.

At certain times the shoals did not come inshore and then the luggers worked to and fro until a strike was made well out to sea, a good indication being the clouds of gulls diving to pick up the small fry swimming near the surface, which had brought in the shoal. The larger Beer luggers rigged out poles on either beam to work six lines at once.

The skill lay in keeping just the right 'drag way' upon the boat to keep the lines clear, never tacking, as the lines might get under the keel, but wearing round before the wind. When the fish were biting well and near the top of the water the lines were shortened to within a fathom or two from the boat. The men never hauled in more than one line at a time or re-baited as long as a scrap was left on the hook; at times mackerel would often bite at a bare hook, attracted by the glint. A morning's catch could be anything from 100 to 500 fish a boat; instances have been known of two men hauling about 1,500 between dawn and noon, when the fleet usually made for the shore. The fish were then sold to the dealers—'jurners'—waiting on the beach.

A fresh southerly wind with a cloudy sky—a 'mackerel breeze'—was preferred to an offshore smooth-water wind, providing there was not too much sea to launch off. The fish were then more scattered, and the fleet worked farther from land, but if it freshened up into half a gale it was an anxious time running in to beach. The boats hauled their wind for a moment just outside the breakers in order to hook a rope into the stem; then in they came, men seizing the rope the moment a boat touched. If it was blowing very hard with the seas breaking over the sea-wall, the boats waited until the tide had fallen sufficiently to expose the Chit Rocks; then they ran in for the end of the beach about a quarter of a mile from the usual landing. Unfortunately there were no capstans here and at high water only a narrow strip of beach was left under the cliffs. Should the gale continue to harden it was necessary to lighten the boats before dragging them along the shore to a safer place.

When a gale coincided with a spring tide everything had to be rapidly cleared off the beach, capstans and all; then as the huge seas thundered in they rushed over the seawall, piling shingle up in the roads and flooding nearby houses. Boats were often well inland in several feet of water, tied up to lamp posts or anything handy. Then was the dangerous time for the collier brigs anchored off-shore; either they had to ride out the blow or slip and try to get into shelter elsewhere.

After such a sou'wester the wind would fly round to the nor'west in a hard squall with heavy rain, and soon the long rolling seas no longer broke shorewards but turned back on themselves, flinging up great plumes of spray; the wind knocked the weight out of the sea and boats could be launched again. In the herring season after such a blow, good catches were frequently made while the sea was still thick with sand and washings from the cliffs.

By the 1880s, the length of the luggers had increased from 18 ft up to 24 ft, but it was rare to carry a third hand, although these boats shot anything from 300 to 400 fathoms of net, taking over two hours to get in.

Harbours were available farther west at Brixham, Dart-mouth and Plymouth, and long lines were worked from the 'hookers', heavily-built cutters of 4 to 5 tons.

In 1833 some 70 hookers worked out of Brixham, fishing up
to 10 to 12 miles off the land according to the season. In
summer, when the mackerel shoals came into Torbay, short
poles were rigged out on either side of the boat with extra lines
attached. When long-lining, the lines, kept in 'spiller' boxes,
carried from 1,000 to 3,000 hooks, the local name being
'bulters'; 'spilliard' and 'spiller' were other names. Hand lines
were chiefly used for whiting, bream and gurnards. In the hake
season, before the coming of railways, Brixham men often
sailed up channel to Portsmouth to land their catches, which
were sent to Billingsgate in fish waggons or light vans drawn by
horses. If unable to catch the evening waggon the fish had to be
thrown overboard as the Devon men were unable to salt them
owing to the prohibitive duty on that commodity; it was not
until late in the 1820s that the restrictions were removed. There
is a story that on one occasion when Brixham men were fishing
in Torbay a disagreement arose concerning the sharing of the
money and the huge catches were dumped over the side; the
fish thereupon deserted the bay and returned no more. When
I was in Brixham in 1950 several old fishermen confirmed this
story.

At one time upwards of 40 hookers fished out of Plymouth,
some long-lining in deep water 40 to 50 miles outside the
Eddystone, where the bottom was sand and shells, closer inshore sand and mud. In 1878 Prosser Germain, a fisherman for
40 years, stated that he had caught hake, conger, halibut, soles,
turbot, red mullet, brill and skate in the fall of the year, going
as far west as Looe. Other men worked 20 miles off Start Point,
in the vicinity of Bolt Head, and on rough grounds inshore
where trawling was impossible, 50 dozen whiting in a tide being
a fair catch just outside Plymouth Sound. The favourite bait
was squid, but pilchards were often used; if bait was scarce
pieces of skate and dogfish were put on the hooks. Bait was an
expensive item, costing about £100 a year, with pilchards from
5s to 50s a thousand, enough for one baiting of a long line of
1,500 hooks. (Picture, p 118.)

There were two classes of hookers at Plymouth; the smaller had a length overall of about 31 ft, a beam of 10 ft, and were half-decked with a small cuddy below and waterways aft. They were cutter-rigged with a short pole mast and an enormous yard laced to the weather of the topsail and hoisted with it. The larger boats ran up to 40 ft 6 in overall, with a beam of 13 ft 4 in and a depth of 7 ft 6 in, and were fully decked with a hatch amidships and a companion aft leading to a cabin. Rig was true 'dandy', a short mizzen mast being stepped against the transom; on it a standing lug was set, sheeting to the end of an outrigger. Both types were square-sterned, deep-heeled and carried a boomless mainsail with two rows of reef points. (Picture, p 117.)

In light weather the big hookers set a huge reaching foresail, a big jib and a jib topsail set from the head of the jackyard which was drawn forward by the pull and presented an extraordinary appearance as the head of the topsail was now almost horizontal.

The dandy-rigged *George & Stanley*, PH 56, had an 8-cloth jib, a 10-cloth foresail laced to the forestay, a 10-cloth mainsail with two rows of reef points, 20-ft foot, a 12-cloth topsail bent to a 25-ft pole standing vertical, and a 4-ft yard at the clew. The lug mizzen had five cloths and sheeted to an outrigger to starboard. The reeving bowsprit went out through an iron collar to port, the bobstay being set up with two single blocks, the jib outhaul fast to an iron traveller.

The deck arrangements were a line reel for'ard of the mast, immediately aft was a hatch, then the stove chimney and companion. The short mizzen mast, raking aft, was stepped to port of amidships to give sufficient play for the tiller.

This hooker was built at Porthleven, as were many others, length being 40 ft 6 in, beam 13 ft 4 in, and depth 7 ft 6 in. The hull was painted grey, the outside of the bulwarks black with a white streak, inside pea green with brown or buff stanchions, spaced 3 ft 6 in apart. The tip of the bowsprit and outrigger, and both mastheads, were green.

The lines of a small hooker 339 PH were taken off by the late

P. J. Oke on behalf of the Coastal Craft Sub-committee of the Society for Nautical Research in 1935. Length overall was 31 ft, beam 10 ft, length of keel 27 ft 9 in. The hull was half-decked with a small cuddy below, access being through sliding hatches in the bulkhead of the well which extended aft for 16 ft. Athwartships was a hand 'wink' with narrow waterways on either side of the well; aft was a 2-ft deck, fish were stowed in wing pockets below and the ballast was under the platform. Floors were very sharp, bilges rounded; draught was 4 ft for'ard, and 6 ft 6 in aft.

The reeving bowsprit was 21 ft overall, 14 ft outboard, diameter 5 to 4 in, with three fid holes, and ran out through the port bulwarks. The mast, stepped against the bulkhead, had a forward rake, but was upright when boat was afloat; length was 35 ft, diameter $7\frac{1}{2}$ in, two shrouds a side. The 21-ft gaff had a diameter of 4 to $3\frac{1}{4}$ in; no topmast was fitted, but the topsail had its luff bent to a 30-ft pole, with an 11 ft 6 in jackyard at the clew to which the sheet was bent. The boomless mainsail had two lines of reef points, and the sheet traversed on an iron horse on the transom. Eighteen floors were centred 18 in. Both types were fishing in the 1930s, fitted with motors, but still retaining sails.

At Hallsands, north of Start Point, the crab boats had one mast with a sprit mainsail laced to it and a jib with a short bowsprit bowsed down with a bobstay. (Picture, p 198.)

According to a Report in 1883, it was the custom at Hallsands and Beesands to use Labrador dogs trained to swim out to boats coming in to beach, seize a piece of wood with a light line attached to it and return with it to the shore. Men then pulled in a heavier rope and the boat was hauled up stern first by a rope through a hole in the after end of the keel.

THE CORNISH COAST

Eighteen miles west of Plymouth, Polperro lies in a deep valley; the harbour, known locally as the 'hauen', is open to the

sea in a SE direction and runs up into the land for about a fur-
long. On the west it is guarded by a natural breakwater, a bold
mass of craggy, pinnacled rocks, 'the Peak'; to the east the hill
descends into the sea, ending in a ledge of wave-worn rocks.
Centuries back the need for greater protection was seen and in
Tudor times Leland mentions an old quay made of parallel
walls of stone, filled in with stones and rubbish. Houses were
later built upon it. Then came the outer or new quay, nearly at
right angles to the old. In 1774 this pier was badly damaged in
a very heavy gale and some two-thirds was rebuilt. In January
1817 a SE gale destroyed much property, the seas breaking clean
over the 90-ft high Peak, cottages were flooded to the ceilings,
the shipyard demolished, sean nets lost and 30 large and many
smaller boats smashed to pieces. The Sand Quay was rebuilt a
foot higher, but to no avail, as seven years later both piers were
virtually destroyed. Rebuilt again, further damage was sustained and the outer pier was lengthened; in 1861 the Duke of
Connaught pier was constructed, at a cost of £627, the money
being raised locally. It projected out about 50 ft from the east
side, but sustained damage four years later. Yet another disaster
occurred in 1891 when practically every boat was wrecked or
badly damaged. Another pier was built out from the east side
in line with the outer west quay and in storms the entrance was
closed by massive baulks of timber, and for the first time the
the harbour was reasonably safe.

In the 1830s about 30 boats fished out of Polperro, besides
several punts used in spring and summer for crabbing. The
larger craft were about 27 ft on the keel, with a beam of 9 to
10 ft, clinker-built, stiff for their size, fast and safe. The usual
rig was one mast, a sprit mainsail, gaff topsail and foresail to
the end of an iron bumpkin, but a lug mizzen was frequently
set, and a bowsprit rigged out to carry a jib. Completely undecked, except for a small cuddy between the first beam and
the stem, the crew lived hard, in calms rowing 10 to 15 miles to
the fishing grounds.

In Cornish waters the lines, known as 'boulters' from at least the days of Queen Elizabeth I, were 120 fathoms in length with 1,000 hooks. The snoods, locally called 'nessels', were made at home on a 'nessel-taker', a crude but ingenious device fixed in a beam. Each deep-sea line was armed with 'ganges', fine brass or copper wire twisted round hook and snood for a foot or more to prevent fish biting through the twine.

The fishermen knew the bottom of the sea as well almost as the fields ashore; prominent landmarks—a church tower, a tall tree or clump of trees, a white house—told the position of prolific grounds. The hills and valleys, steep crags and gullies of weed or sand (each had its especial fish), had been found by armed leads; the names of each spot were of ancient origin and the accuracy with which they could be found was the secret of a man's good fortune. This knowledge is now largely lost.

For hook fishing, the crew numbered two and the catch was divided into fifths, one share to the owner, four between the two men equally. The owner was frequently 'the master fisherman'. 'Rabble fish', such as dog-fish, ray, skate, gurnard, scad and a few others, were shared by the men without any share for the boat. Until well after the mid-nineteenth century hake from its abundance was classed as 'rabble', but it was stated in 1871 that 'from its rarity is classed with cod and whiting, a few years back a dozen were bought for the present price of one'. The men fished for them between shooting and hauling the pilchard nets; in the early days a 10-lb fish would be sold for twopence.

Whiting always found a ready sale, being split through the belly and gutted before being sold to 'jowlers'; if split through the back, salted and dried they were called 'buckhorn' and sold in bundles of six. Whiting were caught with bait of mussels, pieces of pilchard, gurnard or squid; they cease biting soon after sunset and will not take again until after sunrise. although they will sometimes take on a bright, moonlight night. The season lasted from November to January. When whiting were served up at table it was customary to pass the tail through the cavity of the eye so that they lay curled on the plate—the only fish I know to be treated in this manner.

Cod were at their best in December and January; throughout the summer they were 'louning' or 'spent', but the young 'tamlin cod' were eaten. Tongues and sounds were pickled for home use and for export.

Ling were taken all the year round, the greatest quantity during January and February. After the removal of viscera and backbone the fish were salted and dried, the tongues and sounds being separately potted. Dory, turbot and brill were rarely caught in any quantity, hence they always fetched high prices.

Conger was an important item of food in the West Country and large quantities were exported to Spain and Portugal as early as the reign of King John. The trade fell off during the long years of the Napoleonic wars, chiefly because of the scarcity of fish, there not being enough to satisfy the home market. 'Conger douce', as it was called, was prepared by cutting the fish flat through their length and sewing the pieces together with twine to form a continuous sheet. This was then stretched on a framework without salt or other preservative until dried— 'in wet seasons much loss and more offence to the noses of townspeople accrued from so very coarse a process'. This delicacy was grated and used to enrich soup.

Conger rarely take a bait by day or on a moonlight night, and never touch tainted bait. The 'boultys', or 'boulters', had a snood 5 to 6 ft long at every 2 fathoms with a tinned hook baited with cuttle or pilchard. The long line was stretched and moored, its position marked with a buoy, the snoods having many separate cords to prevent the fish escaping by gnawing the line. The best grounds lay 30 to 45 miles from land on sandy bottom; conger were here coloured white and ran to enormous size, many exceeding 1 cwt. In littoral gullies the colour was a rich purplish-black. 'Once a boat not infrequently brought in 1,000 lb in a night's fishing, now (c 1870) two cwt thought remarkable, fishermen consider this is due to trawling.' Off Land's End, conger ran 50 to 60 lb apiece, but only about 10 lb in Mount's Bay. According to the 1878 Report, 'once 6 to 8 cwt was an ordinary night's fishing for two men, and 25 cwt in one

Page 197
Zulu skiffs
at Camp-
belton.
Note length
of sweeps

Page 198 (*above*) Hallsands, Devon, crabber, *c* 1937. Note spritsail is laced to the mast, jib tack is on a bowsed-down bumpkin and heel of sprit in rope snotter;

(*left*) Manx fore and mizzen 'yawl'

Page 199 (*above*)
Morecambe Bay
prawner hauled up on
slipway. Note under-
water lines and beam
trawl with bobbins
threaded on a chain;

(*below*) Loch Fyne
Zulu skiff, *c* 1907, in
Lochranza outer bay

Page 200 (*above*) Fleetwood Regatta with Morecambe Bay prawners racing. The boat to windward with white hull was built at Fleetwood, probably by Armour, the others at Crossfield's yard at Arnside; (*below*) Another view of prawners racing

night by a single boat'. The largest one ever landed at Meva-
gissey was caught by M. Dunn and J. Hicks and turned the
scale at 112 lb, and they had two others taken the same night
weighing 70 and 60 lb. Another landed at Falmouth was 7 ft
4 in long, 2 ft in girth and scaled 72 lb. In January 1875, M.
Dunn had one weighing 54 lb with a 4½ lb roe which yielded
about 7,960,000 eggs. Conger pie was a popular dish in Cornwall.

Conger are very sensitive to changes of temperature; in
severe frosts the air bladders are abnormally distended and the
fish get 'blown', floating helplessly on the surface. During the
pilchard season they leave the holes in which they lurk among
the rocks or wrecked ships, and rise to attack the shoals in the
nets, leaving behind them a mark, or 'suc', where they roll up
a length of net about 1 ft wide and 5 ft long in the shape of a
pine cone, a tangle most difficult to unravel. The newly taken
conger were bought by curers at a price rarely as high as 5s a
cwt, but were often sold at 30s retail.

Monk fish, a species of skate, were also caught on hooks.
Digging holes in the sand, they lie concealed with only their
eyes visible until a victim approaches; then they use their
flapper-like wings to 'fly', eagle fashion, through the water in
swift pursuit.

Whiting-pollack and the rauning-pollack were found in
abundance and 'held in great esteem'. Ling preyed on the
shoals, and one caught in March 1878 between the Scilly
Islands and Land's End weighed 42 lb; in its stomach was a
9½-lb pollack.

About the 1830s the number of drift nets carried varied according to the means of the men, but usually they totalled about
20, each 18 to 20 fathoms long, 7 fathoms deep, making a
'string' about ¾ mile long. The nets were fastened to each other
and to a head line—the 'baulch'—which had a row of corks;
another line ran loosely along the middle of the nets to give
added strength in rough weather or when the nets were
'drawn'. Shot at dusk, the nets were drawn in about two hours,

L

then shot again towards morning as pilchards are most active in the evening and morning. A rope from one end of the nets, fastened to the bow, was shifted to the quarter when hauling, the string floating with the tide. No sails were set, except in very calm weather to prevent the nets from folding together. Later improvements reduced the number and size of the corks and when fixed at the proper distances with the buoy attached the nets sank to a depth of up to 2 fathoms. 'The fishing was prosperous until the coming of seans, then declined until only one boat was fishing. Merchants were also the owners of seans and refused to buy drift fish as being less valuable by being caught by strangling . . . now revived (c 1840) and 17 boats employed.

'The best time for "driving" is in hazy weather with some motion on the waves; in clear moonlight the fish are shy, but on very dark nights the "briming" makes the nets look like a wall of fire.' The season was from July to the end of the year, in lesser 'schulls' as late as March.

The crew numbered four, and the proceeds of the catch were divided into eight parts, the boat and nets taking half, the crew the remainder. A lad was usually aboard; he had what he could save from 'the losses during the draught by his "kieve net" and by the capture of hake etc in intervals'.

A boat and nets then cost about £250, the price of each net being £6 with a life of some six years, but it called for frequent mending as the blue shark 'cut out fish at its pleasure, swallowing net and all'. A big haul might be as much as 40,000 fish.

Mackerel were generally caught by hook and line, drift-net fishing being 'not very successful locally. At the time of the last great storm that destroyed piers and shipwrights' yards, two large boats utterly destroyed in course of building, another boat sent to sea soon after, but not greatly successful. Early in 1850 a much larger lugger with a string of nets 1,400 fathoms long went west to Scilly Islands, not much encouragement. In 1858 four new luggers, 35 ft long, 10 ft beam, cost £110 to £120 each, ready for sea, put to sea with varying success.'

Living conditions in Cornwall were grim before the coming of railways, communications were poor and communities relied on local products. The women spun up cloth at 4d to 5d a lb, which was then sent to 'tucking' or 'fulling' mills for dipping and stretching before being made up by journeymen tailors working for a shilling a day and their food. The suits were practically everlasting and needed to be, for farm labourers had a shilling a day; if skilled, 9s a week with 12s without a cottage. Oxen were used for draught in the fields on the cliffs. The rent of a cottage with garden was from £2 10s to £5 5s a year, but prices for anything brought in from a distance were high, sugar 8d a lb, tea 6s to 10s a lb, and bought in minute quantities from hawkers. Barley bread was half the price of wheaten, but pig-keeping was profitable; at six to eight weeks a young one was worth 16s. Sucking pigs were known as 'veers'. Little wonder that fish was a staple diet; but crabs, lobsters and crayfish were considered too good for home consumption and were sold to the gentry.

The fishermen were a hardy race, but earnings were at all times precarious. Often there were days when they were unable to put to sea; in 1868 those lost days totalled 107. Their principal food was potatoes from the garden or plot up on the cliffs, and well filled 'steans' of salted pilchards. Dressed in guernsey frocks, sou'westers and seaboots they bargained over their catches with loquacious 'jowters' at the 'fish scales' as the market near the 'strand' was called.

Do not make their own nets or spin lines, buy at Bridport . . . women and children expert at mending nets, a more difficult task than making . . . very tenacious of old customs and their rights. Formerly slept at bottom of boat, only covering their thick sea dress and a coarse tarpaulin. Only five or six years back had cuddy in bows of boats . . . also tried sinking drift nets to some depth below surface, thus avoiding danger from ships running across them. . . . Brave and intrepid, in cases of shipwreck and disaster are hospitable to shipwrecked who are often ungrateful for rescue and food and clothes.

By the 1870s the second-class boats numbered ten, 27 to 28

ft long, beam 9 to 10 ft, costing £80 to £90 each, and a further fifteen about 22 to 24 ft long, breadth 8 ft, and costing £60 to £70 each. The smaller boats were all spritsail-rigged, except for two which were gaff-rigged.

The nets were chiefly made of cotton, each about 42 fathoms long, and cost £8 to £9, a boat carrying eight to 13 nets. For mackerel, the nets were of hemp and cotton, chiefly hemp, each 22 fathoms in length and cost £3. 'The nets belong to the owners of the boats, now about 25 drift boats including the luggers, a large one was built last year (1870), nets and boat taking half the earnings, crew sharing the remainder. Nets are barked with catechu, oak bark now seldom used.'

'Surmullet' were rarely hooked but were caught by 'trammel', a net formed of three separate ones fastened to a common headline and footline, the meshes of each differing considerably. In the middle net the distance from knot to knot was sufficiently large to take the head and forepart of the fish. The outer nets on either side hung a little more loosely and had meshes allowing passage of the body of the fish until it was caught in the inner net, 'its struggles make the larger meshes into a bag by which the fish is prevented from falling out when the net is drawn to the surface. The net is set at certain inshore marks where the ground is oozy and strewn with scattered stones, the footrope must touch bottom or the fish will find its way under . . . fish in great repute and makes excellent price.'

For the final development of the cutter-rigged 'gaffers', I turn to many letters written to me by Lieut-Col C. F. Jerram,

> Oliver of Looe built many of the best of the Looe and Polperro boats . . . I saw practically all the changes in the drifters. The original boats were clinker-built and quite open and mainly sprit-rigged. These were practically all wrecked and washed up in Lansallos Street in the great gale which necessitated the building of the outer pier.
> They were replaced by the gaff-rigged, carvel boats with a short cuddy which came aft only to the beam before the mast, leaving a space of about 3 ft between the mast and cuddy bulkhead (in which the boy used to sleep). Few people now remember

this and think the cuddy came back to the mast, it was only lengthened to house the first engines in the 1914–18 war. These boats all had a double mainsheet and I stood on the Peak with a crowd of fishermen to watch the first boat with a mainsheet horse coming in from the builders at Looe. They all rather expected her to miss stays in the harbour mouth. However she didn't and it was not long before all the other boats followed suit.

Colonel Jerram went on to explain the art of setting a loose-footed sail . . .

which no amateur knows . . . I knew it more or less but old Oliver rubbed it in. . . .

(a) The line of extension of the mainsheet should not reach further forward than the outer peak halliard strop, very well shown in your diagram. All amateurs bisect the angle as one does in a fores'l or jib lead.

(b) The head of the sail long, and peaked very well up till it wrinkles. All amateurs have too short a head and NEVER peak it up and then curse the loose-footed sail.

Regarding the topsail, the Polperro man's object was to get the greatest amount of sail on the shortest possible masthead, and amateurs have never been able to see how you could get a 24-ft tops'l pole on a 3-ft masthead without its capsizing. The answer was the 'timmanoggy'—the tack rope reeving through a sheave in the gaff just outside the jaws which gave the tops'l its characteristic kink over the bow. . . . I never remember seeing a jib topsail though I'm sure it must have existed, the boats carried a very long bowsprit which could be reefed according to the jib used . . . the bowsprit had no stays or shrouds and the jib outhaul led through a claw cleat in the cutwater and up to deck, acting as a bobstay. . . . The big jib would go out to the end of the bowsprit, there was a block in the bowsprit end for the jib tops'l tack rope and the sail was set from the tops'l pole to the end of the bowsprit.

The word 'timmanoggy' is a curious one and I've never arrived at its derivation. It was in its origin something quite different and referred to a lugger. Before the high-peaked lug, a very square-headed one was used which made for a long and rather slack luff. A thimble was worked into the luff rope about one-third up and a spar used to push out the luff, like the bowline of a square sail in reverse. If the thimble was the timmanoggy, one can see the reference in the tops'l tack of the Polperro man.

Polperro had a type known as 'day boats', carvel-built and completely open, which carried only the loose-footed mains'l and stays'l . . . about 20 ft to 24 ft in length, mainly employed whiting fishing with hand lines and mackerel. Then there were the small crabbers, but 'crabber' is an anomaly really, for the family were crabbers rather than the boat; for instance one of the largest boats in the place was a crabber. The inshore crabber was a small boat of about 18 ft, either with dipping and standing lug, or sprit mainsail and mizzen and a staysail on a short iron bumpkin according to taste; latterly they had centreboards but always carried a good bit of ballast in ½ cwt pigs . . . clinker-built. The best Cornwall crabber of Cadgwith was and is a different boat, carvel-built from 20 to 22 ft, lug-rigged.

I do not think the gaffer was so called to distinguish it from the lugger, but from the spreeter. In Napoleonic times the big boats were mainly luggers, the small ones spreeters. I knew well in her old age the daughter of Richard Rowett, the famous smuggler-cum-privateer, his boat was a lugger. The spreeters gradually grew to the normal 28-ft boats and when the new boats were built after the gale of 1891 they were given gaff rig. . . . Their ballast, originally ironstone from the Caradon mines, gradually gave way to ½-cwt pigs, cast for the boat . . . every pig had the name of the boat cast in it.

In the old days, the men collected on the quays with their white linen bags of bread, butter and tea, but the engine killed that as they found only a tin would keep the taste out. The motor killed the trade in every way, (a) the pilchard is a very timid fish. When going to sea on a fine summer evening, the skipper of the boat, steering, would go 'briming'—a gentle kick on the side of the boat every now and again. If there were fish about, you'd see them shoot off in the brimming water and the order would be 'down mains'l, shoot away'. Motors would obviously drive the fish off and you'd have to wait till they came back after it had stopped.

(c) Under sail, if you had a bad night, week or month, even if you gained nothing, you lost nothing; with the motor, you had to go in debt for your oil. As the masts and sails had been cut down you couldn't sail much and the poorer fishermen were soon so much in debt that their boats were seized and sold. The wiser, bad fishermen sold them for 'yachts' before the inevitable happened. It is a fact that only one or two families of the best fishermen of the early 1900s are still fishing (1953). 'Moose' Curtis, his

son John, and his son whom I sailed with, are now represented by
the grandson still fishing.

As an example of summer fishing—we used to gather on the
pier about 6 pm, about 50 boats (there are now two), and hang
about till the best men got down to their boats. Quite often old
Tom Mark would suddenly start to preach and as often stop in
the middle of a sentence and drop down into his boat. In those
days there was a continuous line of boats and nets from the Rame
to the Deadman and at night it was like a town. After shooting
and a bit of tea, the skipper and second hand would go to sleep in
the cuddy, the boy in the space forrard of the mast and my
brother and self, passengers, on the fore-deck, rolled up in the
staysail. Later, when we woke up to haul, someone miles away
might start an hymn and gradually the whole fleet would take it
up. At the back end of our holidays most of the nets would be put
ashore and the 1,000-hook boulter taken aboard. Then, with
about one-third of the fleet of nets, we'd shoot for bait and then
sail off to the boultering grounds for conger etc. My job was the
kieve net . . . everybody was very poor, including ourselves, but
I don't think we've improved any since!!!

As regards sail plan, the gaffers also carried a reaching fores'l
and an enormous reaching jib set from the bowsprit end and
sheeting home aft, also second and spitfire jibs; it's amazing
where it all stowed. . . . No Polperro boat EVER had mast hoops.
The luff of the sail was always laced and if you could not get your
peak up in any other way, the lacing would be slackened off to do
so. In any case it was always slacked when getting the sail up and
generally not hauled taut at all, unless on a wind . . . the fores'l
was also laced, no hanks . . . a sculling notch in transom. The
whole object of the Polperro rig is the greatest amount of sail on
the shortest possible mast. The lugger could and did lower the
mast, the gaffer couldn't, and riding in a lop they were *very* lively.
The masthead was kept as short as possible, so short that there
was a definite downward pull on the peak halliards, hence the
necessity for the timmanoggy to set the topsail. Reefing was very
simple. The mainsheet block was fitted with a very long hook,
about 7 or 8 in, and all one had to do was to lower the throat
halliards enough to get the hook in the reef cringle. It was never
unhooked from the clew, but the reef cringle taken in on top of it,
the length of the hook allowing for all reefs. Consequently there
was never any danger of the sail blowing away—I've often done
it alone in quite a strong wind. The reef points were then tied up

without rolling. It was seldom necessary to touch the peak halliards. The hook had a bend in the end which prevented it
shaking out.

I was also lucky enough to get into touch with John F.
Curtis, who wrote:

I have been great friends with the Jerrams as they have taken a
lot of trips with us in sailing days. I am 75 and I went to sea at 11
and finished up when I was 70 . . . my first three years was in a
boat called *Hilda*, FY 213, whiting and conger fishing. Then my
father had a boat built at Looe by Angear called *Two Sisters*, FY
253 (picture, p 157), and I sailed with my father until 1919 when
we sold her and bought a lugger. . . . Fishing in those days was
plenty of work and very little pay. We would take out two oars
when it was calm and pull for hours and then hundreds of times
come in with no bait to put on the hooks. We used to work about
1,300 hooks, start about March and we were always glad when
August came to take in the pilchard nets, as that was the only
season to help pay up some of the old bills that was owing. We
used to carry about 19 nets and a crew of three and the average
price would be about nine bob a thousand, one season they was
only five bob. When October came the pilchards would go away
and then we would take in a few hundred hooks again to catch a
few rays and black conger. If we got a sovereign in those days in
one week we thought it was a big thing.

You asked about the cost of a boat in those days, my Father had
the first one built for £42, a 27-ft boat and all the sail would cost
about £10 for the set and the nets about £2 10s each. With regards to the catches, there would be times when we were hauling
in a nice catch we would say to each other 'Well, boy, we shall
make a good job of this catch', but when we came to harbour the
buyers would say 'You are a day late, it is no good. I cannot give
you more than seven shillings per cwt, and as for rays I have been
throwing them away as there was no sale for them'. So you see it
was living a uneasy existence, but the boats looked lovely with
their lovely barked sails and the fishermen with white jumpers.
You would see about 160 fishermen in those days sail out of
Polperro as there was 40 boats, some luggers about 42 ft long,
but it was a big task to get them out when the wind was blowing
as they used to have big oars as well as sails. Some winters we
would not go out for at least seven or eight weeks, there was no
dole then. Polperro was a quaint little village in the old days,
there was no baulks and they used to pull the boats up the streets.

Seaning first began at Polperro about 1782; as the local men knew nothing of the sean a master was procured from Meva-gissey, 'to have one-sixteenth an "ounce" in addition to a re-gular wage and share of the catch'. A quarrel arose and he left before his second year. This sean was the 'Polperro', the second was the 'Gannet'; both were highly prosperous for many years and the seaners were of such repute that in the early part of the nineteenth century they were employed at eight places along the coast. The cost was a little less than £1,000 and the amount of wages etc considerable, but the net lasted longer than a drift net.

Two boats, carvel-built, 40 ft long and of 10 ft beam, were accompanied by a much smaller boat, the 'lurker'. The 'sean-boat' carried a net of about 220 fathoms in length and 12 in depth, buoyed at the top along the head-rope by a row of corks, with the foot weighted by leads. The second boat—the 'volyer' —had another sean net of 100 fathoms in length and 18 in depth, with a hollow or 'bunt' in the middle.

The master seaner has entire command, quite independent of the 'adventurers'. In August the boats go to the neighbouring bay and anchor, keeping a good look-out for fish, which usually show themselves by a rippling on the surface, 'stoiting' or leaping, or by the colour imparted to the sea. When a schull is discovered, the lurker goes to ascertain its magnitude and the direction it is taking. The depth of water, clearness of ground from rocks, force and course of the tide, enter into the master's calculations before he makes the signal to prepare. Everything done by signs, for the fish are alarmed by noise.

A warp from the end of the stop sean is handed to the volyer and has to be kept all taut. The lurker continues near the fish and points out to the sean boat the space to be enclosed. The boat is rowed by four men, the other three throw or shoot the net, such is their vigour that the whole of the net, rope, cork and lead is in the sea within five minutes. The sean, at first, forms a curved line across the course of the shoal, and while the larger boats are warping ends together, the lurker takes station in the opening and dashes water with the oars to prevent the fish escaping. When the sean is closed, the opposite ends are laced together. If the body of fish is great and sea or tide strong, it is secured by heavy grapnels, laid out in the direction from which danger is feared . . . no more difficult to take a thousand hogsheads of fish than a much smaller number. Larger more easy as its motion is slower, its course less speedily changed through alarm.

When the tide is low the next job is to take up the fish. The sean-net is left as before, and the volyer passes within it and lays his sean—the 'tuck'—round the former on the inner side of its enclosure. It is then drawn together so as gradually to contract limits of the fish and raise them from the bottom. When disturbed the fish become greatly agitated and the greatest care is needed to prevent them from sinking or bursting the net. To hinder their escape back again from the tuck into the stop sean, stones suspended from ropes—called 'minnies'—are continually kept plunging opposite the only aperture. The fish are supported in the bunt of the tuck sean and lifted nearly dry to the surface, the voices of the men being lost in the noise of the fish as they beat the water. Now the seaners, in pairs on the gunwales of the boats, with flaskets lade the fish on board, any surplus to the boats' capacity being left.

The principal mark of a good master-seaner is that he forms a correct opinion of the quantity enclosed and is able to take from it into the tuck net only just so much as can be properly disposed of in the cellar for that day. By the extent of the briming, or light excited at night in sea water by anything that disturbs it, this judgment is formed and is the result of long experience. The advantages, when the quantity of fish is considerable, are: the whole can be salted in a proper condition without fatigue or extraordinary expense, sean is preserved from the risk of bursting, and the fish from the danger of being killed by pressure of their own weight, in which case the whole might be lost as impossible to raise a 1,000 hogsheads if fish drown. The shoal may be left for as long as a week, part taken up every night. An instance known of a ship being sent to France for salt after a sean was shot and returned with it in time to cure the fish.

The crew usually consisted of 18 men and a boy; the wages were 8s to 12s a week for ordinary seaners, and 1s extra for men shooting nets. The master-seaner received a guinea, with a gratuity on each 100 hogsheads taken. The crew in common were entitled to a third part of the fish sold fresh, and a fourth part of those exported; in some places they did not even pay for the casks.

The curing was performed by women, 12 on one sean. The fish was piled up in order, in 'balk', or bulk, against the walls of the cellar—the 'pallace'—a layer of fish, then a layer of salt. Thus they remained for 30 days, the oil and brine draining into pits. Then the fish were taken out and sifted, thus separating dry salt, next they were washed in another sieve and placed in regular order in casks. Each cask measured 50 gallons, and the staves were put together with many crevices in order that the oil on pressure could escape; this was done by levers to which heavy weights were hung. The casks were pressed and refilled for a space of nine days, or until the weight of the barrel was 476 lb when headed up for export. It was then branded with the name of the curer, 'BF' for British Fish, and 3,000, the supposed contents.

The oil was used for outdoor painting by putting it in a clean iron pot over a stove, 'when it begins to heat, skim well, let it remain on fire until it singes a feather put therein. For every gallon, add a small tablespoon of red litharge or other pigment, stir well for about three minutes, take pot from the fire and let mixture cool in the open air, when it is fit for use, dries quickly and becomes solid in a short time on wood or iron.'

This 'train-oil' was used in earthenware or tin lamps fitted with a rush wick, the outer skin peeled off, the rushes being kept in bundles, 'rather evil smelling, in common use up to early 1800s. Old proverbs says "meat, money and light, all in one night" '.

For home curing, the head was broken off the fish and the entrails scraped out with a finger. The fish was then washed, lined with salt and placed in a well-tightened barrel or earthenware pot—a layer of fish, a layer of salt—so becoming covered with brine as the salt dissolved. For immediate consumption the fish were 'scrawed', ie, gutted, split, powdered with salt and pepper, then hung in the sun. Broiled, they formed a favourite food. In earlier days the pilchards were smoked; those prepared by balking were known as 'furmades'.

At Looe, the sprit rig gave way to the lugger about the 1870s, followed by the big mackerel drivers. In the old days the nets were made by hand of hemp and barked, the men going out into the woods to obtain the bark from oak trees. It was then chopped up into small pieces, put into a large copper and kept boiling for hours. Hemp nets had to be dried before and after barking, but when cotton was introduced, cutch from Burma was used and the wetter the nets were the better.

Early in the year the men went crabbing, or collected seaweed for use on the land as manure. The crab pots were made at home. First the men obtained hazel and withies, then the pots were made on a 'stool', a round, flat piece of wood mounted on a post. Hazel was stuck into twelve holes in the seat to form the mouth of the pot, about 8 in wide. Then the mouth was plaited with withies, followed by additional rods, and sections of three were then bent over and tied down before plaiting recommenced.

A crabber shot his pots in fleets, a dozen or more pots on a rope at intervals, and the position was marked with a buoy. They were weighted with stones, but white ones were never used. Early in April the mackerel boats were brought down the river to be cleaned and painted. In the 1860s there were 14 sean-boats and the same number of volyers, manned by everyone capable of being useful. Towards the end of the month 'huers' watched from high ground for any sign of the shoals; each sean-boat had its own huer who directed it by waving a coat, flag or similar signal. When near the fish, he raised it on his telescope, meaning 'stop'. The procedure was then similar to that described for Polperro seaning. Seaning went on until about the end of June when drift-netting for pilchards began, the boats fishing a little outside the Eddystone, but as the season advanced the shoals came nearer inshore; then seaning was again used in the shallower water. The last haul was in 1866, about 200 hogsheads. Women were paid 2s 6d a hogshead for curing. Drift-caught fish fetched about 1s or 1s 3d a hundred, and families stocked up for the winter.

Haking began in October, catches varying from as low as ten

to as much as thirty dozen, sold for 6d to 8d each. The following month some boats went herring fishing out of Brixham and Torquay, working down to Plymouth and Bigbury Bay.

The big Cornish luggers were fully described in my book *Sailing Drifters*.[1]

The boats attending shipping in the Carrick Roads were the Falmouth Quay punts, so called because they worked from the Custom House Quay where the shipping agents' offices, chandlers and similar premises were situated.

In the days of sail, 'Falmouth or Queenstown for orders' was the usual instruction given to a shipmaster leaving a distant port. During the passage home the cargo might well have been sold and resold several times and the final port of discharge could be given to the captain only when he made one of these harbours for orders. Which one it was largely depended upon the direction of the wind when his ship reached soundings. A sou'wester was fair for Falmouth, but a nor'easter was a dead beat to wind'ard and the Irish port would be chosen.

The Quay punts usually left their moorings in the early hours of the morning, stealing away to the west'ard with no lights showing in order not to give their position away to a rival. As dawn came up a keen lookout was kept for any homeward-bounder; the further the punt was down the Channel the better the chance of speaking first, hence the need for speed. In clear weather the first sight might be the royals or upper sails standing up on the horizon, in thick or misty conditions a ship only a mile or two away. Whilst laying-to, the foresheet was pulled to wind'ard and the punt made little headway, but in a moment it could be off, trying to outdistance other boats. Perhaps the ship would be closing the pilot cutter, then mainyards were backed to allow the pilot to come on board. He might have orders with him if the ship had been reported earlier, in which case the yards would immediately be swung and course set up Channel for London, East Coast or Continental ports, up St

[1] *Sailing Drifters*, The Story of the Herring Luggers of England, Scotland and the Isle of Man, by Edgar J. March, 1952, re-issued, David & Charles, 1969.

George's Channel for western discharge in Liverpool, Glasgow, Belfast. No money here for a quay punt. (Picture, p 137.)

What a beautiful sight it was to see a full-rigged ship or barque at sea, canvas straining in lovely curves, a plume of spray at her bows as she rose and dipped in a swell. No rust on her hull could mar her graceful lines, the creak of blocks and a swishing sound was practically the only noise audible. As she came on, a punt bore down on her quarter and the boatmen hailed to see if the captain wanted a boat. If a favourable reply, the punt came up into the Roads where a ship might lie for some days awaiting orders. Meanwhile the captain would go ashore to transact business, the punt would bring out letters, fresh bread and vegetables—all most welcome to men who had lived on salt pork and beef and ship's biscuits for weeks on end.

In the golden years, a hundred or more sail of ships would be a frequent sight and to find a particular one to deliver an urgent letter or telegram could be quite a problem, especially at night.

For such services a special rig was required and mainmasts were kept as short as possible in order not to foul braces or yards when coming alongside a square-rigger. Gaffs were long and high-peaked, and booms just cleared the mizzen mast stepped against the transom stern. On it a 'leg-of-mutton'— jib-headed—sail was set, sheeting to an outrigger to starboard. In winter the foresail was hanked to a stay set up to the end of a short bumpkin; in summer a jib was set on a reeving bowsprit.

The earliest punts were open boats, clench-built, about 18 ft in length and with the foremast close to the stem. A standing lug was set at the foremast, sheeting well aft; the mizzen mast had a jib-headed sail sheeting to an outrigger. Similar boats were used for work in the Carrick Roads long after improved types were introduced. Until the coming of steam, there was little need to go outside to look for jobs; then many punts were lengthened to give increased speed, and the lug rig was abandoned.

By the 1870s length varied from 20 to 30 ft, but the practice of stepping the mainmast well aft made the boats gripe con-

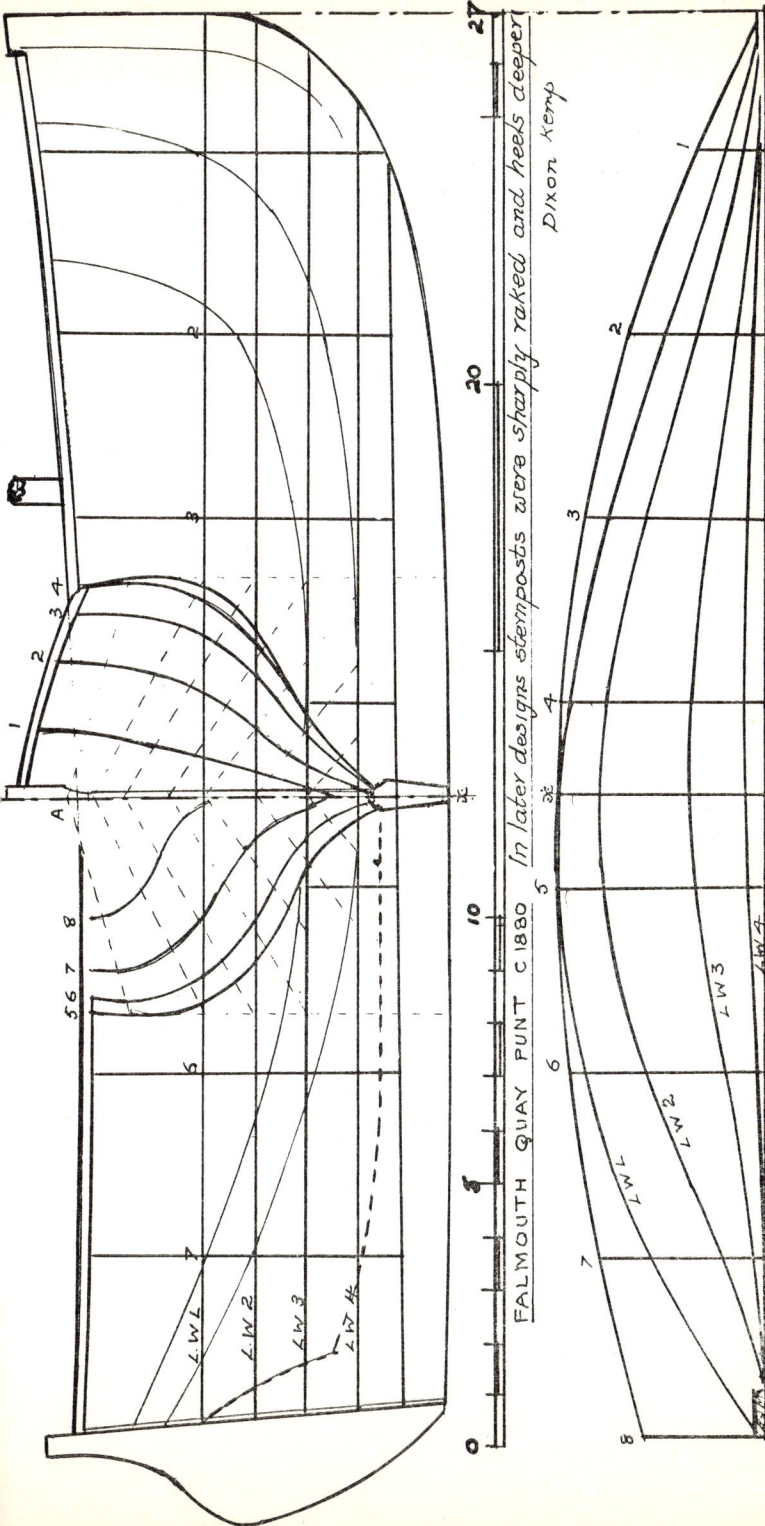

FALMOUTH QUAY PUNT C 1880   In later designs sternposts were sharply raked and heels deeper

Dixon Kemp

Lines of a Falmouth Quay punt, *c* 1880

siderably, and later the mast was moved for'ard to a position about one-third the length abaft the stem. The proportions of masts and spars were largely governed by experience; gaffs were often as long as the boom. This gave a high-peaked main-sail. The hounds on which the shrouds rested were kept as high as possible to give the maximum hoist to the mainsail, making it an awkward job to set up the peak as the blocks on the gaff were higher than those on the short masthead. No topping lifts were fitted. Later practice was to fit a boom to the mizzen and sheet to a short outrigger. The rig was exceedingly handy and a boat could comfortably be sailed single-handed, in heavy weather under staysail and mizzen; the mainsail had up to four lines of reef points and could be reefed up diagonally to give a clear view all round when seeking. Some men preferred to have a big square mizzen in summer in lieu of the leg-of-mutton sail.

Ballast consisted of iron pigs stowed amidships to keep the ends of the punt light, giving easy motion; hulls were invariably carvel-built with straight stems, rounded forefoot, sharp floors and rounded bilges. The hull had a fine run, a deep heel, and a slightly raking transom stern. It was decked to the mast, then came waterways and a short deck aft.

Within the next 30 years modifications based on yachting practice were introduced, the forefoot being well cut away to lessen the time in stays, and more outside ballast provided in the form of heavy iron keels two or more tons in weight, not altogether an advantage. The long, straight keel had made for ease in keeping a course, and the ability to lie comfortably alongside a ship was lost. A heavy sou'wester could send big seas up the Roads and the new boats tended to range wildly, necessitating heavy fenders. Speed, however, had increased, and this was a vital factor as fewer sailing ships now came into Falmouth for orders.

A punt 28 ft 6 in long, 9 ft 4 in beam, had a fo'c'sle extending about 13½ ft, from the stem, waterways 15 in wide and a good locker aft, the cost being around 30s a foot. Ready for sea, a 24-footer cost about £120. Patent blocks and small ropes eased the labour of hoisting sails, as did manilla running gear and wire shrouds. A few boats, built over 30 ft overall, proved too heavy for one man to handle in winter and were the first to be converted into yachts, even though they were the fastest in the fleet.

Masts and spars for a punt 26 ft 4 in overall were: mainmast, deck to hounds 20 ft 6 in, gaff 15 ft, boom 16 ft. Luff of mizzen 13 ft, foot 8 ft.

Sail area for a 28-footer: mainsail 320 sq ft, mizzen 80 sq ft, staysail 80 sq ft, jib, if set, 60 sq ft. Area, winter, 480 sq ft; summer, 540 sq ft.

SCANTLINGS

Keel	English elm, sided 5 in
Stem	English oak, moulded at head 4 in, heel 9 in
Frames	Grown oak, spaced 30 in, sided $2\frac{1}{4}$ in, moulded at head $2\frac{1}{4}$ in, heels $3\frac{1}{2}$ in. Two bent frames of Canadian elm between frames. Some builders all oak frames spaced 1 ft 3 in centre to centre.
Planking	Garboards English elm, remainder pitch pine, 1 in to $1\frac{1}{4}$ in thick.
Beams	Oak, moulded $2\frac{1}{2}$ in at ends, 3 in middle.
Transom	Elm or oak, 2 in thick,
Strings and Shelf	moulded $4\frac{1}{2}$ in, sided 2 in, tapering at ends.

Motors began to be fitted about three years before the 1914–18 war and were soon popular, but not an unmixed blessing. In sail, running expenses were nil and a race to speak a ship cost nothing; now oil etc ate into the meagre takings, perhaps only 7s 6d for a job. After the war conditions had changed; every year saw a drop in the number of deep-sea sailing ships trading, and calls became fewer until, at the end, the arrival of a grain square-rigger from Australia was greeted by the Press and cameramen. By then the day of the Falmouth Quay punt was over.

The oyster dredgers working over the beds in the river Fal

M

are cutters of varying types, few having been built specially;
many were luggers once used for crabbing and general fishing.
It is pleasant to be able to use the present tense as the fleet is
still—1966—under sail, licences being granted only on condition that motors are not used. (Picture, p 137.)

All carry the same rig, mainsail, staysail and jib, pole-masted
with a rather longer masthead than in the Polperro gaffer; in
summer, at regattas, a jackyard topsail and jig reaching foresail are set. As elsewhere, the older dredgermen favour sail as
the dredges can be towed over the quarter instead of astern as
in a power-driven boat. (Picture, p 119.)

The season begins on 1 October and lasts until the end of
March; rules governing the hours of working, size of oysters for
sale, etc, are enforced by a water-bailiff.

In addition to the fleet of some 20 cutters, a large number of
open boats, 14 to 16 ft long, use outboard motors to get to the
grounds—in the old days, lugsails—then oars must be used. In
general, the dredging is similar to that described for the Colne
and Whitstable. At the start of a 'drift' the dredges are thrown
overboard, two if working single-handed, three to four if two
men aboard. Except in light weather, the foresail is dropped
until the limit of the bed is reached, then the cutter sails back
to begin all over again. In the six hours permitted, a fair
average would be eight or nine drifts.

One very old boat, *Zingueneh*, built at Restronguet Creek *c*
1840 and working a century later, was 32 ft 9 in overall. A
draught of a Flushing fishing vessel, 22 ft overall, built in 1905,
shows very sharp floors, rounded bilge, deep keel and heel.
(Picture, p 120.)

Mr Gerald Ruston, a boatbuilder of Restronguet, wrote to
me in 1961 that about 16 cutters were dredging the previous
winter, length 22 ft to 28 ft.

Many of the local families are descended from a legendary
couple called Ferris. It seems that the old girl was as good a man
as her husband. When in the mood, they would go out into a
field with a cartload of timber, several large pasties and a bottle

of rum. Each would build half a boat and when finished, they
would be bolted together down the keel line.

Some of the other famous boat builders were Hitchens, Green,
the Burts and the Jacketts, all of whom built the Quay punts,
fishing boats and the 15–17 ft 'river boats', heavy boats built on
worked frames. These were used for various purposes, oyster
dredging, line fishing and, in the season, ferrying fruit from the
plum gardens up the Truro river to Falmouth market. . . . The
Edith, which was working until a couple of years ago and is still
occasionally seen 'family pottering', must be over 150 years old,
though perhaps not a great deal of the original structure survives.
I myself have a 30-ft pitchpine river launch between 60 and 70
years old, and the hull planking is as hard as flint. The Scilly gigs
are still racing at Newquay and very beautiful things they are . . .
it is good to recall happier times, when men enjoyed and took
pride in their work and thought more of the craft than the pay.

Men were tough in those days, writes the late Wm. Pezzack:

. . . My father never pulled in a race, but on one occasion in
Plymouth, winter fishing, some argument arose about pulling, by
opposing pilots at home. They favoured beer, father belonged to
the Mousehole teetotalers. The beery ones were going to pull
from Mutton Cove, Devonport, to Morwellham, the weir head
of the Tamar, in record time. Father's party let them choose their
six-oared gig at Peter's yard and as soon as they were out of sight
took the next best gig and were off on a stern chase. They let the
first gig land and the crew get at the beer. Then they landed,
stretched their legs after their 29 miles' pull, jumped into the gig
again without bite or sup and started on the return 29 miles. The
others swallowed their beer on being told that the teetotalers had
landed and were off again and started to chase, but never caught
the TT's. I have also known the rival gigs at Mousehole start in the
dark from Mousehole to meet the London steamer, then calling at
Penzance for casked pilchards, and pull around the Lizard in
hopes to intercept her, sometimes to miss her altogether, or if one
got her, the other would pull back, practically never leaving the
oar out of their hand, except that each in turn would have a spell
at steering and baling. Wet, cold, hungry, but took it as part of
the day's work.

Men from many a Cornish cove put out in 20-ft luggers
loaded with crab pots, those from Sennen Cove being parti-
cularly noted. This fishing was often a hazardous calling

among the rocks and fierce tide rips, and hard work for the crew of two, hauling up the pots, taking out the crabs or lobsters, re-baiting and putting the pots over the side again. Generally speaking, the type of boat was similar to those already described. In the early days a sprit mizzen, then a lug and finally the mast was brought more inboard and a bigger sail set; the forelug was now high-peaked, tall and narrow. Despite their small size, many of these open boats went as far as the Scilly Islands in the summer months; being caught out in a gale in the vicinity of such rocky coasts could bring disaster, but the men knew every rock and gully where it was possible to seek shelter and ride it out.

NORTH DEVON COAST

Barnstaple Bay and the ground out to Lundy Island were fished by small cutters from Barnstaple, Bideford and Clovelly. In 1872 Barnstaple had one first-class and 76 second-class boats on the register, Bideford eight and 117. A photograph taken about this time at Clovelly shows seven 'long-boomers' dried out in the tiny harbour, lying at all angles with trawl beams to starboard and nets hanging to dry from topmast heads. Luggers 19 to 24 ft in length, went drift-fishing; fore and mizzen lugs were very square-headed, and top strakes aft had a pronounced tumble-home to meet the heart-shaped transom sterns. Boats were registered at Bideford. (Picture, p 120.)

CHAPTER SIX

PILOT GIGS

THESE beautiful six-oared gigs, used for pilotage, life-saving and salvaging, were owned by small local companies at Falmouth, Newlyn, St Ives, Newquay, Padstow and the Scilly Isles.

Superbly built, many of these gigs still survive, thanks to the Newquay Rowing Club and the enthusiasm of Mr R. H. C. Gillis who, at the age of 14, was rowing bow-oar in the *Dove* and to whom I am deeply indebted for information placed at my disposal.

In these magnificent open boats, able to live in any sea, rival companies raced to secure orders for repair work at their shipyards, boarded pilots, took out cargo samplers; in fact, provided any service required. In the old days the men thought little of crossing to France on a smuggling trip. John Nance, who lived to the ripe age of 84 made 25 trips to Roscoff in an open gig, a round trip of about 250 miles, smuggling brandy, lace and silks. On one occasion he and the crew of six were 30 hours at the oars just keeping the gig head to the seas. No Custom's cutter could catch these swift boats which, if hard pressed, simply pulled to windward; Government regulations forbade the building of eight-oared gigs. In later years they carried potatoes and cut flowers to the mainland from the Scilly Isles, or ferried them from the small islands to catch the steamer. Happy bridal parties were taken to weddings, the doctor was fetched in an emergency, and the dead were brought ashore from a wreck.

At Newquay, rival gigs would row perhaps as far as Lundy, a distance of over 50 miles, in the hope of picking up a vessel bound to their harbour; if lucky, the men provided the large

coir hawsers for mooring and the labour to unload the cargo.
The two shipyards at Padstow always kept a gig swung out on
davits ready to race to a disabled ship and bid for the repairs
required.

In the village of St Mawes, near Falmouth, stands a small
cottage with a 1790 date-stone. When the Peters family were
building this house they received an order for a six-oared pilot
gig to be used as a lifeboat on the North Cornwall coast.
According to Mr Frank Peters, the present owner of the Pol-
varth yard where nearly all the gigs were built, the order was
completed in 1791, and for nearly a century this type of craft
was constructed, first by John Peters, then William and finally
by Nicholas, still on the original moulds but with more beam to
carry potatoes and flowers in the Scillies. His son, Frank, still
builds boats; a wonderful record. He writes:

> The gigs were built of what was called 'narrow leaf' elm from
> trees which the Peters' men selected and felled themselves . . .
> insisted on young trees, seasoned by being chained and buried in
> the creek mud for five years, then sawn into planking in the pits
> by hand-pit saws and stacked for one year. Iron bolts were deli-
> berately used to fasten the deadwoods, because when such long
> and slender boats were being handled on shore, or twisting in a
> seaway, copper fastenings would stretch and not be rigid enough
> in that part of the boat and so cause leakage. A local blacksmith,
> Sam Hooker, is known to have made bolts and other metal
> fittings for the gigs. The copper roves were hand-made, cut from
> a sheet of metal with a pair of snips and a small hole punched to
> take the nails. They were supposed to be square, but often turned
> out diamond-shaped. The ropes used as painters and heaving
> lines on the gigs were also made at St Mawes and descendants of
> these rope-making families, such as the Hitchings family, still live
> in the village. I was given to understand by my father that the
> oldest gig at Newquay was one of three built for shipment to
> Bassein, but owing to shipping difficulties this one was left behind
> and was used in Falmouth harbour. A number of gigs were
> shipped to Bassein for pilotage and use as bumboats. It is de-
> finitely known that some of them were still in use and in good
> condition in 1937. Others were sent to the Isles of Scilly and
> elsewhere for pilotage work. I have recently discovered in the

oldest part of my sheds some of the original moulds from which
the gigs were built, though a trifle worm-eaten now, and also
some parts of moulds from which the boarding punts used by the
Falmouth pilot sailing boats were built. (Picture, p 139.)

The gig left behind in 1812 was taken by Wm Broad & Sons,
Lloyd's agents of Falmouth during their first year after the ap-
pointment was granted on 13 November 1811; later they sold
it to the Newquay company. Her length overall was 29 ft 11 in,
beam 4 ft 9 in, depth 22½ in; name *Newquay*.

All the pilot gigs varied in length, but were usually between
28 and 32 ft. William Peters insisted that no plank should have
more than one scarph, consequently the length of the boat
varied with the length of tree used. All were built to weigh a
little less than 7 cwt so that seven men, the usual crew, could
launch them or carry them ashore without undue effort. Built
two at a time, no two were exactly alike. Each shipwright
carried a bottle of whale oil and every joint had a liberal appli-
cation by means of a feather; all driven copper nails were
notched like a fish hook with a chisel before use. No hog pieces
were fitted and the triangular rabbet into which the garboards
fitted was only $\frac{3}{8}$ in deep, the planks being skew-nailed. This
form of construction gave great flexibility, and despite frequent
launching over rocks or rough shore prevented leaking. Many
fishermen working from small coves demanded similar construction.

Notched timbers only were used; the men knew just where to
cut each before steaming and when placed in position it exactly
fitted every overlap. Planking was $\frac{1}{4}$ in thick, garboards often
$\frac{3}{8}$ in.

About 50 moulds were found in the sheds in 1953; four of a
set of five were an exact match to the lines of the *Newquay*, and
many were fastened by very old-fashioned iron nails made by
the local blacksmith. One mould had a pencil marking 'pilot
gig for Mr Banfield, Scillies', another '*Defiance*, St Ives', a boat
known to have raced in a regatta held at Newquay in 1835.

Thwarts were very thin and supported by a central pillar

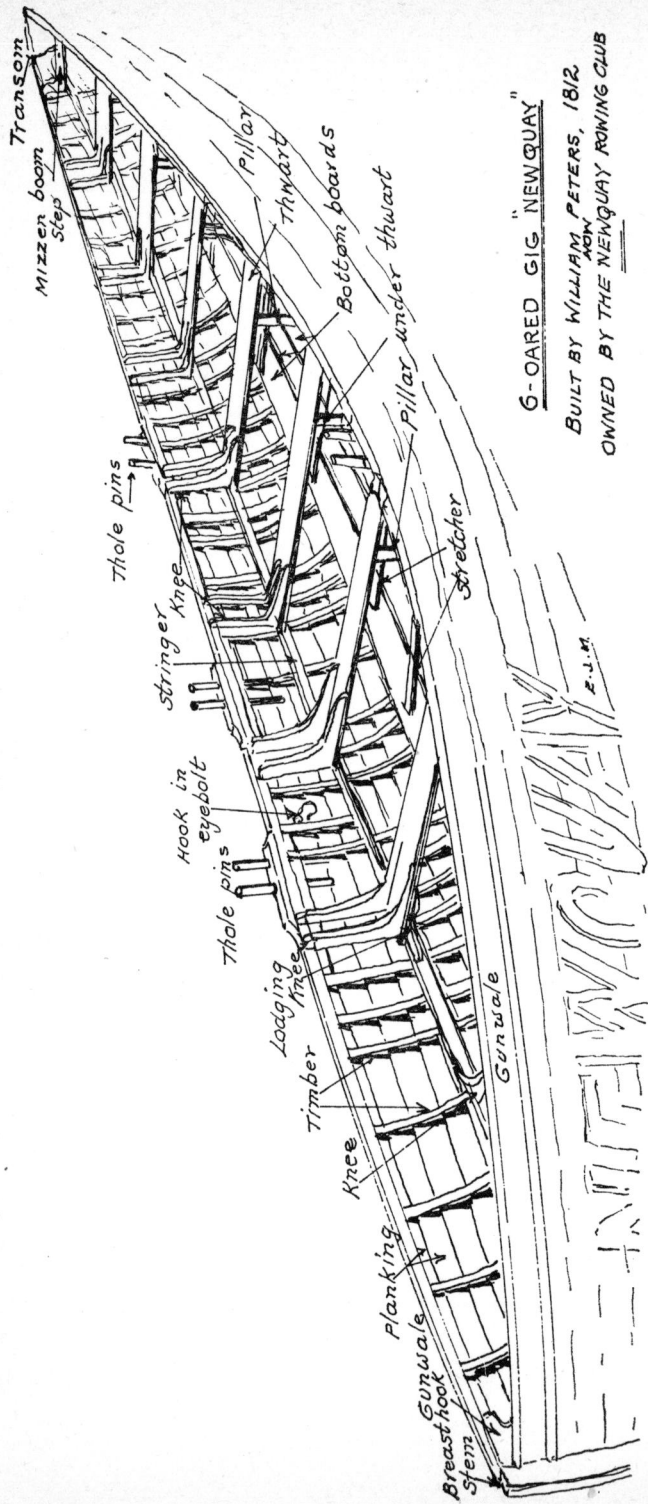

6-OARED GIG "NEWQUAY"

BUILT BY WILLIAM PETERS, 1812

NOW OWNED BY THE NEWQUAY ROWING CLUB

Transom

Mizzen boom
Steps

Pillar

Thwart

Bottom boards

Pillar under thwart

Thole pins

Stringer

Stretcher

Knee

Hook in
eyebolt

Thole pins

Lodging
knee

Timber-
Knee

Gunwale

Planking

Gunwale

Breasthook
Stem

E.J.M.

Sketch of six-oared gig *Newquay*

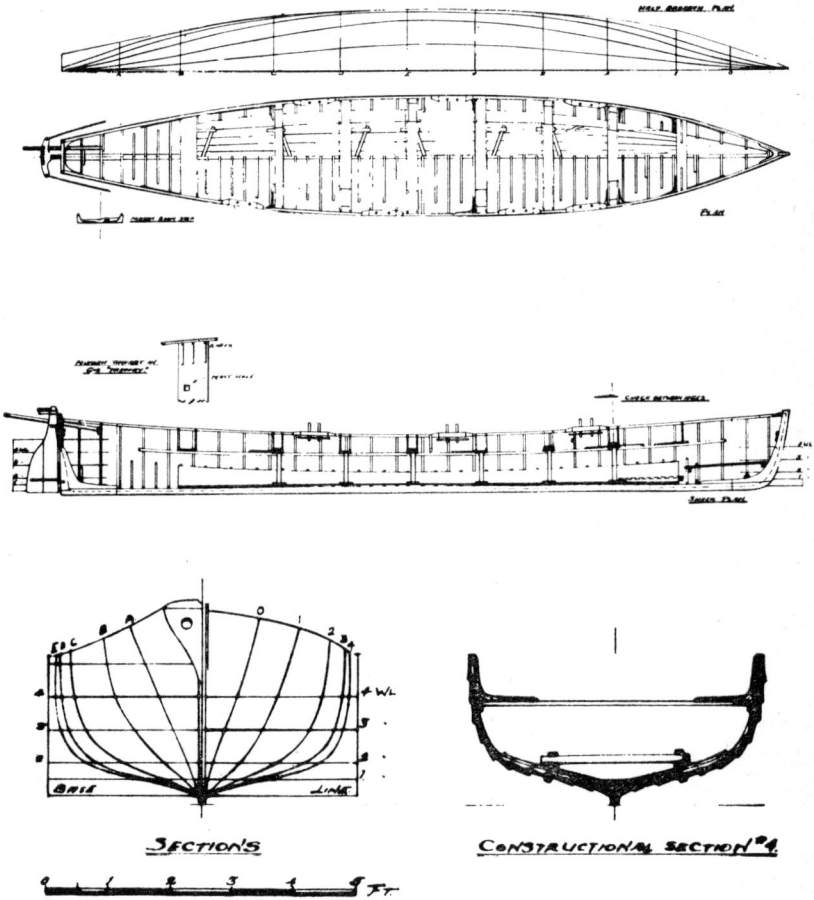

Plans of Newquay gig *Newquay*

which gave them a decided upward curve. In the first gigs
heavy rigid thwarts were fitted and, occasionally, when alongside a ship in blowy weather, a bump would force the end
through the $\frac{1}{4}$-in planking. Thin thwarts of American elm were
introduced with a central pillar and any lateral impact bent the
seat instead of fracturing the planking. It is essential to see that
all pillars are in position before setting out as at times they drop

out through the gig flexing when being carried, the thwart becomes limp and the boat leaks in the bilge planking if the pillar
is not replaced.

Knees fitted were:

		On each side	
		Standing	Lodging
1st thwart		1	1 on aft side
2nd	,,	2	2 fore and aft
3rd	,,	2	
4th	,,	2	1 on aft side
5th	,,	2	
6th	,,	2	
7th	,,	2	1 on aft side
8th	,, (wider)	2	

Distance between thwarts, 28 in; except in *Czar* 1879, $27\frac{1}{4}$ in.

Sail plans differed. In Mount's Bay a sprit mizzen, in St. Ives
a standing lug, and in the Scilly Isles a leg-of-mutton sail. Foremasts were 16 to 20 ft, foreyard 12 to 16 ft, mizzen mast 11 to
13 ft 6 in, yard 9 ft, sprit 10 ft, boom or outrigger 5 ft, spritsail
12 ft.

The late William Pezzack wrote in 1930:

> I have written the grand-daughter of the old smuggler at St
> Martins, Scilly, there are several sisters and smart as men in their
> own boats. They are a good mixture, their father smuggler
> enough for anything and their mother a Pezzack from Mousehole,
> a cousin of mine. The rig of the old pilot gigs was a low lug fore-
> sail and a sprit mizzen. There was a hook in each bow for the
> tack of the foresail which was hooked on the weather bow. The
> sail was too shallow to dip and was lowered and passed in tacking
> . . . the foresheet first unhooked, the halyards lowered, tack un-
> hooked, sail pulled into mast, lee end of yard on the deck, the
> tack would be about 4 ft off the deck, lee end—after end—passed
> around the mast. They sailed in a leading wind but pulled in
> head wind with the mizzen set as a steadier.

Oars were 14 to 16 ft long, stowed blades aft, and rowed in
hand-split oak thole pins. A small thing like a broken thole pin
often caused trouble; it was usual to use an iron pin for'ard, an
oak one aft, never two iron ones because 'catching a crab'

would then mean either a broken oar or a broken gunwale, not just a smashed pin.

Gigs for salvage and rescue work had greater beam and freeboard than those for pilot work. The three Newquay boats, *Newquay*, *Treffry* and *Dove* had an extreme beam of 4 ft 9 in, although *Treffry* had a length of 32 ft, *Dove* 31 ft 1 in, but *Slippen* was 28 ft long, beam 5 ft 4 in. *Campernell* was 30 ft and 6 ft, yet *Queen*, only 3 in longer, had a width of 7 ft. The width of the transom varied from 15 in for *Shah* to $20\frac{3}{4}$ in in *Slippen*, about $\frac{7}{8}$ in thick.

William and Nicholas Peters insisted that all their gigs were painted white, no matter what colour was ordered; the only other finish allowed was varnish. Pilot gigs were generally painted black on service. Gigs built by John early in the nineteenth century were found to be painted in two light colours when the ancient black was burnt off in 1953.

SCANTLINGS

Keel	American elm, sided 2 in, moulded $3\frac{1}{2}$ in.
	3 in × $1\frac{1}{2}$ in tapering to $\frac{1}{2}$ in.
	Height about 3 ft, some gigs 2 in less, others $\frac{3}{4}$ in more.
Stern Post	1 in thick, 20 in high, $3\frac{1}{2}$ in wide at heel, tapering to nothing at head.
Inner Post	$1\frac{3}{8}$ in × $1\frac{1}{4}$ in.
Deadwood	$1\frac{1}{4}$ in thick.
Planking	$\frac{1}{4}$ in thick.
Timbers	$\frac{1}{2}$ in wide, $\frac{1}{2}$ in at thickest, $\frac{1}{4}$ in at thinnest section. *Golden Eagle* $\frac{5}{8}$ in.
	In pilot gigs 1 long, 1 short alternately, spaced 6 in, salvage boats all long.
Thwarts	$5\frac{1}{2}$ in wide, $\frac{3}{4}$ in thick, some chamfered at edges.
Cost	*Czar, c* 1872, *Golden Eagle, c* 1870 and *Sussex, c* 1886, were all built for £1 a foot overall length; oars, masts and sails being extra.

When rowing, bow and numbers 3 and 5 had their oars to port, numbers 2, 4 and stroke to starboard, but bow had rowlocks on both sides and, when rounding a mark, always, or nearly always, tossed his oar to starboard for a quick turn. Oars were known locally as 'paddles'. In 1953 they cost £3 10s each, and were made of silver spruce.

The superlative quality of the planking can be judged from the fact that when *Slippen*, built *c* 1830, was in for repairs in 1953 nearly all the planks were found to be in good condition. One 4-ft length of the bilge planking was removed and it could be bent to a complete circle and returned to normal without damage.

When going fast and being forced over a big sea, about one-third of the length of a gig was out of the water, but hulls were tight as a bottle; any water to be baled out came in over the gunwale. A very ordinary crew would drive a gig at about 8 mph, the fastest time for a gig race in the Scillies was 11 minutes on a straight course from Carn Near to St Mary's Pier, won by *Czar* over about $1\frac{1}{2}$ miles, or 1 mile in 7 min 20 sec. James Nance, born in 1831, was a man of huge stature and it was reckoned he could pull against three others; he worked the gig *Bonnet* in conjunction with the cutter *Queen*. His father, John, of smuggling fame, lived two years longer than his son, who died at the age of 82.

At various times some 30 six-oared gigs were attached to the pilot cutters which cruised around the area of the Bishop Rock lighthouse, putting pilots aboard incoming ships for the road-stead at Scilly to await orders as to where their cargo was to be discharged. If a ship did not come into the Roads, the boarding clerk from one of the shipping agents—Banfield for Lloyd's, Buxton for the Liverpool and Glasgow underwriters—ascertained the nature of the cargo and the names and addresses of the holders of the bills of lading. To transmit this information rapidly to the mainland, carrier pigeons were taken out in the gigs, released with a message, and within a few hours the vessel would receive her orders.

Gigs would go well outside the islands to take off a pilot from a ship outward bound. Gigs from two or three islands would race for a job, and if a boat was frequently beaten the company would order one to be built faster than the crack gig. At Bryher was the gig *Albion*; *March* was built to beat her and in turn *Golden Eagle* was ordered to beat *March*, which she did. *Albion* and *March* were no longer used and old Nicky Peters was asked to build another to beat *Golden Eagle* and he produced *Czar* which was towed across by the yacht *Sea Snake, c* 1874.

Among the many services performed by the Scilly gigs were taking wedding parties to Tresco, fetching the doctor, or at times taking a seriously injured person to hospital. *Sussex*, built in 1886 and stationed on the east side of Bryher, was last used to take a bride on 6 August 1929. Frequently a call for a doctor came on a wild night, with a sou'-west wind and deluging with rain. The crew would be called out, wooden ways laid down and the men would range themselves on either side and drag the gig down until the stern touched the sea. Others fetched the mizzen, kept bent on its spars, put it aboard in the centre of the boat, then ran her afloat, shipped the rudder, and away she went under oars with mizzen set.

A landing was made on Stony Island to pick up about 5 cwt of stone ballast before using the fore lug, usually double-reefed; then the crew crouched down on the bottom boards to trim the gig, which tore along with water slopping aboard, to be immediately baled out. The question was 'where would she fetch'; the nearer St Mary's harbour, the less pulling. Sails and mast were taken in and under oars the gig was run in on Town Beach. One man ran off to knock up Dr Addison, and the moment he was aboard a reef was shaken out for the run to Bryher. Once, when the 3-mile run was made in 15 minutes, *Sussex* was picked up on a sea, which lifted her rudder out of the water and spun her round with her lee gunwale under, all hands baling furiously. Under oars in calm weather, the passage took about 25 minutes.

A wheat sampler, Herbert Prior, who died in 1955 at well over 91, recalled having been taken out to grain ships in a pilot gig. When the Bishop Rock lighthouse was built, the keepers were at first relieved by a gig. A well-known one was *O & M*, named after the Christian names of her owners, Obediah and Mary, and built in the Scillies. In Queen Victoria's Jubilee year the cattle ship *Castleford* was wrecked and the *O & M* was un-lucky enough to have her bow stove in when salvaging a bul-lock. Many cattle were saved from similar wrecks by swimming them ashore with their heads kept above water by rope halters secured inboard. The gig rescued five people from the ss *Schiller* ashore in fog on 7 May 1875, when 331 persons were drowned, also the captain of the Italian barque *Barnato*, sole survivor when it was wrecked near Annet.

Such work in heavy seas meant much wear and tear on the gigs. On one occasion a bale of cotton was being rolled into a boat at Samson when it slipped and went right through the bilges.

From Falmouth, the gigs often went seeking well down Channel and if unlucky the crew would run their boat ashore and sleep by her, in bad weather turning her upside down.

Many of the Scilly gigs were built locally by Samuel Tiddy who served his time in the Peters' yard at St Mawes; among them were *Hope*, *Sultan*, *Leo* and *Gipsy*. When the latter was bought by the Padstow Rowing Club in 1955, one of the planks halfway along the port side still had a patch over a hole made by the horns of a bullock swum ashore from the ss *Castleford* some 70 years earlier. Her condition was so good that she only required to be repainted. *Zelda*, purchased by the same club, was built by Nicholas Peters and named after the ship which was wrecked on the rock, Maiden Bower, in 1873. This gig was last used in the 1920s when taken to the wreck of the *Isabo* on Scilly Rock, arriving just as the last survivor had been taken off by a rival gig, *Czar* from Bryher. A new keel was fitted in 1955. The last six-oared gig built by Peters was *Wingfield*, and the final three four-oared gigs were *Mabel*, *Sally* and *Como*.

At Padstow, *Warspite* was built by local men employed in Devonport Dockyard, *Vixen* in Rawles' yard, *Peace* in Lowere yard, and *Constance* by Dennis. *Rival* was painted green, *Rescue*

blue, *Constance* black, and *Gazelle* white. *Victor* was varnished, as
was *Peace*, and *Warspite*, *Hero* and *Teaser* were black.

Regattas have been held for very many years, and a trophy
still in the Scillies is a silver bowl with George III florins as
embellishments. For races under oars a triangular course,
rowed anti-clockwise, was traditional. Frequently ten or more
gigs would engage in friendly rivalry, and similar events took
place around the Cornish coast.

At Newquay, the races gave £1 a man prize money. In 1857
there were six competitors, *Treffrey* covering the 7-mile course
in 46 minutes, beating *Circe* of Truro by 1¼ minutes; *Dove* came
in ¾ minute later, followed by *Girl I Love*, *Newquay* and *Arrow* of
Padstow. A challenge race between *Newquay* and *Zoe Treffrey*
was won by the latter, and on her bow next morning was
roughly painted *Teazer* and so she was called until sold in 1915
to be used, keel-up, as the roof of a fowl run. This evidence suggests that six gigs were then stationed at Newquay.

During the search of the boatshed at St Mawes, one set of
moulds had pencil writing 'Pilot grig—*Arrow* and *Sursey*'—the
man knew what the name *Circe* sounded like, but couldn't spell
it.

In 1888 Charlestown men in *Treffry* beat Fowey men in *Dove*
by one yard only; the following year Padstow were the victors in
Constance. In 1891 the Fowey crew brought their own gig but unfortunately it was too rough to race and the regatta had to be
abandoned. *Constance* won again in 1892 and 1895, with *Rose* of
Hayle second. Next year *Dove*, with a Fowey crew, was the
winner, 2nd *Treffry* with Charlestown men, 3rd *Rose* from
Hayle, 4th *Newquay* with a Par crew.

Treffry would race in any heavy sea and come back with
scarcely a drop of water aboard. In 1893 she was rowed some 22
miles to Hayle where she took first prize. On another occasion,
when taken overland to Penzance, the trophy was awarded
without her going into the water; all the other crews refused to
race against her!

Treffry, built by Peters in 1843 to the order of a Newquay company, was always considered to be the finest pilot gig they ever built. She had been specially ordered to be 'the fastest one ever' and for that reason was given extra length, 32 ft, with a beam of 4 ft 9 in, against the 30 ft of *Newquay* and the 31 ft of *Dove*. When finished, she was such a beautiful job that Peters refused to paint her; instead she was polished with linseed oil. This was verified in 1952 when members of the Newquay Rowing Club burned off the many coats of black paint. After a ceremonious launch the crew, wearing top hats, rowed round Falmouth harbour, passing a warship whose captain ordered the ensign to be dipped in salute. Later, she was rowed up to Truro and carried by waggon to Newquay where her design was proved to be well nigh perfect; the harder she was driven the more she would lift.

Two men still living at Newquay in 1956 had taken part in the 1893 Regatta at Hayle—James Gill, 85, and Will James, 83. After they left work on the Friday afternoon they, with others, rowed up in fine weather, the pull from the bar to Hayle being the hardest part because the gates of the pool had been opened to clear as much mud out as possible for the regatta next day. The men got ashore about 11 pm and search was made for lodgings, but nobody was around at that time of night. Eventually a policeman directed them to the house of an old lady 'who puts up you sort of sailor chaps', but she needed some persuasion before taking in the crew and giving them tea or cocoa. When she heard the men were a gig crew from Newquay, she remarked, 'I hope you win, but I don't think you will because Falmouth always win the gig race here.'

Next morning, on seeing the Falmouth gig *Dido*, the Newquay crew were of much the same opinion because she was a much lighter craft, almost a skiff. The draw for berths gave *Treffry* the centre one, a great disadvantage in the confined space of Hayle Pool, and she was second around the first mark; the St Ives boat, *Richard*, with a Hayle crew, lay third. Gradually *Dido* was overhauled and the race, four times round the Pool, w as won.

The finest rescue work in the annuals of the Scilly Isles gigs was undoubtedly at the wreck of the iron-screw steamship *Delaware* in December 1871. On the 18th she left Liverpool for Calcutta laden with a valuable cargo of cottons, silks, sheet lead and tin. Early on the morning of the 20th the ship was seen from Bryher, obviously in distress, and her position worsened as the nor'west gale increased in violence. She was making no headway against the huge Atlantic rollers, and drifting in closer and closer to the outer rocks. By noon it was clear she would be driven ashore between Mincario and Seal Rock towards Fearing Ledge. The ship was now unmanageable owing to the engines overheating and having to be stopped. The captain ordered a jib to be hoisted to bring her through the channel between the rocks, but it carried away; attempts were made to hoist a staysail but it blew clean away as soon as hoisted. If only the sails had held, the ship could have been got before the wind and brought into more sheltered waters. As it was, she turned broadside on a mountainous sea and the bridge vanished; another broke right over her and the steamer disappeared.

The watchers ashore reckoned that any survivors would be carried towards White Island, uninhabited, with a fairly flat but very rocky shore, and lying some quarter of a mile to the westward of the largest uninhabited island of the Scillies, Samson. A keen watch was kept from South Hill and two men were seen on half a boat, two on a spar and one on a piece of wreckage.

The gig *Albion*, held to be the best boat, 30 ft long and of 5 ft 6 in beam, was carried ½ mile overland to Rushy Bay where she could be launched from the boathouse at the Great Par with a following wind and sea. Six oars were placed across the gig and lashed to the thwarts to enable 12 men to carry her by taking an oar in the crook of their elbows and using one hand on the gunwale to hold the boat steady. The arrangements were that 10 men went on the rescue, aged from 21 to 50, including the two acknowledged leaders, Patrick Trevellick at the yoke lines, and Richard Ellis. Ellis was to be left on the North Hill

N

of Samson to give signals back to Bryher by 'swaysing' his jacket if help were needed; in which case the six-oared gig *March* was to be taken to Rushy Bay. Gigs are constructed for running before huge seas, and between each sea *Albion* was gradually edged towards Samson and made the lee of North Hill. Some of the crew scrambled ashore and went to the top of the hill where, with telescopes, they could see the two men on the half-boat nearing White Island. As it struck, one jumped into the sea and, grasping a rock, was left high and dry by the backward surge. The other was washed up soon afterwards and also reached safety.

The two men on the spar were cast ashore 100 yd farther out on a point covered at high water; they managed to get on to the rocks but were washed off and drowned. The man on the wreckage came in at the same spot as the first two, but made no attempt to get up and was lost. No more survivors being seen, the crew decided to take the gig farther down to the East Par of Samson, carry her across the 200-yd isthmus, and launch from West Par. If they reached White Island, four men were to jump ashore, leaving five in the gig to keep her in the shelter of the island. It was an appalling task to carry the heavy boat over the seaweed-covered rocks, grass and scrub against the full force of the gale whipping sand and spray into their faces, then to surmount the most formidable obstacle, a bank. And if control was lost as the men lifted *Albion*, to drop her on one stone would fracture the planking. The gig was taken out of the slings, held by the thwarts, and lifted over the bank and boulders to rest on the beach. She was then launched into the full force of wind and sea. Standing almost on end, very slow progress was made until about halfway; finally a landing had to be made on a stony brow. The men waited for a smooth, then ran the gig in quickly on the back of a sea; as it receded she was left almost high and dry. Four men jumped out, and on the next wave *Albion* floated off. The youngest, John Jacob Jenkins, was first to reach the survivors. He used to relate that the men had collected stones on the approach of the rescuers and were ready to throw them to defend themselves as they had heard that the islanders were little better than savages. One man had no jacket and was bare-footed, the other had no trousers, but the crew gave the first socks and a jacket, the second a jacket to wrap round in place of trousers. Search revealed no more survivors, so all made for the gig which was run in on a wave; the men jumped out and pulled her ashore.

While Richard Ellis was signalling for help to come in the gig *March*, the *Albion* crew struggled across the isthmus and placed the survivors in the shelter of a rock on East Par, where all huddled together for warmth and rest. A crew from Bryher carried *March* ½ mile overland to Rushy Bay and came into East Par; here the two survivors were placed on board. The *Albion* crew then took over and fought their way back to Bryher where the rescued mate and the third mate of the ill-fated *Delaware* were given hot drinks and put to bed. The crew left on Samson remained there all night and then had the job of getting the *Albion* back across the isthmus to the shelter of the East Par.

After this service *Albion* and *March* were no longer used for pilotage as the newly-arrived *Golden Eagle* had proved to be the fastest gig. *Albion*'s owners then had *Czar* (picture, p 139), built to take her place and to beat their rival, which she could always do under oars; but *Golden Eagle* was exceptionally good under sail. *Albion* was sold to A. Watts, boatbuilder at St Mary's, who later used her planking to build a dinghy.

Incredible as it may seem the men taking part in this gallant and hazardous rescue were never acknowledged or rewarded in any way, save for the recorded fact that their efforts had saved two lives.

In January 1882 the German barque *Excelsior*, anchored in St Mary's Roads in a strong NW gale, began dragging her anchors. The Bryher men launched away from the east side of the island to save lives if necessary, and earn salvage money if possible. In heavy squalls, the oars kept blowing out of the thole pins, but with the weather oars double-banked and mizzen set they managed to reach the upper side of the Roads. Here a terrific squall made them consider heaving-to, but a shout, 'A St Mary's gig has nearly reached her,' made them push on. This gig had got out of St Mary's Pool and across the Roads, every oar double-banked. Both gigs ran against opposite sides of the barque at the same time and their cox'ns leapt aboard, only to find the captain very drunk. The crews agreed to work together, the gigs were cast off with only three men in each and ran to leeward into comparative shelter until they could beach and drag their boats above high-water mark. The men left aboard slipped the cables, hoisted a jib and wore off, but running out of Crow Sound there was insufficient water on the bar; the vessel struck and started to leak so they ran into Higher Town Bay of St Martins and beached. The local men then launched their gig and as the barque was deep loaded with rice, she was lightened until she refloated, while being towed to St Mary's, however, the ship capsized, filled through the hatches and sank, the wreck being marked by a buoy for many years.

During the summer of 1911 the steam trawler *Roche Castle* struck rocks in dense fog at the back of St Mary's and began blowing for assistance. *Czar*, *Golden Eagle* and *Sussex* set off from Bryher to St Mary's Sound and spoke the local gig *Dolly Varden* (picture, p 139), which was returning from a search at the back of St Agnes. *Czar* went along the back of St Mary's, found nothing, returned to the Roads and saw a light, and there was the trawler anchored, having been brought in by *Shah*, pilot Dick Legg. As no salvage was likely, the Bryher men decided to go home. *Golden Eagle* pushed off first, followed by *Czar*, and for sport the bow oarsmen of *Sussex* caught hold of *Czar*'s stern and jokingly asked for a tow home. The reply was that only by towing would *Sussex* be likely to come in with the others. This rankled her crew, who threw off their jackets and jerseys and whaled into a race. The night was a flat calm, with a full moon shining, the sweat ran freely, so much so that soon the thwarts were marked with dye from the men's clothes, but they got

Sussex ahead and kept her there, beaching 100 yd in front, and jeered when *Czar*'s crew came ashore.

On 17 December 1885, the ss *Sussex* was wrecked. Some of the crew were rescued by *Golden Eagle* and the gig was used in the salvage of 200 bullocks, flour, lard, tinned beef, frozen geese and turkeys. In 1898 she saved the crew of the ss *Brinkburn*, laden with cotton for Harve, and the following year she was at the wreck of the ship *Eric Rickmers*, bound from Bangkok to Antwerp, with rice. On the same night she also rendered assistance to the French barque *Paranee*, ashore with coconuts from the West Indies. On 15 April 1910 she rescued lives from the big Atlantic transport liner *Minnehaha* ashore on a sunken ledge in dense fog after having been in thick weather for three days. On board were 66 passengers, 177 crew and 234 head of cattle, in addition to over 8,000 tons of general cargo, including silk stockings and typewriters. Five soundings, taken between 10 pm and 12.15 am, when the ship struck the Crim Rocks, gave depths of 60, 65, 52, 55 and 47 fathoms; boats had been swung out when weather had become foggy. Captain Leyland had had to rely on dead reckoning for three days and at noon on the 17th had altered course to pass clear of the Bishop Rock by 7 miles; unfortunately he was north of his estimated position, and the fog signal from the lighthouse was not heard until three hours after stranding. Standing orders of the company were to keep 10 miles from the Bishop Rock in foggy weather; the master was held to blame and his speed of 6 to 7 knots was considered excessive.

Golden Eagle was bought by the Newquay Rowing Club in 1953, but was damaged by a very high tide in the autumn, keel, deadwood and garboards being broken near the stern. Every rivet had to be replaced as it was found that the middle portion of each was eaten away to the thickness of a pin, the reason for her leaking. When gigs were painted black it was customary to blacklead below the waterline; this was supposed to shine better if mixed with vinegar and it was assumed that this acid ate the bolts away. Built by Peters *c* 1870, *Golden Eagle* was paid for with part of the £100 salvage earned for services to the ship *Award*, wrecked on her maiden voyage on Gweal Island.

Dolly Varden was built at St Mawes in 1873 and when the crew of the pilot cutter *Presto* went to collect her they reported seeing a very fine-lined gig, 'too fine for Scilly waters'. This boat had been built to the order of a St Ives company, practically identical to *Newquay*, but they refused to take delivery, alleging she was too fine and quite unsuitable for work on the North Cornwall coast. Nicholas Peters then contacted the Hicks family, all noted pilots, and three came over in their cutter to inspect her. A long argument ensued, Abraham did not approve, and Jacob said that if they bought her she would be their coffin; finally Abraham James Hicks bought her and the gig was taken to the Scillies on the deck of the cutter and named *Shah* (picture, p 140.) Despite her lines the gig was only once in serious danger and then not through rough weather. The St Agnes pilots saw a naval vessel towing a disabled sailing ship, and *Shah* and *Gipsy* both launched and raced to put a pilot aboard. *Shah* first went to the warship to board a pilot, intending to go next to the towed vessel, thus getting two jobs. By an unlucky chance just as she went alongside the ash chute opened and cinders filled the bow to overflowing. The crew leapt aft to save *Shah* from sinking, while their rival, *Gipsy*, got both jobs.

For her first two races for pilotage *Shah* failed to be first and considerable misgiving arose as to the wisdom of purchasing her; no doubt 'I told you so' was frequently said. However, she soon proved her worth. Once the cutter *Agnes* left St Mary's in a SE gale with a reefed trysail and foresail to go to a brig flying the pilot jack. *Shah* was launched in heavy seas and won the race; after putting a pilot on board the seas were so big that the crew did not dare turn the gig, so they returned safely by backing all the way. She was easily the fastest gig ever seen in the Scillies; with four oars she would beat her rival *Bonnet* pulling six, often having this smaller crew because a normal share for a row of several miles was only 4d with seven men. A match arranged with *Czar* over a triangular course of more than the usual length saw the two gigs pulling side by side but, turning the last mark, *Shah* gained a length and held it to the finish.

Czar, fitted to pull seven oars, was kept in first-class condition and in 1954 was still well painted and housed at Bryher. She was kept ready for immediate use, with a very sharp axe lashed to a thwart, and Mr Henry Stideford was then her guardian. She was employed for three weeks in 1910 on salvage work from the ss *Minnehaha*.

Dove, built *c* 1830 for the Newquay Company, had finer lines than their *Newquay*, to give increased speed. This she certainly has in smooth water but in rough she pushes her bows into heavy seas and ships a great deal of water. After the first war she, with *Newquay* and *Treffry*, was taken over by the Newquay Rowing Club and all have been raced ever since. In 1953 when *Dove* was refitted, Frank Peters was astonished to find that broad leaf elm had been used instead of the usual narrow leaf for planking which is more flexible and lighter. This may well account for her being a 'dirty' boat, and it is interesting to speculate if her name derives from 'the diver bird, so called from its habit of ducking its head', vide Brewers Dictionary, rather than the 'emblem of peace' belonging to the pigeon family.

In 1928 *Dove* was rowed by a Newquay crew over a course from Harbour Gap towards Blowing Hole at Porth until the cox'n had sight of Porth post office. The record of 6 min 30 secs set up in 1908, was beaten by 15 seconds, the time being taken by the cox'n and checked by a watcher on shore as the bow oar was tossed immediately the mark was sighted.

When *Newquay* was examined by Mr Brabyn, of Padstow, in 1955, he found that the forward 20 ft of oak keel had been cut down level with the planking and the keel built up partly with elm and part ordinary deal. At the stern 6 ft had been renewed with badly fitting oak bedded on the deadwood with a mixture of white lead and putty; the bow deadwood on pitch and the iron bolts had rusted to the size of matchsticks. A piece of plank had also been renewed with deal instead of elm.

Treffry and the recently purchased *Shah* were also due for major repairs and a search was made for a suitable baulk of timber for new keels. The length of 32 ft made timber merchants raise their eyebrows; moreover, oak, narrow-leaf elm or American elm without blemish was required. Finally Mr Henry Moreland, of the Gloucester timber and match firm, a great supporter of the club, took up the quest and eventually located a suitable baulk at the Castletown sawmills of Messrs Venables in Stafford, who offered to cut from an oak in their possession. Mr Moreland wisely advised taking sufficient to do all the remaining keels whilst such a large oak was available. The tree came from the Clanna Estate in Gloucestershire and the baulk, weighing about 9 cwt, was sent to Mr S. B. Brabyn.

Mr Moreland had seen only one gig race but was so profoundly impressed by the keenness and stamina of the crews that he wrote to Mr R. H. C. Gillis:

> I shall be glad if you will accept the baulk and the delivery charge as some little token of esteem and respect for men who in these changing days find interest, sport and pleasure in the pilot gigs and the welfare of the Newquay Rowing Club and, if I may say so, out of very great regard for your good self and your unremitting support in aid of the club.

Shah was bought from eleven shareholders whose consent had to be obtained before agreeing to part with her for £36. Five old men took her from her house on a November night, rowed to the bar connecting St Agnes and Gugh, and moored her for transport the next morning. At 9 am she was towed to St Mary's, and although it was her first trip for four years she leaked less than two bucketfuls on the run of 3 miles. Unfortunately, she was badly damaged on passage in RMS *Scillonian*, the pillars got released, knees broken and garboards damaged. Transport to Padstow and back to Newquay, plus the sea trip, came to as much as the cost of the gig. Nearly a wheelbarrow-full of paint was burnt off, and 54 new timbers, eight new thwarts with knees and a new keel were put in without removing the garboards. Moulds were taken every 2 ft along the length, known as 'he' and 'she' moulds to shipwrights, one for the hog and one for the keel. *Shah*'s keel is slightly curved and a hog of American elm had to be put in in three pieces and scarphed together, one piece being slid in from the bow, another from the stern; the third was easily fitted. A stone had gone through a garboard plank about 40 years earlier, making a long fracture which had been patched by doubling. This section, about 12 ft long, was removed to fit the third piece of the hog and was the only piece of planking that needed renewing; in fact, very little was replaced in any of the gigs. The keel was fitted in one piece, and both garboards doubled with pine to make certain *Shah* would not leak. The hog is nailed to the keel and riveted to each garboard and each garboard is skew-nailed to the keel. A hog is new to gigs; none was ever fitted originally.

I have before me as I write a piece of the garboard, $\frac{1}{4}$ in thick, Cornish narrow-leaf elm, as tough as the day it was fitted in 1873. What stories it could tell, of wild nights at sea, joyous trips with brides, boarding pilots in sunshine and storm, tense struggles at regattas!

Finally *Shah* was painted royal blue, with white below water and a white strake and name in gold leaf given by Frank Peters; in all, £120 was spent on repairs and renovations and £39 on oars. (Picture, p 140.)

Having fitted this new keel Mr Brabyn was ready to tackle *Newquay*, a much older gig, cutting away the old keel 6 in at a time. This had just been done when he was taken ill and his 22-years-old assistant, Donald McBirnie, recently home from fighting in Korea, did the job, instructed by Mr Brabyn from his bed. *Newquay* has not leaked since; before this nothing could prevent her taking in water. The hog was fitted in two pieces; in each case the keel was slightly chamfered where it met the edges of the garboards to form a caulking seam.

Bonnet, bought from Tresco in 1953, required 32 new timbers, each taken up to the gunwale. A good, strong boat, her iron keel band was replaced with a hardwood false keel, as was done to all the gigs when refitted. When built, beam was 5 ft $0\frac{1}{2}$ in, but subquently she was retimbered and 'hove-home' to try and make her faster, her beam being now 4 ft 9¾ in, but the timbers were spaced too far apart and the hull, being limp, was subject to leaking. After repairs, *Bonnet* was painted bright green, but was very uncomfortable to row in as the gunwales and thwarts had not been lowered when the beam had been reduced at Tresco, and pulling her in had given too sharp a turn in the bilges.

In 1956 *Bonnet* was sent to Brabyn to take off a strake, put in new risings and lower the thwarts; at the same time a new keel was fitted, cut from the baulk presented by Mr Moreland.

Slippen, built *c* 1830, was owned by pilots at St Martins until 1869 and named *Bernice*. The gig was then moved to St Agnes to be nearer the shipping lanes, and so started a long line of famous Channel pilots, Hicks and Legg, who would take a ship as far as Antwerp. About this time her stem was broken and a repair made, which was still there in 1955 when it was streamlined by Brabyn.

On 14 December 1907, three survivors were rescued from the wreck of the seven-masted American schooner *Thomas W. Lawson*. The gig was launched in huge seas, each oar double-banked, 12 men instead of six—'at times she came backwards almost turning end over end'. Later she went out to collect the dead bodies from Annet and brought them to St Agnes for burial, the crew then including six members of the Hicks family, one Legg and a Trenary. (Picture, p 138.)

Twenty-six lives were saved in a NE gale from a French ship in 1925, the crew receiving decorations from the French government. On 10 November 1931, *Slippen* was washed out of her house at Periglis and carried as far as the road. The Newquay Rowing Club bought her in 1953. Her planking, in good condition, was fastened with copper nails over small squares of the same metal, but many of the timbers were broken, 23 long and 16 short ones being replaced and a new breasthook fitted, as well as other repairs. Painted bright yellow with a narrow blue band round the gunwale and blue below the waterline, her refit cost about £60.

On trial, all three gigs did not leak even the smallest amount and in April 1954 it was the first time since 1857 that six gigs had taken part in a race off the North Cornwall coast and *three of the same gigs were competing*. On Sunday, 11 April, the New-quay Rowing Club's fleet of six rowed the 16 miles from Pad-stow to Newquay after their first major refit in 100 years, the first, *Slippen*, arriving in 2 hr 40 min. Now they give pleasure to rowers and spectators, at regattas racing over a course of about 6 miles. The principal trophy is a solid silver scale model of a pilot gig, presented by the late T. A. Reed in 1922. Average winning time is just over 40 minutes.

Zelda and *Gipsy* were acquired from Tresco and St Agnes by the Padstow Regatta Committee. *Gipsy*, built by Tiddy in the Scillies, has less sheer than the Peters'-built gigs. Her last trip for pilotage was on 22 December 1938, when she went to the vessel *Foremost* and put aboard the Trinity pilot Jack Hicks, one of the 11 shareholders who subsequently sold her to Padstow.

On the night of Friday, 21 January 1955, the 7,176-ton Panamanian steamer *Mando* went ashore in dense fog on rocks between the Menavaur and Golden Ball rocks off the north end of Tresco. The Round Island lighthouse keepers saw the flares and called out the St Mary's lifeboat; the 90 inhabitants of Bryher were alerted by the siren, and the men, playing billiards in the recreation room, at once ran down to the beach and launched the gig *Sussex*, built in 1886. In spite of her age she was considered the best boat to take because of her shallow draught and absence of any propeller to foul when taken in among the rocks. She had not been used for twenty years since a wedding party was taken to Tresco, but Vernon Hicks, one of the crew of eight, said the gig was as tight as a drum and did not make as much as a cupful of water. Other men went with lanterns to guide the lifeboat, the visibility being about two yards.

Most of the gigs died through neglect when sail passed, the few remaining being scarcely ever used, except on Regatta Day, when they were both rowed and sailed. *Guinivere* was lost off the

Bishop Rock lighthouse, pulled to pieces through being towed too fast after putting a pilot aboard a ship. Her crew were saved. *Gleaner* was broken up in 1954, but her planking was good enough to be used in the building of a small boat, the wood being in perfect condition after nearly a century's use. *Queen* and *Empress* lay at St Martins, the latter with a motor, as had *Emperor* at St Mary's.

In Mount's Bay, Lord St Levan has the six-oared St Aubyn state barge, 27 ft 2 in long, 7 ft 4 in beam, and another gig is also in his boat shed. Frank Peters said that one was not their build, but the other was. Matthews stated that one was built on the Mount 'a beauty with a cod's head and a conger's tail'; Peters replied 'they say the same of their beautifully tucked gigs with a narrow transom, but say 'mackerel' not 'conger'. He reckoned the barge was nearly 200 years old, planked with Cornish elm, notched timbers, square roves.

The late P. J. Oke measured up the gig *Mabel* at St Michael's Mount in August 1937; length 24 ft, beam 5 ft 5 in, depth inside 1 ft 11¼ in, built by J. Burt *c* 1867. The hull had twisted longitudinally and the stemhead was approximately 3 in out of centre. The gig was painted white with a red strake below the rubber, inside was white from gunwale to thwarts, red below. The mizzen was a spritsail, sheeting to a 6-ft outrigger.

At St Ives, he took off the lines of a gig 26 ft 6½ in long, beam 6 ft 4 in, depth inside 2 ft 6 in, draught 1 ft for'ard, 2 ft aft, five pairs of thole pins a side, and oars 14 to 15 ft long.

There were 13 strakes of planking, two half-round rubbers and two square runners at the bilge. The sail plan differed from the usual gig custom, the foremast, 20 ft long, was stepped more for'ard, and the dipping lug, bent to a 16-ft yard, had the tack to the stem, not the weather bow. The mizzen mast, 13 ft 6 in long, was raked for'ard with a stay, set up with a whip purchase. The standing lug was bent to a 9-ft yard and sheeted to a 12-ft outrigger. There were two lines of reef points on the fore lug, but none on the mizzen.

Many Mawes-built pilot gigs were once stationed at St Ives.

Guide was lost when putting a pilot aboard a steamship through the vessel rolling on her. *Richard* was sold to north Somerset and taken there on the deck of a ketch in the late 1890s. *Silver Spray* was badly burned in a fire at the pilot's boathouse in 1917 and had to be condemned. *Branch* was blown off the quay in the early twenties of this century and had to be written off, but for *Teazer* and *Forester* no records remain. *Cetewayo* was sold to the St Agnes pilots, who later owned *Shah*.

The pilot gigs in Mount's Bay were smaller. *Evelyn*, built in 1888 by Simmons of Penzance for Crouch of that town, was reputed to have been designed by G. L. Watson. The length overall was 19 ft 3 in, beam 5 ft, depth 2 ft 1½ in. The floors amidships were flat with well-rounded bilges; 12 strakes of planking, four thwarts and rowing six oars in double thole pins. The gig was painted black above the waterline with a white 'list'—sheer line—below was red.

The foremast, 16 ft 6 in long, was stepped in a chock on the floors and secured by an iron collar to the after side of the for'ard thwart. The high-peaked, dipping lug was bent to a 10 ft 3 in yard, tack to weather bow, and had three lines of reef points. A spritsail was set on the 8-ft mast which went through a hole in seat to step in a chock on the floors. The sprit was 8 ft 6 in long and the sail sheeted to an outrigger, 5 ft 6 in overall, which went out through a hole to port in the transom—the normal fashion in Cornish gigs.

Photographs taken in March 1924 show the winter rig to be a short mast with a standing lug fitted with a boom, a staysail hanked to the forestay with the halyard to a single block at the top of the mast. A small spritsail on the mizzen mast had the sprit set to port. When the gig was measured up in 1937 by the late P. J. Oke she was owned in shares by Penzance pilots.

The Newlyn gig PZ 689 was painted white to the waterline, black below, and black sheerstrake. The sail plan in July 1921 was a high-peaked standing lug, 10 cloths, fitted with a boom, set on a short mast stepped through the second thwart. A staysail was hanked to the forestay and the standing lug mizzen was fitted with a boom and sheeted to an outrigger.

NOTE. The old name 'Scilly Isles', as shown on charts and other documents, has been used as being more appropriate to the period than the modern Isles of Scilly.

CHAPTER SEVEN

PILOT BOATS

SHIPPING lanes were unknown in the days of sail. Being entirely dependent on the wind, a deep-sea vessel might strike soundings—the 100-fathom line—almost anywhere and make a landfall on the Bishop Rock lighthouse, the Lizard, Start Point, or the Fastnet lighthouse, to name a few. Pilots had to go 'seeking' any ship requiring their services. In the early days coasts were ill lit and buoys few and far between, but the men knew the waters and, when inshore, had their own landmarks to guide them up and down intricate channels. A cast of an armed lead told them their position by the nature of the bottom—sand, shells or mud. On a dark winter night with hands so benumbed with cold that they could not tell the marks by touch, placing them to their lips instantly gave the information; white, a piece of canvas, indicated 5 or 15 fathoms; red, a scrap of bunting, 7 or 17 fathoms; blue, a piece of cloth, 13 fathoms, and so on.

Pilot stations were established when steam began to oust sail, but for years afterwards men continued to cruise in their cutters hoping to pick up a 'call'. By day they flew the Pilot Jack, at night a blue flare was fired every 15 minutes. Steamers using specified lanes now sought a pilot on station, so that these big cutters or ketches remained in a certain area, boarding a pilot by boat, the next on the rota taking any ship, whether it were small sailing vessel, or a big liner. This was not altogether a satisfactory arrangement, and the custom soon began of certain shipping lines having 'choice pilots'.

The Trinity House cutters were powerful vessels, able to ride out most gales, as it was then that their services were most re-

247

quired. At Dungeness was *Vigilant,* 69 tons, built at Wivenhoe
in 1879 as a cutter and later converted to ketch rig, when she
acted as tender to the steam pilot boat, taking out pilots and
stores. She was lost by striking a mine in the first world war.
Pilot Parish was once washed along her deck in heavy weather
and jammed under the windlass. He had to be extricated with
handspikes, badly injured with several ribs broken.

A 'freelance' schooner, *Kindly Light,* built of oak at Bremen in
1879, had been purchased from the Weser Pilot Service, 'she
was very sluggish, needing half a gale of wind 'to quote one
man's remarks; and she drew 12 ft 6 in. The men failed to make
a living and the vessel was laid up in Dover Harbour, eventually
being sold to the Scarborough Sea Cadets who renamed her
Masie Graham, and sailed her over 14,000 miles in six years.

The cutters had an enormous sail plan. From details given in
the ledgers of Finnis, sailmaker at Deal, a mainsail cut for No 4
had a leech 54 ft 6 in, head 29 ft, mast 29 ft 6 in, foot 43 ft, 23
cloths, 362 yd No 1 coker, head gores 8 in a cloth. For a ketch
264 yd; mizzen leech 37 ft 8 in, head 16 ft 6 in, mast 19 ft 6 in,
foot 18 ft 9 in, with two lines of reef points, sail 85 yd, linings
24½ yd, total 109½ yd No 3 canvas. Mizzen topsail No 6 canvas
13 ft 3 in, 21 ft 3 in, 18 ft 8 in. 'Philip made it too small, put
two more cloths in it.'

In 1875 he cut a squaresail for No 4 cutter, 'M. cutt 33 ft
3 in, head 20 ft 10 in, foot 30 ft 10 in. First cutt straight, 1 reef
6 ft. 173 yd No 7 coker.' Four years later he cut another for
'new cutter' of similar size, '20 thread holes, ¼ cloth along the
foot, 164½ yd, gore on the two leeches'.

Two jibs, leech 27 ft, stay 36 ft 6 in, foot 18 ft.

For *Princess,* 1883, a storm foresail had 65½ yd No 1 canvas,
cringles in the stay, 25 thimbles, '26½ boltrope' weather 32 ft
10 in, leech 29 ft 6 in, foot 16 ft 6 in. For the gaff topsail,
Finnis only gives 'First cutt 23 ft 6 in', followed by the gores for
eleven cloths, 'foot seams 3 in run up 6 ft to 1⅜ in body, head
1½ in'.

Only one costing is given:

	£	s	d
Mainsail			
263 yd of No 1 Royal Navy canvas @ 1s 0½d	13	14	–
58b of rope @ 25d	1	5	–
Twine @ 6d		6	–
Labour 16¼ days @ 5d	4	2	6

June 1884 £19 7 6

In the Isle of Wight area, many first-class branch pilots for the South Coast lived at Yarmouth and kept their cutters in the harbour, one of the finest in the early years of the nineteenth century being *Pallas*, owned by John Long. A heavy sw gale had been blowing for days before Christmas 1820, and all the pilots decided not to put to sea, except John Long who left on the first of the ebb early on Christmas Day to seek any vessel off the Needles at daybreak. The wind had shifted a little with heavy sleet and snow squalls when, under trysail and storm jib, the cutter went out into the storm to beat down to the Needles in pitch blackness. As dawn was breaking a large ship was sighted coming up Channel, obviously out of her reckoning as she was heading for the Shingle Bank on which huge breakers were leaping. Long immediately made for the vessel and hailed for her to heave-to with her head to the south'ard. As the wind came abeam, the mainmast went by the board, the cutter threw out her boat and with two men pulling had difficulty in getting alongside owing to the wreckage. Eventually Long managed to get on board and gave the proper course for the Needles, to the utter astonishment of the captain. For twelve days he had been without any observations and by dead reckoning thought he was in the vicinity of Falmouth.

The ship was a valuable West Indiaman, crowded with passengers, including many women and children. Course was shaped for the Solent and the disabled vessel finally anchored in Cowes Roads, the pilots earning good salvage money.

John Long died at the age of 82 in 1842. In October 1855 John Brown was killed falling from the masthead of *Pallas* in which he had served for 17 years. In 1868 the cutter *Blonde* was

o

sunk with all hands by the P & O steamer *Syria*, the two pilots and crew of two being drowned. *Agenoria* was in the pilot service until 1905.

I am indebted to the late Captain A. G. Cole for this information and I enjoyed many a yarn with him before his death when well into his 90s.

About 1910 Trinity House put two very fine auxiliary ketches, *Solent* and *St Helen's*, on station. Built of steel at Leith to special survey, 100 A1 at Lloyd's, they measured 68 ft overall, 18 ft beam, 11 ft 6 in depth. Straight-stemmed with a moderate cutaway forefoot, they had high bows, a good sheer and freeboard and cruised under sail in all weathers.

To the westward, in the Scilly Isles, were four large cutters 65 to 75 ft overall, and seven smaller ones 45 to 50 ft, owned and manned by pilots and crews from St Mary's, St Martin, St Agnes, Bryher and Tresco. *Atlantic* was 67 ft LBP, 16 ft 4 in beam, and drew 9 ft of water. Mainmast was 61 ft deck to truck, boom 48 ft. Sail area was about 800 yd, summer rig; 360 yd winter. *Rapid* of Bryher had a registered tonnage of 46.

At Falmouth was *Arthur Rogers*, 72 ft LBP, beam 15 ft, while *Verbena*, built by Jackman at Brixham in 1879, sailed out of Plymouth, and *Allow Me* and *Leader*, designed by W. H. Prigg, were reckoned to be the fastest cutters on the sw coast.

Design varied according to owner's requirements; some favoured yachting practice with hollow bows in lieu of full-bodied sections, but all insisted on straight stems and keels, a deep heel and good rise of floors. Beam varied considerably. *Ferret*, one of the smaller Plymouth cutters, had a beam of 15 ft 6 in, practically the same as in hulls 8 to 10 ft longer. The entrance was sharp, with a good run aft, but draught was 9 in more than in the bigger boats. Her sailing qualities were good off the wind, but poor beating to wind'ard.

One requirement was paramount—good seakeeping ability. Construction was on the heavy side, elm keels 60 to 70 ft long, often in one length, floors moulded 15 in, frames sawn oak and doubled, spaced 19 to 29 in, garboards 3 in, planking 2½ in thick, fastenings trenails and spikes and, in accordance with the then common practice, every hull was 'salted'.

Deck fittings were kept low and as near the centre line as possible, leaving plenty of space for launching the small boat. There was a reeving bowsprit, and small horse on the taffrail for sheeting the trysail set in heavy weather. In winter, a short topmast with a smaller topsail was carried and it was then customary to lace the weather of a topsail to the mast. For a cutter 62 ft overall the main boom was 43 ft 6 in, much the same length as in the Dover cutters, mast, deck to cap, 41 ft 6 in, masthead 8 ft, topmast 29 ft 2 in, fid to sheave.

As many as five jibs were carried, two foresails and a short gaff mainsail for winter use—usually called a 'storm trysail'—with a spitfire jib set on a short bowsprit and the storm foresail.

Some cutters were renowned for speed in light weather, others in hard winds, although the quality most desired was to be good in any wind. Ghosting ability in very light summer breezes was especially valued. A good average speed in a moderate wind was around 9 knots, but 10 was not uncommon. The smaller cutters did not set a topsail in winter, only a short mast to carry the pilot flag, and the mainsail had no boom. The bowsprit had a bobstay and shrouds, both set up with two single blocks. A short iron on the starboard side of the masthead carried a white light when the cutter was on its station for pilotage duty; then the statutory lights were not shown, but sidelights were kept ready lit to display on the near approach of other vessels. (Picture, p 158.)

Falmouth had a fine fleet of pilot cutters. Masts there were stepped farther aft than the usual distance of one-third the length, and until the decline of square-riggers towards the end of the nineteenth century Falmouth pilots made a comfortable living.

Much of our western coast lies fully exposed to every gale from the prevailing quarter, sw, and huge seas roll in unchecked by land for some 3,000 miles until they break in fury on the rock-bound shores of Ireland and sw England. These coasts have seen countless shipwrecks as wind-driven vessels, off course, have sighted ahead that dread of all seamen, a lee shore against which white-capped seas surge in endless succession.

How welcome to a shipmaster was the glimpse of a tiny pilot cutter, riding the waves like a gull, head-reaching a little under a scrap of canvas and having on board a man whose knowledge could guide a ship to safety.

The Bristol Channel opens between Hartland Point on the south and St Ann's Head, some 48 miles distant to the north. The shores of the channel now run in eastward for about 100 miles, gradually converging until they meet the river Severn pouring out its waters gathered over a length of 180 miles. This funnel shape, and the swift tidal movements meeting the fierce current from inland, kick up vicious seas, and the channel is noted for its great tidal range, 48 ft in places at springs, the second highest in the world.

These conditions demanded a very fine type of pilot boat, one easily handled in crowded waters yet able to face the full force of an Atlantic gale and, above all, having easy motion when laying-to on station.

Six miles up the narrow, winding reaches of the river Avon lies Bristol, in the Middle Ages a port second only to London. From here sailed many of the early explorers seeking new lands in the West and for centuries trade with America was exceedingly valuable. Tradition states that James Georges Ray was appointed by the mayor and corporation in May 1497 to pilot Cabot's ship *Mathew*, and James Shepherd later in the same year, names still connected with the pilot service today. In 1837 George Ray piloted the pioneer Atlantic steamship *Great Western*; seven years later William Ray took out the larger *Great Britain*, probably as far as Lundy Island.

Bristol Corporation long claimed the right to appoint pilots, in 1611 delegating their authority to the Society of Merchant Venturers who retained control for 250 years. This vested interest was challenged when other seaports developed along the coast of South Wales. In 1791 Swansea obtained a Harbour

Act to allow the newly-elected trustees to appoint pilots for their own bay and port, a claim vigoriously opposed by Bristol. Cardiff tried in vain to obtain similar privileges in 1836; by 1860 the number of their pilots had increased to 40, only a few less than those of Bristol. In the following year Cardiff, Newport and Gloucester finally succeeded in gaining their independence. The Society of Merchant Venturers gave up their interest and Bristol pilots were again appointed by the Corporation. Barry obtained similar concessions in 1885.

For much of my information I am greatly indebted to Mr Grahame Farr for his permission to make use of his valuable researches in Customs' registers, and to Mr H. B. Watkins, pilot, whose late father knew the days of sailing cutters and on whose notes I have freely drawn.

Most of the Bristol Channel ports are in a voluntary pilotage area, but Neath and Briton Ferry, the Bristol group of ports, and Gloucester, with Sharpness and Chepstow, have compulsory pilotage. The compulsory outward limit of Bristol pilotage was formerly Lundy, 80 miles distant, but was withdrawn to Flat Holm, 25 miles distant, in 1891. The pilots still made the area of Lundy their principal seeking ground, until in 1914 they were forbidden to 'seek' owing to war risks. An amalgamation of pilots resulted in 1918 and a steam-cutter service was established in 1922 with the *Queen Mother*, owned by a limited company of 30 pilots. At Swansea a steam-cutter service was begun in 1898 with the *Beaufort*, at Cardiff in 1912 with the *Edmund Handcock*, and at Newport in 1920 with the *Fancy*. As far back as 1908, a steam cutter had been proposed for Bristol but the local pilots were dead against the scheme and were the last to give up sail.

On the Somerset bank of the Avon is the village of Crewkerne Pylle, usually known as Pill, where generations of pilots have lived and moored their craft in the creek, always retaining their independence despite every effort by Bristol to bring them within the jurisdiction of the corporation. The massive slip was probably built by the Portbury monks and during the sixteenth and seventeenth centuries Pill grew in commercial importance;

the bay formed by the curve of the river between Pill and Sum-
merhouse Point—Hung Road—has long been an excellent natural harbour where vessels moored to iron steeples and ringbolts
in the rocks.

The pilots' cruising ground from London, Ushant, 100 miles
west of Fastnet, Glasgow. This is a large area but Bristol Channel
pilot boats would be found cruising there. A pilot would obtain
information about a ship and, timing her arrival, would sail away
to intercept her anywhere he thought he could do so. Of course
there was a lot of keenness and several pilots would race for the
same ship but not always would the fastest one board her. Light
winds, heavy winds, fog and rain would very often be the cause
of a ship being missed and a boat nearer home would have the
prize. After boarding the ship, the men left in the boat would bring
the cutter to Barry, Ilfracombe or Pill as required, sometimes
two men, sometimes man and boy and at times two boys.

I was apprenticed in 1908, [writes the late Captain H. S.
Watkins] and from that date until steam started to replace sail,
which it did at Cardiff in 1912, there was a fleet of about 100
cutters serving the ports of Cardiff, Barry, Newport, Gloucester
and Bristol. Bristol in 1908 had about 30 boats, the largest I
would say was the *Pet*, owned by the late Mr F. C. Ellis. Built by
Mr Rowles at Pill in 1904, she was 53 ft overall, 13·6 ft beam,
draught 9 ft 6 in, and powerfully rigged with a pole mast, sliding
bowsprit, wire rigging and patent reefing mainsail, a large one for
the summer and a smaller one for the winter. Headsails were
changed as required, and plenty of light canvas carried, spinnaker, balloon foresail, jib topsail, large topsail. Low bulwarks,
raked stern, big watertight cockpit. The punt used for boarding
was 13 ft × 5 ft × 2·6 ft and was kept on the port side abaft the
rigging. A section of the bulwarks was made to unship, the punt
was launched through this opening and towed astern until in a
position to board the ship to be piloted. There were usually two
pilots in each boat, two 'westernmen' and an apprentice, sometimes one westernman and an apprentice. The westernman was
paid 3s in the £, the apprentice by arrangement.

Very little is known concerning the early pilot boats. Mr
Grahame Farr writes: 'Diligent search has failed to produce
pictorial evidence of the type of craft employed by the Bristol
pilots in the eighteenth century and earlier.' Probably small

open boats were employed, but in a 'Register of Ships', begun in 1795 by Bristol Corporation, particulars are given of twelve 'skiffs' belonging to pilots. *Success*, 24 tons, and *Hero*, 23 tons, are the largest, each carrying a 'master, mariner and apprentice'. The four smallest, registering 14 tons, also had a crew of three, and one, *Elizabeth* of 15 tons, had two apprentices, making four in all. The description 'skiff', rather than cutter, was was always used in the service in the days of sail.

It is probable that most of the pilot skiffs were also registered with the Customs authorities under the Act of 1786, the first Act to make possible the universal registration of British shipping of 15 tons and upwards. The earliest surviving records for Bristol are for the years 1814 to 1820, 1822 and they are intact from 1824.

In searching these records [writes Mr Grahame Farr] I was able to trace five eighteenth-century craft which were in use as pilot skiffs, although it cannot be said with certainty that they were built for the purpose. . . . *William and Jane*, built at Bristol 1768, rebuilt in 1789, and lengthened in 1831. She was listed as a pilot skiff 1837–45 (James Rowland) and broken up in 1852. In a register of 1825 she was owned by John Rowland, mariner, tonnage 18, dimensions 36 ft × 11 ft 2 in × 5 ft 5 in. After 1831 she measured 20 tons, dimensions 36 ft 9 in × 11 ft 6¾ in × 5 ft 9½ in. *Betsey*, built at Bristol in 1786 . . . sold to Barnstaple 1840. . . . *Bristol Endeavour*, built at Pill in 1791 . . . sank in Morgan's Pill, raised and repaired . . . owned by James Buck, pilot 1817, but sold in the same year and afterwards sunk in the Channel. . . . *Tartar* built at Bristol in 1794. . . . *Fancy* built at Bristol in 1796 as an open boat, rebuilt and decked in 1801 . . . broken up in 1831. Tonnage 13 and dimensions 33 ft 9 in × 9 ft 8 in × 5 ft 9 in.

The 1807 Act did not lay down rules for the size of skiffs, but was content to stipulate the markings to be carried, as follows:

'Each pilot's skiff shall be marked with the number appointed for her by the Haven-master, in black paint on the three lower sails, such number to be at least four feet in length; the hull to be painted black, with a white streak under the gunwhale; to be also numbered on the bow and the pilot's name on the stern, and to carry a flag constantly at the masthead, with blue and white horizontal stripes, of the dimensions four feet by five feet.'

By a stroke of good fortune there have been preserved the lines of the skiff *Charlotte*, built by the Hilhouses of Bristol in 1808 for John Berry, pilot. The plans, drawn up by George Hilhouse, have been preserved among others by Charles Hill & Sons, shipbuilders and successors to the Hilhouses. This skiff was a medium-bodied little craft with a forefoot rather shallower than in later examples ... a clean run except that it was slightly interrupted by the tuck under the square stern. Her timbers give the impression of great strength. Dimensions given on the plans: length from the fore part of the stem aloft to the after part of the post on the keel, 33 ft 2 in; length extreme aloft 38 ft; breadth extreme 11 ft 8 in, depth from skin to skin 6 ft 4½ in, admeasurement 18 88/94 tons; mast (including 7 ft head) 43 ft; boom 32 ft 9 in, gaff 20 ft, bowsprit 34 ft.

There is no sail plan of the *Charlotte*, but the following advertisement, dated 1812, gives a clue to the sails and equipment carried by the skiffs of the period:

'For Sale, the skiff *James and Samuel*, 14½ tons, at Pill, with furniture, etc, consisting of 2 anchors, 2 cables, 1 mainsail, 2 fore-sails, 4 jibs, 1 square-sail, 1 gaff-topsail, 1 topmast-steering-sail, 1 pont (sic)—James Craddy, sr.'

With the aid of the annual issues of the local directory, we can list all the Bristol pilot skiffs from 1837 until 1917, together with their owners (usually one pilot, rarely two or three). . . . From these sources I have listed 162 pilot skiffs and 10 other examples which may have been reserve craft, though possibly yachts. There were 25 in use in 1837 and the number gradually rose to a maximum of 45 in the years 1863–6, then a decline to 33 in 1880 and 26 in 1890, down to the level of 16–17 in the years 1893–1901. Numbers then slightly increased to 26 in 1907 and fell again to 18 for the years 1912–17.

In the period 1814–35, the two largest skiffs were *Echo* built by Hilhouse in 1835, 44 ft 4 in length, and *Albion* built at Bristol in 1825, 45 ft 6 in long, the smallest being *Fancy* 33 ft 9 in.

After 1855 the largest were *Pet*, 47 ft long, built at Scilly in 1843 and purchased in 1862, the *Unexpected*, 49 ft 6 in, built by H. S. Trethowan at Falmouth in 1878, and the *Pet*, 53 ft long, built by Rowles at Pill in 1906. The latter is still with us (1953) and is considered to have been the largest skiff ever used in the Bristol service. After several years as a relief boat, fitted with an auxiliary engine, the *Pet* was sold out of the service in 1949 and purchased by Mr T. W. R. Ellis, for whose uncle she had been built. The smallest skiff was probably the *Wave*, 10 tons, built by Cooper at Pill *c* 1867.

Among the builders at Pill were:

James Phillips, who built his own skiff, *James*, in 1809.
William Morgan & Thomas Rowles, *c* 1815–17,
William Morgan, 1822–40, Thomas Price had been building small craft at Weston-super-mare when he came to Pill 1854.
Charles Cooper, 1862–1879. His property devolved to George Cooper, then building at Penarth, but the Pill yard was carried on by John Cooper until 1905.

Edwin Rowles, a shipwright at Bristol 1877–8, began building skiffs at Pill in 1887, the last commercial builder there, his business closing down in 1910.

The Hilhouses of Bristol built many of the earlier skiffs, others came from Bideford, Ilfracombe and Padstow; in 1851 two were built by R. & J. Tredwen at Padstow and seven by William Patterson at Bristol. After the Act of 1861, Charles Cooper opened a yard at Penarth; other builders then were John Williams, Newport, William Williams & Sons, Newport, Davies & Plain, Cardiff, Mordey & Carney, Newport, Jeens and Levison, Gloucester.

The greatest rivalry existed among pilots who demanded faster boats, some going as far away as Fleetwood, Hamble and Porthleven, hoping to secure better craft than those built locally.

The late Captain H. S. Watkins wrote:

We had all shapes and sizes sailing the channel by 1912, boats up to 60 ft long, small flat-sterned boats, boats with sharp raking stems, spoon bows, hollow bows. The *Alpha* of Barry had no forefoot at all, straight stem to the waterline, then a curve to the heel: some full-bodied, some had hollow bilges, fitted topmasts, pole masts, steel booms, cross-cut sails, hulls mostly painted black, some near black, one belonging to Barry was blue, the bottoms were treated with anti-fouling black, white, red, green, all the colours of the rainbow. Each expressing the ideas of the owner within the limits of the local bye-laws.

Mr Cooper had the reputation of building the better boat regarding construction, condition of timber, but also and very important, better sea-going qualities. They were not always as

fast as Rowles' boats but having a straight stem and a deep forefoot would heave-to for hours and never 'fall off' in the trough of
the sea. The foresheet would be hauled to windward, the tiller
lashed (as required) a little 'down' and the boat would be with
the luff of the mainsail gently lifting; rarely would any heavy
water come aboard.

Rowles' boats were a little finer in the bottom, not so much
draught forward, and unless allowed to make more headway
through the water would 'fall off' in the trough of the sea and
probably take water aboard and throw the pots off the cooking
stove. However it spoke well for the construction of these boats
that we still have two boats in our service (c 1928). The *Pet's* rig
is reduced and a petrol engine installed, but the accommodation
remains the same, and we use her when it becomes necessary to lay
our steam cutter up. The *Bertie*, our houseboat at Portishead, we
believe to be over 60 years old, built Penarth . . . after stripping
her out completely, little had to be done to her frames and
planking before rebuilding her inside, and so far as we know she
is still in good condition.

The Pill builders, backed by the local pilots, introduced
their changes gradually. The old square stern developed into an
elliptical counter in the larger skiffs, or a flat raking transom
with outside rudder head in the smaller ones. They never de-
parted from the straight stem, long experience having shown
that a clean forefoot and broad shoulders meant good seakeeping in the seas met west of Lundy. The roller-reefing gear
was introduced in the 1890s, a mixed blessing; although it eased
labour, the set of the mainsail was ruined and the strain broke
many a boom. Plans were never used, hulls were built by eye
from a half-model which had previously been approved by the
owner and his many unofficial advisers. (Picture, p 177.)

A departure from the traditional design was made in 1904
when *Faith* of Barry was built from lines draughted by H. Clay-
ton, with a spoon bow running into a curved forefoot sweeping
down aft to a short keel. Built at Penarth, length was 50 ft 6 in
and her accommodation was unusual in having a separate
owner's cabin. Two cutters built by Armour Bros at Fleetwood
in 1911 were *Alpha* of Newport and *Kindly Light* of Barry, on

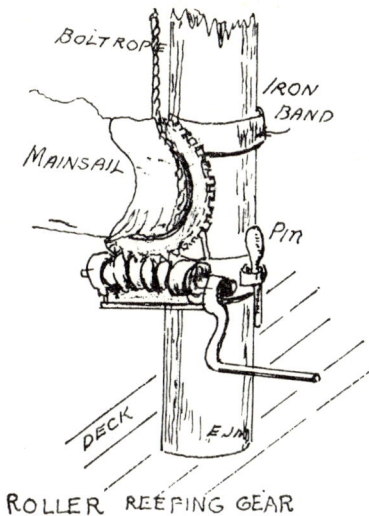

ROLLER REEFING GEAR

Sketch of Skiff's roller reefing gear

similar lines to the Morecambe Bay prawners and noted for speed in light weather. Slade of Polruan built *Cornubia* for £350 ready for sea.

The skiffs of the 1870s were sturdy cutter-rigged craft, 33 to 40 ft on the waterline, flush-decked with high bulwarks, and tarred hemp rigging set up with deadeyes and lanyards; 'I have heard some had chain rigging, a mainsail that had four reefs, foresail with two reefs and different size jibs.' Later vessels had a cockpit, wire rigging, three shrouds a side and patent reefing mainsails. Running gear was the best manilla and all blocks had patent sheaves. A large cotton canvas mainsail was carried in summer, a smaller flax one in winter. (Pictures, pp 158–9.)

The keel was 6 in thick, varying in depth up to 18 in, 40 or more ft long, elm and in one piece. Stem and stern posts of oak, frames of oak, natural grown, 4 in to 6 in by 3 in double amidships, single at the ends. Planking was oak, elm and pitchpine, 2 in to $1\frac{3}{4}$ in, in varying widths, decks pine 2 in to $1\frac{1}{4}$ in thick, $3\frac{1}{4}$ in wide.

The mast was pitch or Oregon pine, standing rigging wire, set up with lanyards, some boats had rigging screws . . . port side of mainsail had the number painted on it, also the starboard side of foresail. All other boats had their port initials instead of numbers, on the bulwarks forward would be the number, aft would be the name, name of owner and port painted on the stern.

Accommodation consisted, from aft forward—steerage, for sails, stores, lamps, ropes, paint etc; next, the pilot's cabin with two built-in bunks, a settee each side running the full length of the cabin, about 12 ft long, cupboards, drawers etc all finished in varnished pitchpine and a mahogany table in the centre. Forward again would be the crew's forecastle, built-in bunks, lockers, sail racks, water tank 60 gallons, chain locker and food stores. No ports, deck lights gave us light, at night of course paraffin lamps. Summer time the boats would leave home for a couple of months and call at Barry or Ilfracombe to pick up their pilots and stores after boarding a ship. . . . The hull had to be painted black, usually black varnish. Ilfracombe was the best port to go to do this and the boats would have legs bolted to each side so they would stand upright on the hard sand. The rudder pintles and keel band etc would be examined and overhauled as required.

Approximate costs at the turn of the century were £350 for a medium to £450 for a large skiff. *Hilda*, built by Cooper with assistance from one boy, cost, complete with ballast, £350 in 1899. Her dimensions were:

	ft	in
Length overall	49	0
Length waterline	43	0
Breadth	13	5
Draught	8	0
Freeboard at bow	5	0
do stern	2	9
do least	2	3
Rail	1	6
Ballast, iron with concrete between floors		
Copper fastened		

Hilda was run down by the tug *Brunel* on the night of 4 November 1912.

Design reached its culmination around the turn of the century, the spoon bow, known to pilots as the *Valkyrie* bow—having been introduced in the Cup challenger owned by the Earl

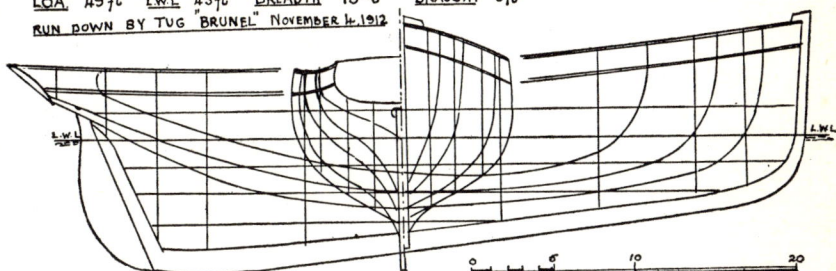

BRISTOL CHANNEL PILOT BOAT "HILDA" Nº 2 BUILT BY J. COOPER AT PILL 1899
LOA. 49 ft   LWL 43 ft   BREADTH 13'-5"   DRAUGHT 8 ft
RUN DOWN BY TUG "BRUNEL" November 14, 1912

L.W.L.   L.W.L.

0   5   10   20

Traced from plans lent by Captain H.B Watkins, Pilot, 1966.

Edgar March
1966

Lines of Bristol Channel pilot boat *Hilda*

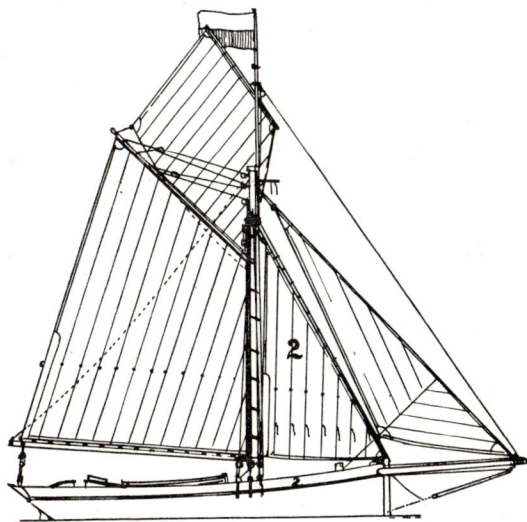

2

NOTE Topsail is shown to port for clearness, usually set to starboard

Sail plan of *Hilda*

of Dunraven—was favoured by Hambley of Cardiff, a long curved forefoot by Armour of Fleetwood. These innovations made a boat handier in stays and improved speed, but the wonderful seakeeping qualities of a long straight keel were lost to a great extent, and many pilots refused to adopt them. Neither were they keen on outside ballast, bobstays, backstays or runners, holding that a mast should have plenty of play, and preferring deadeyes and rope lanyards to rigging screws even after the introduction of wire for shrouds. They selected their bowsprits with the greatest care trusting to the spring of the long spar to give life to their skiff, and considered a bobstay interfered with the natural play. The older men held that any additional standing rigging, other than vitally necessary, should be done without, as taking all life out of a boat. And who can deny they were right? Few indeed were the cutters lost at sea over the years; many were run down by steamers but a mast going by the board was unknown.

Every man had his own ideas on the disposition of ballast, always seeking an easy roll. Shifting a little forward when running helped to increase speed by making the stern more buoyant. Pilots, living afloat for nine months and more in a year, desired comfortable motion at sea, a dry vessel which could be left to look after herself if necessary when hove-to and able to keep her course without attention. They abhorred weight in the ends, and every halyard and sheet had to be within easy reach of the helmsman.

Choice of underwater lines was highly individual. Some liked plenty of beam, full forward sections, a fine run aft. Others wanted a fine entrance. All liked plenty of freeboard and a good rise of floor, but some skiffs were rather round-bottomed. A loose-footed mainsail with many rows of reef points and a boom ending at the taffrail, or just outside, was customary until the introduction of the Appledore patent-reefing gear, early in the 1890s, which reduced the labour of reefing in heavy weather. A worm gear turned by a handle engaged in a set of cogs round the boom which could be revolved several times, thus rapidly reducing the area of the sail. The great drawback was the terrific strain on the spar when several turns were on; the leech was now several feet inboard and the boltrope, being thicker than the canvas, more came down, resulting in a baggy sail. Worse still, the boom, held by the gooseneck at the mast and the sheet outboard, now tended to buckle and frequently broke at any weak spot.

Peak and throat halyards had their purchases alongside the mast and the falls led through bulleyes to belay round bitts in the deck at the sides of the cockpit. The sheets of the headsails also led aft; the mainsheet often had rubber buffers or a strong steel spring in a cylinder to lessen the effect of a gybe all standing. The larger skiffs had crosstrees or spreaders, but in winter a stump topmast was carried. Staysails generally had two sets of reef points, the first 4 ft, the second 6 ft from the foot. A number of jibs were carried, the storm or 'spitfire' for heavy weather, a 'slave' slightly larger and so called because it was almost permanently set, a 'second' and a 'spinnaker' which went to the topmast head from the end of the bowsprit, the sheet being led outside the shrouds to belay aft of the mast. Some set a big foresail with its sheets also led aft outside the shrouds, and a small jib topsail above a big jib in light weather.

A wide variety of topsails were set, varying from an almost square gaff topsail to one with a very long pole laced to the luff, and a short jackyard at the clew projecting beyond the gaff, a jib-headed one, or a similar sail with a short headstick. In the palmy days, or when racing at regattas, the sail was always set a'weather. Later practice was to carry it to starboard and to make the sail set better some men had the luff hanked to a 'leader'—a jackstay fast to a ring sliding freely on the topmast and belaying to a cleat at the foot of the mainmast.

Naturally the regattas saw the keenest of racing, the pilots using every device known to them to obtain extra speed, including moving heavy weights to positions known to give the best results under certain conditions of sailing. For years *Polly*, built by Davies & Plain in 1878 at Cardiff for Pilot Williams, was first at many a hard-fought regatta, her owner moving a heavy anvil to selected marks to obtain the best trim, as well as enough iron pigs to ballast a schooner. *Marguerite*, built by Rowles at Pill in 1893 for another Cardiff pilot, F. Trott, proved to be faster, winning in 1895, 1896 and 1897, and again in 1905 and 1907. When racing, she carried a huge mainsail with its boom extending 6 ft beyond the taffrail. (Pictures, pp 158 and 159.)

On service, speeds of 9 to 10 knots were attained. Pilot W. J. Russell recalls an incident during the winter of 1907 when he was westernman in *Hilda*, No 2, Enoch E. Watkins, hanging on to a Watkins tug because the wind made it impossible to anchor with safety. Cruising nearby was *Emma*, No 20, Edward Rowland, under four rolls of mainsail, reefed foresail and storm jib. At about 4 pm they saw *Emma* increase canvas, hoist her pilot flag and stand towards the south end of Lundy; soon after she showed the Anglo-American private signal and the tanker *Potomac* came into sight to be boarded by Pilot Rowland. During the night the wind increased, with heavy rain, but still west of south. At 8 am the next day *Emma* came up, reefed mainsail to five rolls, reefed staysail and kept under way. At dinner time she boarded an Elder Dempster liner. Between boarding the tanker at 4.30 pm, the skiff had sailed for home with the tide under her, reaching Avonmouth at the same time as the *Potomac* was in the Old Dock locks. Pilot Rowland rowed over to his cutter and just as the tide began to ebb made for Lundy, knowing the liner was due. The tide was a neap, 2 to 3 knots, the wind on the beam and strong, and the total distance of about 150 miles was covered in a little over 15 hours, or about 10 knots over the ground. *Emma* had been built by Rowles at Pill in 1902.

On another occasion four years later Russell was in *Freda* No 8, W. Selway and S. Buck. They set out from Pill soon after the 8 am train had brought the Bristol papers with their shipping intelligence, the wind fresh northerly and a beat out of the river. On clearing the mouth they were in company with *Lily* No 24, William Hunt, built by Bowden at Porthleven in 1905.

The wind freshened and by midnight both skiffs were off Pendeen and Pilot Buck boarded the ss *Nymegen*. When rounding Land's End they were in sight of the *Lily*, and also at 8 am the next day when they were 3 miles south of the Eddystone, both having missed the New Zealand steamer they were seeking. The distance covered in two ebbs and two floods with a strength of 3 to 5 knots was approximately 236 miles in 24 hours.

When boarding a pilot, the procedure differed according to weather conditions. If fine, the skiff was sailed alongside the steamer; if bad, the cutter got under her lee and one hand took the pilot across in the boat. If short-handed, the pilot would go alone, and as he gained the ladder he would kick the punt off, to be picked up by the skiff.

Punts were heavily built with flat floors and transom sterns, launched through a portion of the bulwarks made to unship, and got on board again without the aid of any halyards or tackle. The knack of heaving up in a confused sea was knowing how and when. The boat was brought up to the lee side, the lad jumped aboard and joined his mate, and both waited until the keel of the cutter was at the right angle. Then the sea did most of the work against the broad transom and as the skiff rolled to leeward the bow lifted on deck and was hove down to a cleat; the next roll brought the rest of the punt in with very little effort.

The two men worked watch and watch, and deemed it unseamanlike to have to call for help unless absolutely necessary; all the work of sailing and handling the canvas could be done by one hand. Out of each guinea received for pilotage the westernman had 3s, the boy 1s 6d, the owner finding ship and food. In the old days, once a pilot had received his 'parchment' he was exempt from any further examination by the authorities. A few unlicensed men known as 'yawlers' used to seek for jobs, keeping well out of the way of the certificated men, but had little hope of securing pilotage if the master demanded the production of a certificate.

In 1880 three 'choice' pilots were picked by certain ship-

P

owners and this action aroused such high feelings that the 37 other pilots put a chain across the creek at Pill and a two months' strike ensued. By 1890, 31 pilots were handling some 965,000 tons of shipping entering or leaving Bristol.

Pilotage fees in 1809 from Lundy to Kingroad were 3 guineas for vessels under 100 tons, 4 guineas if 100 to 200 tons, 5 guineas up to 300 tons, and over that tonnage 6 guineas.

Pilots were then and for many years afterwards responsible for towing arrangements in the river, vessels being handled by one 'yaul' and three or four men if small size. Larger ships might require the services of up to three yauls and 14 men. The standard fee for the usual tow from Kingroad to the 'bason' was 3s 9d per man, 3s for the yaul, plus an allowance of beer. When horses were employed, the charge was 5s per horse and 1s for the driver. Steam tugs were not introduced until 1836 and riots occurred when the tug *Fury* started work.

An account book kept by Pilot James Cox from 1831 to 1838, and now in the possession of Mr M. P. Buck, gives his fee for piloting the French brig *Julia* in October 1838 from the Bason to Kingroad at 10s, and from that point to Lundy, £2 10s. He piloted a brig from Lundy to Liverpool for £5 5s, and when quarantined on board a ship he had brought in he was given 7s 6d a day. Forty-one jobs in 1832 earned him £80 12s 9d, but four years later 29 jobs brought in £162 14s 6d, and two years after that, 30 jobs brought £186 8s 11d.

In bad times a man might cruise for several weeks without earning a penny, but the ever increasing number of ships loading coal on the South Wales coast brought better prospects. After boarding a steamship a pilot could reckon on being in port in a matter of hours; not so with a sailing vessel. Pilot T. Thayer tells how he was 11 days bringing a local barque from a position only 10 miles west of Lundy; also he once boarded a German barque off the Lizard, was blown back into the Bay of Biscay and reached Bristol 15 days later.

The risk of foundering was probably not nearly so great as being run down. On 1 November 1859 the *Diligent*, George

Gilmore, was lost with all hands off Lundy. Seven years later the *Ellen*, Charles Porter, foundered in the same locality, but Porter escaped as he had earlier boarded a ship. At times the hazard was that the ship boarded itself went missing.

The yearly increase in the number of steamships brought boom conditions. In 1850 the total tonnage entered at the Port of Bristol was 643,217; 30 years later it had practically doubled and in 1910 was 2,134,592 tons. The opening of the new docks at Avonmouth in 1908, capable of taking large vessels, brought the question of pilotage rates to a head. A demand was made to establish a steam pilot-cutter service at an estimated cost of £12,000, a proposal strenuously opposed by the pilots. The main purpose of the Corporation was to reduce pilotage rates on ships over 2,000 tons; as they stood, they would militate against attracting big steamers to use the New Dock, the charges being 8s 6d per 100 tons. The pilots agreed that the rates were too high and a compromise was effected.

Similar conditions prevailed at the South Wales ports where the export of coal, excluding bunkers, rose fantastically; from Cardiff the tonnage cleared was greater than that from Liverpool, and on nine occasions greater than that from the Port of London, reaching 15,405,059 tons of coal in 1912. Bunker coal was sent to stations all over the world to be priced at 26s a ton at Port Said, 35s in Singapore.

It must always be remembered that as the draught of ships increased, so did the responsibilities of the pilot, who could have in his charge a vessel and cargo worth a million pounds and more.

The Barry Docks were opened in 1889 and the following year 1,733 vessels loaded 1,692,223 tons, in 1910, 3,267 vessels loaded 4,314,023 tons.

When the steam cutters went on station the majority of the skiffs came on the market. Some were sold foreign, others for trading, but their lines prohibited the carrying of much cargo, and after freights took a downward plunge early in the 1920s they were laid up or resold. Many yachtsmen bought the more modern boats and found them eminently suitable for cruising, but in many instances the removal of the 10 to 12 tons of inside ballast in favour of heavy outside keels tended to spoil their easy motion in a seaway.

The development of Swansea began early in the eighteenth century when the copper smelting industry was established there in 1717. Lying adjacent to the South Wales coalfield, it later had a practical monopoly of the export of anthracite, and no other part of the world could compete with Swansea tinplate. It can be understood how irksome it was that Bristol Corporation claimed the right to appoint pilots. In 1791 the Harbour Trustees were appointed; their duty was to deepen and widen the entrance to the river Tawe. One stipulation was that each pilot should have a boat of 21 ft stowage, 6 ft 6 in beam, and a depth of 2 ft 7 in with six oars for towing purposes. Hulls were clench-built and the rig differed from any seen elsewhere, being similar to the shallops depicted by Dutch artists in the seventeenth century. The foremast was stepped close to the bows, the mainmast raked well aft, both sails having very short gaffs about 6 ft in length with the luffs laced to the masts. The main boom projected outside the stern for almost half its length, and no headsails were set.

Such a rig was unique in British waters and no doubt was suitable for local conditions. The harbour drying out at low water, all ships and boats had to take the ground, so it was as well that the tonnage laws then in force produced flat-bottomed, deep-sided hulls well adapted to sit upright on the mud. Unfortunately, Swansea faced south-west and the prevailing wind was a dead muzzler for ships leaving the port, but the pilot boats had to be weatherly to go outside into the bay to secure the pilotage of vessels running in for shelter, especially as the holding ground was poor in the Mumbles Road. Their sails could be easily handled and the short gaffs reduced weight aloft.

As trade increased, so did the need for larger pilot boats, and average length was now about 30 ft. Hulls were carvel-built and a jib was set on a running bowsprit. Transom sterns prevailed but a few had counters by the 1850s, masts and boom were approximately the same length as the waterline, and there was no standing rigging other than a bobstay when the bowsprit was out. The open boat was giving place to half-decks and a cockpit aft. Ten pilot boats were now in service.

The coal trade prospered with the coming of railways, and the opening of the South Dock permitted large ships to use the port. Copper ore was brought in small barques from Chile until the discovery of sources nearer home brought about a decline in the 1890s. These conditions increased the competition among pilots, who ordered new boats with hulls similar to those of the Bristol Channel skiffs. Deep draught was no longer an obstacle as their boats berthed in the basin and remained afloat at all states of the tide, draught being from 6 to 8 ft. The rig, however, remained the same, and hulls varied in length from between 41 and 50 ft. By 1890, 11 modern boats, built between 1859 and 1875, had taken the place of the old half-open craft, the majority built locally by Bevan or Bowen, with two or three by builders at Bideford. Mast hoops replaced the old-fashioned lacing and booms were shortened. A steam cutter went on station in 1898, but the best two sailing boats, *Grenfell* and *Benson*, were kept in reserve until sold in 1904.

The late P. J. Oke drew up plans of *Benson*, S 4, based on data found in a sailmaker's notebook and such information as remained available in 1936.

Built by Bowen at Swansea in 1870, the hull was 50 ft overall, beam 12 ft, depth 9 ft 8 in. Frames were 3 in square, spaced 1 ft.

Bowsprit	25 ft, outboard 17 ft 6 in
Foremast	51 ft 9 in
Fore gaff	9 ft 6 in
Mainmast	52 ft 10 in
Main gaff	10 ft
Main boom	34 ft 3 in
Sets of reef points: jib, 1; foresail, 3 or 4; mainsail, 3	

The top of mainmast plumbed on the rudder head, the main-

Plans of Swansea Bay pilot boat *Benson*, S 4

sail was loose-footed. The pilot flag was carried on a short staff
at head of foremast. At the regattas held until the turn of the
century these schooners could hold their own with the cutters.

The rise of Liverpool began in the eighteenth century and by
1800 the number of vessels entered was 4,746, tonnage 450,060;
30 years later 11,214, tonnage 1,411,964, practically doubling

by 1860. Numbers then remained fairly constant but tonnage of ships increased until, in 1910, it amounted to 18,654,071 for 24,961 vessels.

An authorised pilot service was established in 1766 and sloops used to wait in Almwch harbour to board approaching ships. The schooner rig was adopted subsequently and in 1875 No 11, *Mersey*, 79 tons, was built at Almwch. Frequently in very bad weather, when it was impossible to board a pilot, the schooner would hoist the signal 'Follow me' and lead a fleet of ships across the Bar, up Crosby Channel to Sloyne.

The No 6 pilot boat was sold when a new steel schooner took her place, and after being laid up for a long time she was sailed out to Dakar in December 1879.

The Mersey Dock Board ordered a schooner in November 1891 to be built by Philip & Son, Dartmouth, to the design of Alex Richardson who had designed the crack yachts *Iverna* and *Irex*. The dimensions were: LOA 104 ft, LBP 102 ft, extreme beam 21 ft, depth moulded 11 ft 2 in. The steel frame composite hull was constructed to Lloyd's highest class, 21 years A1, with a short clipper bow and elliptical stern, 80 tons of iron kentledge, all inside, accommodation for 40 pilots and crew, and larger than any existing pilot boat by about 15 ft.

This fine schooner, named *George Holt*, sailed from Dartmouth in November 1892 and was off South Stack in 47 hours, 50 min. Fitted out like a yacht, her draught was 11 ft, and her tonnage, 196. (Picture, p 178.)

At Barrow, the pilot boat for many years was the once famous cutter yacht *Mosquito*, built of iron in 1848 by Mare & Co on the Thames in conformity with the theories of Scott Russell, the naval architect. She was one of the first vessels to have a long hollow bow and a short after body of great beam. In 1851 *Mosquito* sailed in the race for the Queen's Cup won by the US yacht *America*; 13 years later her keel was lengthened 8 ft and the head of the sternpost brought in 21 in on deck. Her last racing season was in 1870, when she won three firsts. Subsequently sold and re-rigged as a schooner for the pilot service,

Mosquito cruised in the vicinity of Morecambe Bay lightvessel, or lay at moorings near Piel Island, Barrow Channel before being sold by auction on 4 March 1896.

To be a pilot, or 'lodesman' to use the old name, is to follow an ancient and honourable calling, entailing great responsibility and severe penalties if negligent. Fortunately the penalties are not now so drastic as those defined in the Laws of Oleron during the reign of Richard I. Then, if a pilot from ignorance or otherwise lost the ship entrusted to him and the merchants incurred losses, he had to make full satisfaction if he had the means, if not, he forfeited his head.

CHAPTER EIGHT

THE WEST COAST: WALES, LANCASHIRE AND SCOTLAND

FOR centuries, oyster dredging was carried on in Swansea Bay from a village variously known as Oystermouth or Mumbles. The boats used were originally open rowing skiffs, but lug sails were adopted as the size of boats increased, also the peculiar short gaff sails seen in the Swansea pilot boats. Hulls were clench-built, bluff-bowed and transomsterned.

The beds were free to all, and smacks from Kent and Essex dredged for brood which were relaid in their own layings. Local sales were made from the 'perches', principally to Bristol. By 1844, the intensive dredging was arousing protests and demands that the local council should interfere before the beds were entirely destroyed, but little was done. During the following 20 years about 9 million oysters were dredged annually by a fleet of some 200 smacks, and thousands of spat oysters went to restock the beds in Colne and Blackwater, and at Whitstable and Faversham. The Welshmen could see their livelihood going and, impressed by the Essex cutters, a delegation went to Colneside in 1855 to study local smacks and methods, finally ordering many small cutters of around 12 tons and costing about £300 complete. The first to arrive at Mumbles was the *Seven Sisters*, but the name skiff was retained to the last. Soon, similar cutters were built for local owners at yards in Devon and Cornwall, only repairs being done in the neighbouring boatyards; Brixham copied the rig in the 'Mumble Bees'. The open boats retained the dipping fore lug and sprit mizzen, and in 1872 the number of fishing craft registered at Swansea was three first class, and 184 second class (under 15 tons).

The new decked skiffs, being fine seaboats, were able to work on more distant grounds, at times as far north as the Solway Firth. Out of season the men went trawling, using the normal beam trawl; for oyster dredging the crew of three handled two dredges, and shares were one quarter to the boat and the same to each man. The oysters were brought in and laid down on 'perches', plots marked by stones, for which rent was paid to the owner of the foreshore. Industrialism brought increased pollution and in January 1913 the Fishmongers Company requested samples of oysters after easterly winds had been blowing; Mumbles faces east and rough seas were preventing obnoxious matter from getting away with the tide. During the 1914–18 war disease brought great mortality and soon the end came to an age-old fishery; the last sailing skiff *Emmeline* ceased working a decade later.

The decked skiffs varied in length, 40 ft being about the maximum; if too small they were not powerful enough to tow the dredges, but bigger cutters tended to lift them off the bottom and were, of course, heavier for a small crew to handle.

Fortunately the skiff *Emmeline* was measured up by the late P. J. Oke and the plans reconstructed from details given by H. David and J. C. Evans, the previous owner. Built by William Paynter at St Ives, *c* 1865 for William Burt, the length overall was 40 ft, keel 31 ft, beam 10 ft 7 in, depth 5 ft 8 in. Straight-stemmed and deep-heeled, the draught for'ard was 3 ft 6 in, aft 7 ft. The sternpost was well raked, and the square overhanging counter stern with low freeboard aft made for ease in working the dredges. (Picture, p 178.)

Steam capstans were first fitted early in the 1870s; previously the dredges were hauled by the mast winch. The hull was fully decked with a hatch abaft the mast giving access to the hold below, with sail racks on either side; for'ard was the fo'c'sle. Ballast was copper dross stowed below the platform.

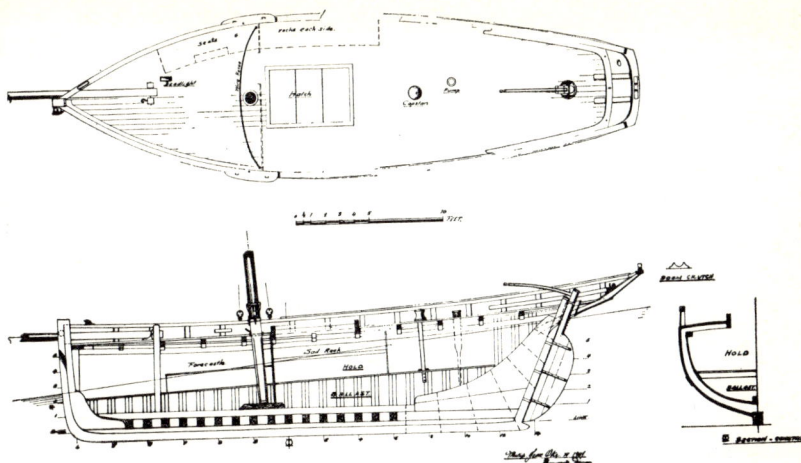

Plans of Mumbles oyster skiff *Emmeline*

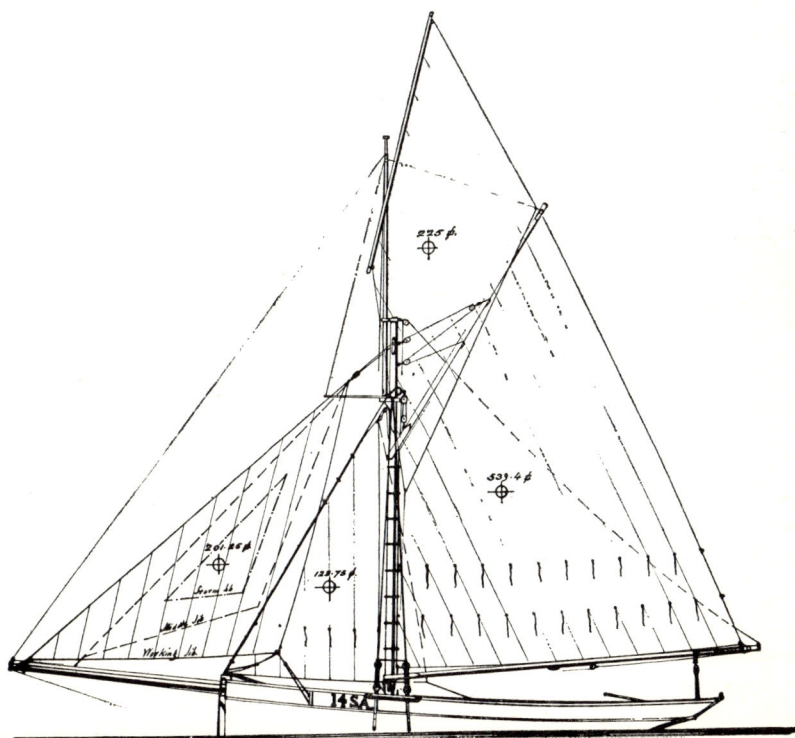

Sail plan of *Emmeline*

Spar dimensions were:

Mainmast	Deck to cap 30 ft, dia 8 in, masthead 6 ft.
Topmast	Fid to sheave pin 18 ft, dia 5 to 3 in.
Gaff	22 ft, dia 4½ to 3 in.
Boom	29 to 30 ft, dia 5 to 4 in.
Bowsprit	LOA 24 to 25 ft, outboard 16 ft 9 in, dia 6 to 5½ in.
Topsail Yard	20 ft 6 in, dia 2½ to 3 in.
Crosstrees	8 ft spread.

The bowsprit, to starboard of the stem and stepped in small bitts, had a bobstay but no shrouds; to port was a roller. The mast was supported by two shrouds a side, set up with deadeyes and lanyards, and a forestay, usually wire, led over a groove in the stemhead, back through a hole in the stem to a deadeye secured to the bitts. On account of the narrow beam, chain plates were usual. The topmast shrouds led over crosstrees to blocks and tackle secured to the bulwarks; the stay led to a block on the end of the bowsprit.

The lead of the running gear was 'skipper's choice', some preferring spider bands at the foot of the mast, others belaying pins in the rail on either side. Throat halyards went to port, peak to starboard, and topping lift to port. Staysail halyards went to starboard, jib halyards were usually double with one end belayed on either side. The staysail was sheeted to an iron horse across the foredeck, the jib sheets, double, led in through a hole in bulwarks to cleats inboard. The topsail sheet led through a cleat at the gaff down through a block on a long pendant fast at the hounds, belaying on the starboard rail. In summer a large gaff topsail was set, in winter a jib-headed one. A large, small, or spitfire jib was carried according to the weather; the foresail had one row of reef points, the mainsail two, and the sail was loose-footed with the luff secured to mast hoops, although earlier cutters may well have used a lacing. When the mainsail was stowed, the boom rested in a crutch in the centre of the taffrail.

Although Tenby has a long history, fishing was never on a

very extensive scale, but fishermen acted as pilots when sailing ships were forced to seek shelter, and the harbour was frequented by Brixham trawlers and Mumbles oyster skiffs.

In the sixteenth century a favourite ground was Will's Mark, an area about 3 miles by $1\frac{1}{2}$ miles between Caldy Island and Lundy, consisting of a shoal patch with 12 to 16 fathoms over it, deepening away to 32 fathoms.

Open boats engaged in line fishing inshore until late in the nineteenth century, but numbers seldom exceeded about 30, and sean nets were used off the beach for herring and mackerel. The boats, rigged with a dipping fore lug and sprit mizzen, carried a crew of two or three, the larger ones going drift-netting for herring. Oyster beds lay about 2 miles off Caldy Island and were dredged over during the winter months; a few small cutters went trawling.

The luggers had a keel length ranging from 15 to 25 ft, hulls were clench-built, straight-stemmed with raking transom sterns, and open except for a short foredeck extending to the mast with a low cuddy about 5 ft long and 3 ft 6 in high, entered by a sliding hatch in the bulkhead. This was used as a sail locker, but could afford some shelter to the crew; inside ballast was usually iron pigs—kentledge—stowed below the floorboards.

The foremast, stepped on the floors, was clamped to the 'crosspiece', the mizzen followed the rake of the transom against which it was stepped to starboard of the rudder head, and the sprit mizzen sheeted to the end of an ash outrigger passing out through a hole in the transom.

In the 1930s *Seahorse*, one of the few remaining under sail, was measured up by the late P. J. Oke and I have several photographs of her under sail, taken by my friend H. Oliver Hill. This lugger was built at Tenby by James Newt, *c* 1886, as *Three Sisters*, length overall 24 ft, beam 8 ft 10 in, depth 3 ft $8\frac{1}{2}$ in, three thwarts and one aft with side seats extending to No 3 thwart, oars rowed in thole pins. Floors flat, bilges rounded, good sheer, light spars, no standing rigging.

Spar dimensions were:

Foremast	LOA	24 ft 8 in, dia 5½ in to 3 in.
Foreyard		12 ft 4 in, dia 2¾ in to 1½ in.
Bowsprit		15 ft 6 in, outboard 8 ft 10 in, dia 3¼ in to 2½ in.
Mizzen mast		12 ft 4 in, dia 3 in to 2¾ in.
Outrigger		9 ft 6 in, dia 2½ in to 2¼ in.
Sprit		14 ft 8 in, dia 2 in.

The mainsail had three rows of reef points, three jibs—the big, working and winter—were carried, and a trysail, laced to the mast, was set in bad weather. The bowsprit went out through a gammon iron to starboard of the stem and stepped in a small, square, iron bitt near the foremast. The sprit was set to port; the fore halyards belayed round a pin on the weather side and were moved over when the lug was dipped, the jib halyards went to a cleat on the crosspiece. In bad weather, when the bowsprit was run in, the jib tack hooked to the stemhead. There were no bowsprit shrouds, only a bobstay with two single blocks purchase, the lower block being shackled to a short chain on the stem.

During the summer, the boats were mainly used for taking visitors on trips; when dried out in the harbour the hulls were kept upright on legs.

In Cardigan Bay records of herring fishing at Aberystwyth date back at least to the tenth century. The boats were small but numbers and size increased until, by the 1750s, they registered about 12 tons, many trading vessels going fishing and vice versa. Harbour facilities were poor until the building of a stone pier about a century later. A few trawlers, cutter-rigged, had clench-built hulls, chiefly half-decked, and in 1872 only six second-class boats were registered compared with 70 third class, classified as rowing boats; but Cardigan Bay was frequented by smacks from Lancashire ports.

Drift nets were 5 fathoms long, 4 fathoms deep, attached to the 'upper tant' suspended below the buoy rope by lines whose length regulated the depth at which the nets fished. Stones on the 'lower tant' kept the nets upright in the water.

The smaller boats carried six to eight nets which were shot at sunset; after an hour or so the first net was hauled and if the catch was good, the remainder were hauled. Fish and nets were bundled amidships and cleared ashore, the herring generally being sent by rail to Liverpool or hawked locally. The measure was a 'long hundred'—126 herring, a 'meise' being a nominal five hundred.

The cutters were similar to the Morecambe Bay boats fully described later, hulls being clench- or carvel-built, many by Crossfield at Arnside and Armour at Fleetwood. Other boats were three-masted, no headsails; the fore and main sails had short gaffs, no booms and two lines of reef points, sprit mizzens. Keel length varied from 23 to 25 ft, with transom sterns, four thwarts, and shingle ballast. Spars were light, the foremast was stepped close to the stem, the mainmast against the foreside of the middle thwart, the mizzen raked at the same angle as the transom. There was no standing rigging, but peak and throat halyards were always set up on opposite sides. The later double-ended boats were generally used to take visitors for trips round the bay, a more profitable occupation than fishing, which was ever a precarious calling.

The fisheries on the Lancashire coast are of great antiquity, records going back to the time of the Norman Conquest. North Meols Bank, a long sandy flat some 20 miles north of Liverpool, was then and for centuries after only a desolate shore backed by sand dunes. During the fishing season the men lived in log huts where Southport now stands.

By the end of the eighteenth century a few trawlers were selling their catches at Liverpool, taking as many as 100 pairs of soles in a few hours, selling at 3d to 4d a lb, shrimps fetched a few pence a quart, herring about a shilling a hundred.

Before a lifeboat was stationed on the coast about 1860, the fishermen saved many lives from the numerous ships wrecked on the dangerous sandbanks; in later years they manned the life-boats. The great disaster of 9 December 1886 was still spoken about when I was in Southport 40 years later. The barque

Mexico was driven ashore in a fearful storm on the Birkdale Sands; three lifeboats from Southport, Lytham and St Annes launched to the rescue. In a short time the Southport boat capsized, drowning 14 of the crew, the St Anne's lifeboat lost every man of her 27 crew, but the Lytham boat kept on and saved 13 lives.

Shrimping thrived as resorts sprang up on the dunes and by 1900 about 70 boats were employed, many only a few years old. Takings were divided into five shares, one going to the boat, two to each of the crew of two. Over a year a fair average was around 30 quarts per boat for every fishing day. Unfortunately the channels frequented by shrimps were constantly changing and silting up, a condition aggravated by the construction of training walls in the estuary of the Ribble. Finally Southport became practically inaccessible, the lifeboat was removed, the fleet of shrimpers sold and most of the fishermen moved elsewhere, except for a few who continued shrimping as best the tide allowed.

The early smacks, 'nobbies' to use the local name, were about 36 ft long and drew 4 ft of water, the later vessels ran up to 40 ft, but draught had increased to 5 to 6 ft. Hulls were fully decked with a cockpit aft, cutter-rigged and fished with a beam trawl. In the palmy days, three boatbuilding yards, a sailmaker and three ropewalks had flourished, but many fishermen made their own sails.

When 'boat-shanking' for shrimps four nets were streamed, the 'forward', 'tack', 'quarter' and 'hindmost', the first and last being boomed out with a long pole. Among other methods was 'putting', in which a man on foot pushed a 'power-net' in front of him in shallow water, seeking shrimps left behind in the sand ripples. Another method was 'cart-shanking', when two nets were streamed from a pole across the shafts behind the horse, a dangerous job should the horse drop into one of the many holes in the sands, when it might be necessary to cut the harness to save man and beast. A good haul might yield as many as 100 quarts.

The best time for shrimping was from August to November, the heaviest catches being made when the water was cloudy. Few shrimps were caught in cold weather or when 'snow water' was coming down the rivers.

Before the silting up of many channels boats left at any convenient time, but in later years only around high-water neap tides, and an hour before and after high water springs; this meant being 12 hours at sea, and catches had to be boiled on board instead of ashore, as was the case with shrimps caught by putting or cart-shanking. Then the catch was washed, boiled in coppers and finally picked—'shilled'—by women who could shell about a quart an hour, the work being easier if the shrimps were boiled in fresh water. The shelled shrimps were then delivered to merchants, known as 'badgers', for potting and distribution to distant parts of the country.

The original Lancashire boats often had transom sterns, and until the end of the 1890s had an almost plumb stem with a small round at the forefoot and a little rocker at the forward end of the keel. The ballast was almost all inside and the bows had a very hollow entry. Boats of this type, but with counter sterns and moderately raked sternposts, were still being built in 1906 when the cutaway model was well established. The older form was preferred for channel fishing, for which the newer form was not so well suited.

The Southport and Fleetwood boats ranged from about 34 ft to 40–48 ft in the largest type, whose draught was 6 ft to 6 ft 6 in. At these ports the men favoured a stem fairly plumb to the waterline, but cut away rapidly below into a well-rockered keel to which was fitted an iron keel of from 1 to 3 tons weight, as well as considerable inside ballast.

They were very wet boats in a seaway and steered hard off the wind. Much of this hard steering was due to lack of trouble over arranging the sail plan to balance the hull, aggravated by the very hard-bilged quarters which many had. The very long gaffs were also a disadvantage as the jaws were often strained badly by the twisting of the sail in a hard breeze.

Q

Sometime late in the 1890s the midship section of many of the boats became more and more hollow and this was almost universal after 1902. Many of the boats at Lytham and St Annes had rounder sections with little hollow in the mid-section. This feature of hollow sections became rather exaggerated. At least one deep-sea smack from Fleetwood was built on these lines and was so fast that she challenged any craft to sail against her for money. The term 'smack' was applied only to the ketch-rigged trawlers working from Fleetwood and Liverpool.

An average size would be 35 ft overall, beam 10 ft 6 in, with a draught of from 5 ft to 5 ft 6 in, $1\frac{1}{2}$ tons of iron on the keel and about $3\frac{1}{2}$ tons inside ballast in pigs. The sail area was around 900 sq ft, with the mainsail about 500 sq ft; the rig was heavy to work. Many suffered damage to their counters and were fitted with a bulkhead, known as a 'tuck', inside the counter to make a watertight compartment. No bobstay was fitted. There were two shrouds a side and a forestay, the staysail hoisting on a single whip. Three working jibs were carried, the halyard being led through two blocks on each side of the mast-head, and the fall going down to the port pinrail; the standing part was set up to starboard. The topping lift was double and a fish tackle from the masthead was used to get the net in. The contents were poured into large baskets and later sorted on the side decks.

Some of the Morecambe crews sported bowler hats at sea, and during the summer many of their boats were hired out to business men from the cotton towns for weekends and holidays, the skipper remaining in charge. Trips were made to the Isle of Man or the Solway Firth.

A few boats, such as *Eureka*, built by Gibsons at Fleetwood in 1905, had a centreboard. Many of the craft built by Armour of Fleetwood were designed by W. Stoba. John Leather writes, 'I do not know who he was but have had reason to examine the ex-pilot boat *Theodora* designed by him and built by Armour as the *Kindly Light*. She is a most interesting shape and shows the theories of the better-known Lancashire type carried out in a craft 50 ft long.'

The inshore waters along the Lancashire coast and in beautiful Morecambe Bay called for a special type of craft, able to ride out the fierce sou'westerly gales with a 'fetch' of over 120 miles to the Irish coast, yet capable of working in the shallow water where shrimps and flat fish were found in abundance.

These arduous conditions produced the handsome, counter-sterned vessel, pole-masted with cutter rig, known as the Morecambe Bay prawner, or 'nobby', whose length varied from 32 to 38 ft overall, with a beam of from 9 to 11 ft and a draught around 4 ft. These fine craft were well able to face the short, steep seas rapidly kicked up in blowing weather, while the sweet lines and big sail plan gave the speed required to race the tides and bring the catch fresh to market. The handiness of the rig allowed the boat to be sailed by one man if necessary, although a man and a boy were the usual crew.

In the earlier boats the sails were 'coated' by first wetting them, then brushing one side with coal tar, three pints for the mainsail of a 28-ft keel boat. Next the sails were coated with boiled oil and red ochre, after the sail had been well wetted so that it took little oil, then a dressing of boiled oil alone until the sails got so polished as to shine.

Prawners took the ground on their bilges, rising to the flood tide without difficulty.

Morecambe Bay looks a vast expanse of water at high tide, but appearances are deceptive and much of the ground consists of large sandbanks drying out at low water, leaving innumerable channels between them, many with cliff-like sides, and in these deep gullies shrimps are found in myriads. Between hauls the catch was riddled and the small fry thrown overboard. In the 1860s 25 to 30 quarts a day was reckoned a fair catch for a boat, and about 150 shrimpers were working compared with eight or nine 50 years earlier. The coming of railways had led to intensive development of land along the coast, and seaside resorts sprang up like mushrooms. The hordes of visitors from the manufacturing towns inland, spending a few days holiday by the sea, soon created a demand for the succulent pink shrimp, and when families returned home what better to take as a gift to gran'ma than a jar of potted shrimps with the lid decorated by a coloured picture, now cherished as 'collector's pieces'? Thus another local industry was created, the wives and daughters of the fishermen boiling the shrimps, then dexterously separating 'shruffs' from edible portion and making up a tasty paste. Modest fortunes were made and better boats built locally; and where could a more lovely background be found for work?—the calm waters of the bay reflecting the white clouds overhead, in the distance the beautiful wooded slopes around Arnside and Grange, backed by the majestic line of the hills and mountains of the Lake District.

This was a visitor's impression, but it was a very different story in winter when the great sou'west gales, driving deluges of rain before them, whipped the short seas into white-capped fury. Then the fishermen blessed that short pole mast which did away with a long, naked topmast aloft, and half-decks kept the water out of hulls smoking along, three reefs down in the mainsail and one in the foresail.

Never shall I forget the amazing contrasts I saw in the bay long years ago when smiling winter mornings gave place to wild afternoons and fierce squalls blotted out every landmark. Another astonishing sight was several horses and carts going out across the sands into the shallow water; the men threw out small trawl nets and the horses plodded along, knowing as well as their masters what to do. As far as my memory serves, the mouth of the net had two beams kept apart by short sticks or light iron rods. Closer inshore were men pushing a shove-net, and with three lines of shrimpers a prawn had to be pretty lucky to survive, as farther out were the cutters.

Fishing with line or net had been practised for hundreds of years, mostly from open boats whose design had marked Viking characteristics; not surprising as the Norsemen held sovereignty over the Isle of Man until 1265, founding many settlements on the mainland where a few local dialect words remind one of those distant days. The cutter rig was favoured in Manx waters until the coming of the Cornish luggers to the herring fishing during the early years of the nineteenth century, and undoubtedly similar vessels were seen in Morecambe Bay.

Some of the first cutters had a long mast and topmast, setting an almost square-headed gaff topsail, heavy hulls with straight stems and keels; but the later tendency among fishermen was for a shorter polemast and a long yard on the luff of the topsail, peaked well up. Bowsprits, run out through a gammoning iron to port or starboard of the stem, had no bobstays, and main booms rarely extended beyond the taffrail. (Pictures, p. 200.)

The constant call for speed and more speed led to builders adopting yachting features, and the zenith was reached at the turn of this century. The most noticeable feature was the change from the long, straight keel to a graceful cutaway stem with a rounded forefoot sweeping down to join the rockered keel in an unbroken curve from the waterline almost to the raking sternpost and making the boats very quick on the helm. The lines were easy, garboards hollow, floors sharp with well-rounded bilges, a fine entrance with bold, high bow, the sheer was brought down to give a low freeboard aft for ease in working the gear, but the somewhat narrow counter had ample buoyancy to keep the stern well up in a seaway. (Picture, p 199.)

A nobby was very weatherly, working to within four points of the wind in the hands of fishermen well versed in the art of making a boat *sail*. Many a fine 'prawner' came from Crossfield's yard at Arnside near the mouth of the river Kent. I was fortunate enough to get into touch with Mr F. J. Crossfield who checked my draft notes and added further information.

The practice was to build from a half-model made up of six pieces of $\frac{1}{4}$-in pine to a scale of $\frac{3}{4}$ in to 1 ft, or 1 : 18. This gave the deck plan with the sheer line screwed above at right angles; below were four sections, the first about 5 ft 4 in from the stem, the second 10 ft 8 in, the third 16 ft 8 in and the fourth at 22 ft.

The keel, of elm or oak, sided 4 in, moulded 8 in, was laid down on blocks, the oak stem with natural curved forefoot boxed to it, with a heavy knee inside to strengthen the join, aft,

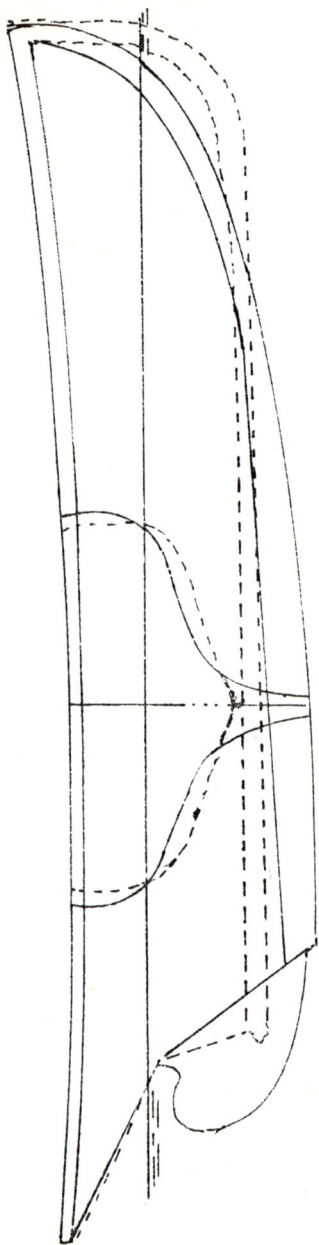

MORECAMBE BAY PRAWNER 40 ft L.O.A BUILT BY CROSSFIELD

OLD TYPE ------ NEW TYPE ————

Sketch plan of old and new type Morecambe Bay prawner

the raking sternpost was erected. Oak floors, sided 3 in, moulded 6 in, were spaced 11 in; the futtocks, butt joined and bolted together, were 3 in sided, moulded $3\frac{1}{2}$ in amidships, $1\frac{3}{4}$ in at ends.

The four station frames, sawn out to the mould taken from the half-model, were set up at right angles to the keel and a stringer and ribbands run round from stem to stern. The shape of the remaining frames was found by the 'chain'; this was something like a glorified cycle chain, the links being short lengths of wood riveted together with copper nails and rooves. After being soaked in water, the wood swelled sufficiently to make the chain stiff, but remained pliable enough for it to be pressed against stringer and ribbands from the top to the keel, thus making the shape of the frame required. The chain was then laid on a suitable piece of oak, natural-grown with the grain following the required curve; the outline was chalked in and the frame sawn out.

The oak deadwood aft with a heavy knee inside was through-bolted with galvanised iron bolts to keel and sternpost. The oak counter framing was 4 in sided, 6 in moulded; beams were usually larch, 3 in sided and moulded, with 5 in camber. Inside the frames at deck level a stringer, 1 in sided and moulded $6\frac{1}{2}$ in amidships, 5 in at bow and stern, was bolted and in way of fo'c'sle and mast a shelf piece of larch or oak, 6 ft long, 6 in wide and 2 in deep, was fastened at right angles to the stringer; on it the beams rested. Bearers bolted to the frames carried the platforms.

A larch or pitchpine keelson, about 15 ft long, sided 3 in, moulded 7 in, extending from the deadwood aft, was bolted to the floors; on it the mast was stepped. The planking, carvel built, was 1 in thick, fastened with galvanised spikes; the bottom planks were larch, topsides pitchpine, with a $1\frac{1}{4}$-in oak plank, 12 ft long, at the turn of the bilge amidships, and a 3 in by $1\frac{7}{8}$ in hardwood rubbing strake or wale one plank below the covering board.

Deck planking was 3 in by $1\frac{1}{4}$ in spruce, tongue and groove jointed and nibbed into an oak covering board, a light 5- to 6-in rail forming the very low bulwarks. Abaft the mast was a long narrow cockpit, about 13 ft 6 in long, 3 ft wide, with 6 in by 1 in oak coamings and rounded ends. Aft was a small steering platform about 1 ft higher than that in the cockpit; in the middle was a thwart, kneed on either side, and the half beams under the deck were supported by short turned pillars bolted to this thwart.

For'ard of the steering platform a small hatch gave access to the store below where the anchor, cable and gear were stowed. A cleat was bolted to the underside of the half beams on either side of the cockpit within easy reach of the helmsman; here the head sheets were belayed, or to pins in the middle thwart.

Two and a half tons of iron ballast were stowed amidships between the floor timbers. To port was the pump made entirely of wood, the casing 4 in square with the suction boarded in both sides between two frames, thus eliminating piping. At the for'ard end of the cockpit was a bulkhead with a sliding door opening into the cabin where the floor was in three levels owing to the upward sweep of the rockered keel. In it was a stove, with a built-in seat on either side from the bulkhead to the first step in the floor, a small glass decklight being the only source of illumination. Except for the cockpit, the deck was unbroken, there being no hatches or companion.

The rudder stock of 2-in iron, passed through the deck and counter in an iron tube, its lower end working in a hole in the 'skeg' where the $3\frac{1}{2}$ in by $\frac{3}{4}$ in iron keel plate turned 1 ft up the sternpost. An iron gudgeon, 3 in by $\frac{3}{4}$ in, was bolted about 2 ft up the sternpost and the wooden rudder was secured by two iron straps a side, bolted to the wood and riveted to the iron stock. The upper end of the stock was cut square to take the tiller, which was through-bolted.

On deck on either side of the rudder head were two 3-in sq posts bolted to the beams and stern timbers. 'These were for trawling uses. The trawl rope is made fast for'ard and passed outside the rigging, and is then put behind these "knogs" or timber heads. The ship is steered by these when trawling by means of a spring rope,' to quote Mr Crossfield. Six feet from the stem were two similar posts, bolted to beams, stringer and shelf piece and used for belaying when hauling the trawl. The bowsprit bitts were bolted to a 4-in sq beam, and to starboard was a mooring post. For'ard of the mast a pinrail was bolted to two bitts; in some boats there was one on either rail under the shrouds.

A 30-lb anchor was carried and 15 fathoms of 5/16-in chain led in over a roller on the side opposite to the gammoning iron and stowed below the platform right aft, 'usually under the ballast boards or floor, rather unhandy but very seldom used as they ride to moorings when in harbour'.

There were two yards in Arnside, both Crossfield's, and building time was approximately six weeks with four men working. In 1912 the cost for a 32 ft by 9 ft beam hull, including blocks, mast and spars, was £60. 'We rarely supplied sails, as at that date the fishermen usually made their own and made quite a good job. Running gear was manilla, throat and jib halyards for 32-ft class, 9/16 in diameter and peak and other gear a size lighter.'

Mast and spar dimensions were:

Mast	27 ft from deck to top, dia 6½ in at deck.
Bowsprit	14 ft overall, 10 ft outboard, dia 6 in at gammoning iron.
Main Gaff	17 ft 6 in, dia 3½ in at jaw's end.
Main Boom	20 ft 6 in, dia 3½ in at mainsheet strop.
Topsail Yard	19 ft 6 in, dia 3 in tapered.

Shrouds were wire, of 7/16 in diameter, set up with deadeyes to straps bolted outside the hull. The forestay, of similar size, set up with a shackle to an eye on the iron strap on the foreside of stem. The topping lift was to port, the fall belayed on the pinrail, peak halyards went to two blocks on the mast and belayed on the pinrail. Main halyards went to the throat double block and belayed on the pinrail. The main sheet went from a single block working on a short iron horse on deck,

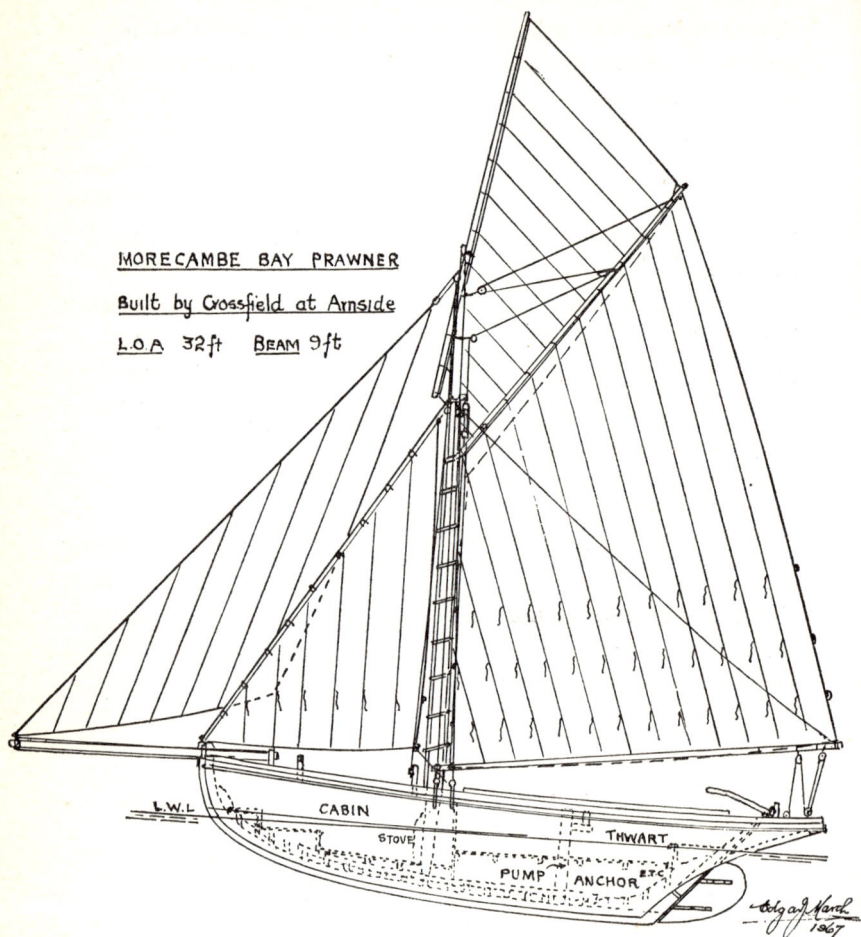

MORECAMBE BAY PRAWNER
Built by Crossfield at Arnside
L.O.A 32ft BEAM 9ft

Sail plan of Morecambe Bay prawner

through a single block on the end of the boom, down through a
sheave in the first block up to a single block strapped to the
boom about 15 in inside, down to a single block and the fall
belayed to a cleat on deck.

The topsail halyards were bent to the yard about 7 ft from
the lower end and led through a sheave in the mast to belay on
the pinrail. The tack went to the foot of the mast and belayed

to an eyebolt bolted through the deck. The sheet led through a sheave at the end of gaff, down through a block under jaws and belayed to an eyebolt in the deck.

The foresail was hanked to the forestay, the halyards led through a single block hooked to an eye on the iron band round the mast and belayed on the pinrail; the sheet went through leads in the deck to belay on a pin through the thwart. The jib was hooked to an iron traveller on the bowsprit, inhaul and outhaul belaying round the bowsprit bitts. The halyards were fast to a single block hooked to an eye on the foreside of the masthead, led down through a single block hooked in a cringle in the head of the sail, back through an upper block and the fall was belayed to the pinrail. The sheets led through fairleads on either side of the deck and belayed on a pin through the thwart.

The loose-footed mainsail had three lines of reef points, the upper ones 3 ft deep, and the lower 2 ft. The foresail had one one line 2 ft 6 in deep. (Picture, p 179.)

FISHING GEAR

Trawl beams were usually of ash, 20 to 25 ft in length, the nets being up to one and a half times the length of the beam, $\frac{1}{2}$-in mesh. The short ground rope was threaded through wooden bobbins, 10 in in diameter in the middle, down to 6 in diameter on either side; these eased the drag on a hard bottom. The warp was manilla, $1\frac{1}{8}$ in diameter, approximately 60 fathoms long, shackled to two manilla bridles which, in turn were shackled to the foreside of the trawl irons. The gear cost about £15. (Picture, p. 179.)

Trawling was usually in 6 to 15 fathoms and the net was hauled approximately every 50 minutes. No capstan was used before the engine days, but now worked by the engine off a shaft through the foredeck. Can tow off either side, but can only haul from the same side as you shoot from without changing the trawl rope round. The favourite grounds were mostly at the foot of Lune, a fisherman goes round with the clock like the tides, fishing day and night . . . The ironwork was made by a local blacksmith who made a very good job. Catches were boiled on board in an ordinary copper set in an iron case and standing as far forward as bulkhead will permit.

Mr Crossfield mentioned that the hardwoods were mostly local grown and sawn by a steam saw. Hulls were painted in various colours. Arnside was a lovely spot as I knew it 40 years ago, with well-wooded slopes, and on the foreshore several prawners lay, some with clinker-built hulls.

Others builders were W. Armour at Fleetwood, R. Ingram at Walney Ferry and A. Anderson at Millom, but the majority of the prawners were constructed by Crossfield Bros.

THE ISLE OF MAN

As the Isle of Man owed allegiance to the kings of Norway until 1265, the local boats bore a marked resemblance to Viking ships, fragments of which have been found in ship graves in the north of the island. One such mound, dating back to about AD 900, contained a lead sinker for a hand-line, probably the earliest evidence of fishing in Manx waters. In 1577 there is a reference to 'boates that fish either in England or in Ireland, either for herring or gray fish', a general name principally given to cod, but including hake, conger and ling. These boats, no doubt built by men steeped in the Norse tradition, carried a single square sail. The smaller craft used for line fishing were known as 'balk-yawls', balk being derived from 'baak', a long line, and yawl from 'yol', Scandinavian terms. In the early nineteenth century the name was spelt 'balc' and the boats were described as being long and open with a light gunwale cut to receive the oars which were squared at the point of bearing to fit the notches in the gunwale. A short mast, stepped for'ard of amidships, carried a tall, rather square dipping lug used when the weather permitted. These boats were easily beached above high-water level, either in harbours or on shingle banks. By the middle of the century the design had been modified, copper

taking the place of iron fastenings, and a square transom re-
placing the sharp stern.

Line fishing was carried on more or less throughout the year,
except during the herring season. The small boat fishing which
began about about late October was known as 'low sea' fishing,
being carried on fairly close inshore. It continued until about
the end of January when the larger boats fitted out, lines were
now shot in deep water some distance from land, cod being the
principal catch on hooks baited with whelks. This fishing
lasted until April, then conger were sought until the beginning
of the herring season in June. Handlines were used in Douglas
Bay for whiting.

Mr John Lace, of the Lhen shore, who sailed in 'baulk-
yawls' in the 1880s stated that the average size was 17 to 18 ft
keel, with a beam of 5 ft 8 in, the boats being clinker-built with
elm frames inserted. The stem was fairly straight but the transom stern raked considerably, an asset to boats launched stern
first from the shore. Two pairs of oars were worked, four
thwarts being fitted; against the second the mast was stepped,
its length being about that of the boat. A broad lugsail was set,
the tack going to a hook in the bow, the halyard to a hook and
cleat on the second thwart against the weather gunwale; there
was no other stay to the mast.

Balk-yawls were usually manned by seven men who baited,
shot and hauled the lines, rowing the boats to and from the
fishing grounds if there was insufficient wind to use the sail.
Some boats went as far as the Lancashire coast where fish were
once abundant, 600 cod being a day's catch on occasion; and a
big fish fetched a shilling on the quay.

Many of the transom-sterned yawls were rigged with an 8-
cloth standing lug, with the clew hauled out on a traveller to the
end of a boom fitted with a gooseneck. There were three rows of
reef points, the four upper knittles reducing the sail to about
half-size. The 4-cloth foresail had the tack hooked into a short
iron bumpkin at the stem; the head went to the top of the mast.

A very fine model of the Ramsey cod boat *King Orry* RY 75,

made by Thomas Brayden, one-time harbour master at Ramsey, was awarded a medal at the International Fisheries Exhibition of 1883. It is now in the Manx Museum and Mr Basil Megaw, the director, kindly had a photograph taken for me by Mr W. A. Mackie in September 1949. (Picture, p 180.) The clinker-built hull has very fine lines aft, oars worked in swivelling rowlocks; the boom projects over the stern and the sheet traverses on a short iron horse above the short tiller, the fall belaying round a pin on either gunwale. The lug halyards are set up to starboard, those for the foresail to port.

Eighty-two second-class boats were registered in 1872 in the Isle of Man. (Picture, p 198.)

SCOTLAND

In the Upper Solway, the Annan trawling smacks fished for flounders in winter, shrimps and prawns during the summer. Their design closely resembled that of the Morecambe Bay prawners which came to the Firth in the 1850s. Hulls were carvel-built, keel length 23 ft, length overall 30 ft, beam 9 ft to 9 ft 6 in, draught 2 ft for'ard, 3 to 4 ft aft, fully decked except for a narrow open hatchway with high coamings. Carpenter's work on the hull was around £45, and the fishermen usually made their own sails and trawls but, ready for sea with sails and rigging, £80 was a fair price. The crew numbered two in winter, but often only one in summer; line-fishing for codling was carried on inshore. When shrimping, the boats left Annan on the ebb and fished down with the tide and back on the flood, working an 18-ft beam trawl and cooking the catch in a copper in the hold.

The lower reaches of the Firth of Clyde lying exposed to the prevailing winds, made it essential for the fishing boats to have good seakeeping ability, be handy under sail, easily rowed and light enough to be beached.

The skiffs from Saltcoats, Millport and Largs had a length of around 19 ft, beam 5 ft 6 in, depth inside 2 ft, double-ended but rounder in the stern than in the bow, with a good sheer. Hulls were clinker-built of pine $\frac{5}{8}$ in thick, ballasted with bags of sand or stone which were invariably shifted up to windward if making a passage.

The fishermen were fine, hardy seamen, and keen racers at local regattas, many becoming yacht hands and sailing masters. Ninian of Largs was renowed for building fast boats, his *Kate*, 288 GK, the winner of over 30 races, being beaten in only two events by his next best boat, *Marjorie*. In the early days a square-headed standing lugsail with two rows of reef points was set; a jib on a running bowsprit was a later innovation.

By the middle of the nineteenth century yachting had become a popular sport on the Clyde and many a man of humble birth steered big cutters and schooners to victory during the summer months. Three Largs men, Blair a tailor, McKirdy a weaver, and Houston a fisherman, became crack skippers, all men of strong principles and never afraid to stand up for them if occasion demanded, despite all blandishments.

The owner of the 53-ton cutter *Cymba*, built at Fairlie by William Fife, wished to challenge *Mosquito*, to be sailed by Nicholls, to a sailing match for £500 a side, but McKirdy flatly refused to take part in any race for a wager. Sunday sailing was unheard of, but there seems to have been little objection to hard drinking.

John Houston started life in fishing boats with an occasional day in yachts, and soon showed his prowess at a tiller, finally becoming skipper of big cutters and schooners, including the famous *Fiona* at the age of 41, racing her in the Solent with conspicuous success for some 20 years. So autocratic did he become that it was not unknown for him to threaten to lock the owner in the cabin if he continued to interfere with the sailing of his own yacht!

The Marquis of Ailsa spent much of his time as a lad sailing in fishing nobbies, and such was his regard for the sterling qualities of the fishermen that, when he succeeded to the title, he had the 35-ton cutter *Foxhound* crewed by local men and skippered by Sloan for her first racing season.

On the West Coast, the season for herring fishing depended upon the locality, and along the Ayrshire shores and in the Firth flounders were caught in a few fathoms of water after the herring season had finished, beam trawls being used. Hand-lining for whiting and haddock was carried out inshore, long-lines were used in the deeper parts of the Firth. The Ballantrae banks, 3 to 4 miles off the coast of Ayr, 8 to 10 miles long and 3 to 5 miles broad, teemed with cod and turbot during the herring season; they were caught in nets or on long lines, the hooks baited with herring. At times large numbers of ling were taken; a favourite ground for setting long lines lay from 8 to 10 miles offshore. Voracious feeders, as many as 15 herring have been found in the stomach of a turbot, 30 to 35 inside one codfish.

In September 1849 John Wood wrote:

I have to state that we have no fishing boats here (Port Glasgow) but in Gourock or Largs there are some good specimens of boats used in Loch Fyne. They are by no means handsome, but are very stiff under sail and weatherly. Their form is spoiled, I think, in order to get them with a short keel for working in narrow waters, as well as for saving the cost of building, the price being reckoned by the length of keel. They are all open, and in these sheltered lochs that is, perhaps, attended with no inconvenience.

There are two classes of boats in use on this coast.

Class 1: 27 ft overall, 11 ft breadth, is getting numerous and is, I think, a decided improvement as compared with the old boats. The stern is upright, the bow narrow, resembling a yacht, and they sail fast by the wind, most part build at Rothesay, Fairlie, and Ardrishaig, many in Gourock, Greenock, Campbeltown and other places. Until of late years they were built entirely open and rigged with two heavy gaff sails and jib. In fishing, they used to unship the mainmast and work entirely with the foresail, by degrees the smack rig has come almost wholly into use, as well as a half deck. These boats make long voyages with only two men, in fishing they have more.

On the Ayrshire coast is a numerous class of boats, about 25 ft by 8 ft, entirely open. They have a very broad, round stern and narrow bow, rigged with one large lugsail and jib. They are handsome and work and sail well. . . . A new boat built at Rothe-say and comes very near the usual form of the Loch Fyne boats. They are, however, a good deal varied, principally in the midship section, some having more hollow in the floor than others. They are all pinched for length of keel because the price is constantly made at so much per foot keel.

Another has an improved bow, introduced by Mr Fyfe of Fairlie and I have no doubt it will get into general use, as being better adapted to the cutter rig than the full bow, as the jib lifts the bow, while the after leech of the mainsail depresses the stern, whereas the schooner—or wherry rig as it is called—required a full harping and narrow stern, to keep the bow up under the weight of the foresail, the foremast being close forward and up-right.

A clench-built, smack-rigged boat, built by Black at Rothe-say, had an overall length of 27 ft, keel 22 ft, half decked, 3 tons of ballast, capacity 5·3 tons, crew six, hull weight 3·4 tons, cost ready for sea £35.

A similar boat 28 ft overall, keel 25 ft, half decked, a hull weight of 4·2 tons, capacity 5½ tons, ballast 3 tons, and a crew of six, was built by Fyfe at Fairlie for £35.

The herring shoals entered the Firth of Clyde on the western side early in the summer and worked northwards, at times frequenting Loch Long and the Gareloch, but their movements were by no means certain from year to year, hence catches fluctuated considerably. In 1873 there was a marked scarcity in Loch Fyne, always noted for the excellent quality of its herring.

The principal stations on Loch Fyne were Tarbert, about 6 miles from the entrance where the width is from 4 to 5 miles, Ardrishaig where the loch narrows to 1 to 2 miles, and Inverary at the northern extremity.

In the mid-nineteenth century there were four classes of herring boats in Loch Fyne, chiefly built at Fairlie, Rothesay, Tarbert and Ardrishaig.

First class. Length of keel 21 ft, half-decked, one mast, rig mainsail, jib and foresail. Cost of hull, sails, mast and oars, £60. Complement of herring nets, fully mounted with buoys and buoy ropes, £40. Total cost, £100.

R

Second class. Length of keel 19 ft, half-decked, similar rig. Cost of hull, sails, mast and oars, £50. Complement of nets, £35. Total cost, £85.

Third class. Length of keel 18 ft, one half of this class half-decked, one mast, rig mainsail and jib. Cost complete, £39. Complement of nets, £30. Total cost, £69.

Fourth class. Length of keel 17 ft, all open, one mast, rig lugsail. Cost complete, £20. Complement of nets, £25. Total cost, £45.

According to the 1849 Report:

> About one-fifth of the boats used in fishing are open . . . northwards from Loch Crinan they are generally all open, and southwards to the Mull of Galloway about one-fifth are open. The half-deck is not considered any inconvenience, and the introduction of the deck has been within the last 25 years. The fishermen live on board the boats while engaged in the fishery, the half-deck affords them protection from the weather, a sleeping and cooking apartment.
>
> They prefer lying afloat when the harbours will admit of it, particularly so on account of drying their nets on board. The Loch Fyne boats do not take the ground easily, being sharp built. They generally last from 15 to 20 years.
> The boats employed in Loch Fyne and its vicinity in 1848 were:

Inverary and Lochgilphead	1,283
Campbeltown and Islay	546
Rothesay	219
Greenock and Ayr	478
	2,526

> Manned by 7,933 men and boys.

The boats used were small cutters for drift netting and open 'skiffs' carrying one lugsail and a jib. Although it was illegal, some men used a form of Larsen trawl, towed between two sailing skiffs for catching herring in the season.

The lines of a Largs line skiff, then fishing in Loch Fyne, were taken off by the late P. J. Oke in October 1936. Length overall was 17 ft 11 in, beam 5 ft 1 in, depth inside 1 ft 11 in. The hull was built by Boag of Fairlie, c 1890, double-ended

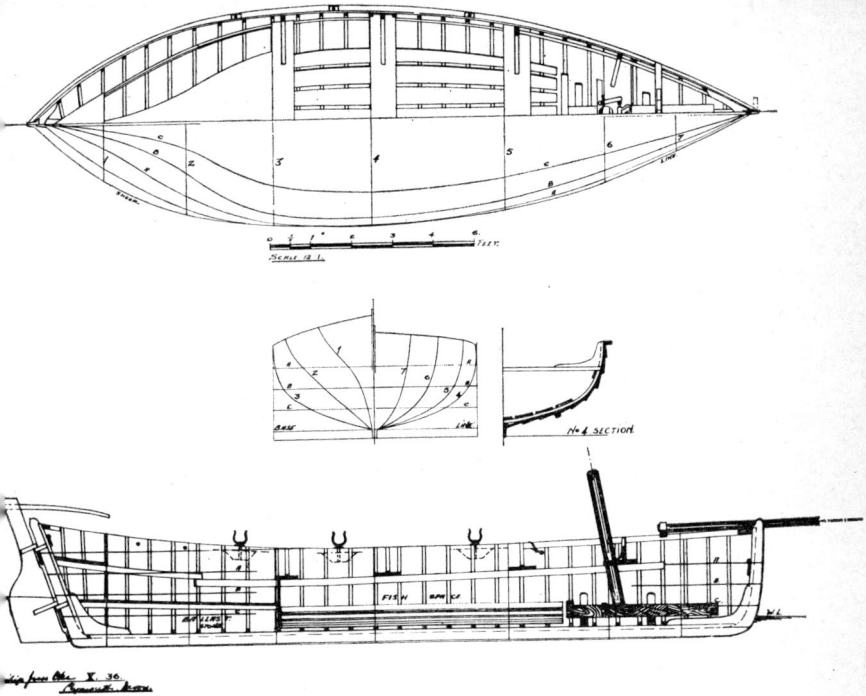

Plans of Largs line skiff

with straight stem and raking stern, entirely open with three rowing thwarts. The 18-ft mast, diameter $2\frac{1}{2}$ to $3\frac{1}{2}$ in raking well aft, was stepped on the floors and secured against the after side of a thwart in a recess and clamped with an iron band. Fore yard 11 ft 3 in, diameter $1\frac{1}{2}$ to 1 in, bowsprit 7 ft 3 in, outboard 4 ft 8 in, diameter $1\frac{3}{4}$ to $2\frac{1}{2}$ in, draught for'ard 6 in, aft 1 ft 3 in. The well-peaked lug sail had four lines of reef points, two in the early days when the sail was more square-headed.

The Loch Fyne line skiff *Snowdrop*, TT 177, built at Ardrishaig by Archie Munro in 1901, had a length overall of 22 ft $6\frac{3}{4}$ in, breadth 6 ft 4 in, depth 2 ft 7 in, keel 20 ft, iron thole pins. Mast 21 ft, rake 1 ft $2\frac{1}{2}$ in over 5 ft, yard 13 ft 8 in. Area of standing lugsail 197·6 sq ft, 18-in cloths, 4 reefs 2 ft deep.

125 0"

27 6"

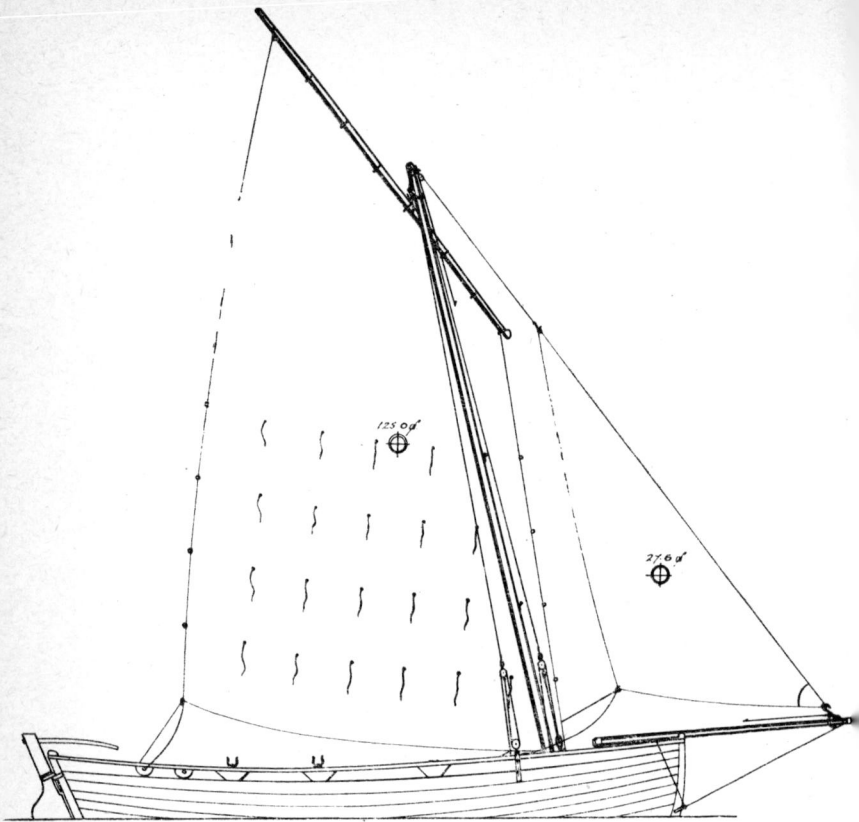

— OLD TYPE SQUAREHEADED LUG — (No Jib).
— AND COLOUR SCHEME. —

Sail plans of Largs skiff

SCANTLINGS

Keel	Elm $2\frac{3}{4}$ in × 2 in iron keel band.
Stem	Sided 2 in, moulded at scarph $2\frac{3}{4}$ in.
Sternpost	Sided 2 in, moulded $1\frac{3}{4}$ in at head, $4\frac{1}{2}$ in at heel.
Planks	Pitchpine, bottom larch, $\frac{5}{8}$ in landings $\frac{1}{2}$ in.
Floors	On every fourth frame, amidships $2\frac{1}{2}$ in deep, $1\frac{1}{2}$ in thick. 1 ft 9 in long. After floors 6 in × $1\frac{1}{2}$ in.
Frames	Spacing 7 in amidships, $1\frac{3}{8}$ in × $\frac{7}{8}$ in, at deadwood aft $\frac{3}{4}$ in × $\frac{1}{2}$ in.
Knees	Oak, $1\frac{1}{2}$ in thick.

The bigger boats, the 'Zulu skiffs', were open except for a short foredeck with a cabin below about 4 ft 9 in high and fitted with two berths and a stove. Hulls were clinker-built and in the 1880s were usually rigged with two standing lugs and a jib on a bowsprit; later they had one mast raking well aft on which a high-peaked standing lug was set, the tack working on a short iron horse at the foot of the mast. (Pictures, pp 197 and 199.)

Those used for line fishing had a keel length of from 24 to 28 ft, overall 32 to 34 ft. A 27-ft keel skiff cost £100, sails £20 to £30; the mast was usually the same length as the boat over the stems. Crew numbered three or four.

Brittaina, TT 154, had a length overall of 35 ft 6 in, keel 26 ft, beam 10 ft 3 in, four oars, 22 to 25 ft long, 3 in diameter. The 33-ft mast rested in a slide 1 ft 3 in long, 2 in deep and $1\frac{3}{4}$ in thick, three-sided, on a 2 ft 6 in by 7 in step in which were three holes of 3 in diameter, 2 in deep; the for'ard was for the mast right up in light winds, centre moderate breezes, and the aft very raked for hard weather.

The foreyard was 24 ft long, and the standing lug was made of 21-in cloths with $4\frac{1}{2}$ rows of reef points. Jib 3 reefs, 2nd jib 1 reef, a big jib was set in fine weather. Bowsprit was about 10 ft outboard.

Hulls were generally varnished to the waterline, red or black below, floors on the foreside of every second frame, spacing 1 ft $1\frac{1}{2}$ in, 20 planks a side, 1 in thick.

In 1872 the number of second-class boats registered at the principal stations were: Campbelton 277, Greenock 1,687, Ardrossan 178, Ayr 160, Dumfries 93.

With the coming of the internal combustion engine early in the twentieth century the long day of sail and oar, which had lasted for thousands of years, was drawing to its close. No longer do fleets of sailing boats set out to fish on grounds once prolific, but now largely denuded by intensive fishing with modern methods.

The extent of the decline can be realised from the returns of 1872 when 16,765 fishing boats were registered in Scotland; of these 12,510 were under 15 tons. In England and Wales the number was 15,331, with 9,353 under 15 tons. It is doubtful if today anyone fishes commercially under sail and oar, so ubiquitous is the power-driven vessel.

Men skilled in the knowledge of how to make the best use of wind and tide are rapidly passing away, but I shall always be proud to have known many of them and to have recorded something of their way of life before it was too late.

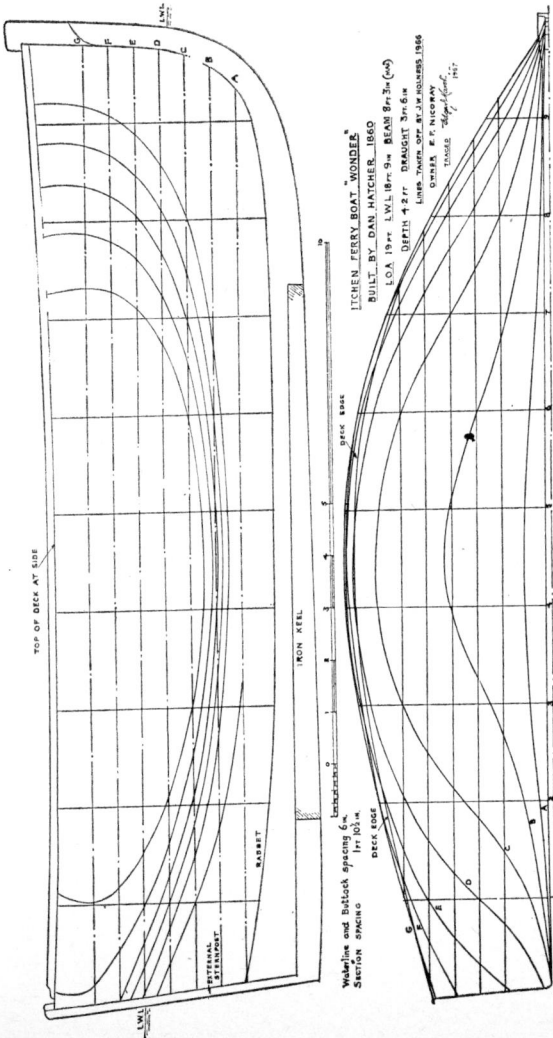

Lines of the Itchen Ferry boat *Wonder*, drawn by J. W. Holness

ITCHEN FERRY BOAT "WONDER"

BUILT BY DAN HATCHER 1860

L.O.A. 19FT L.W.L. 18FT.9IN BEAM 9FT.3IN (MLD)

DEPTH 4.2FT DRAUGHT 3FT.6IN

Lines taken off at J.W.Holness 1966

OWNER E.T.McCRAY

TIMBER ____ ____ 1917

TOP OF DECK AT SIDE

IRON KEEL

DECK EDGE

RABBET

DECK EDGE

EXTERNAL STERNPOST

Waterline and Buttock spacing 6IN 1FT 10½ IN
SECTION SPACING

TOP OF DECK AT SIDE

INDEX

305